WHITE RACISM 2nd Edition

2nd Edition

WHITE RACISM

The Basics

Joe R. Feagin
Hernán Vera
Pinar Batur

ROUTLEDGE
New York and London

Published in 2001 by
Routledge
29 West 35th Street
New York, NY 10001

Published in Great Britain by
Routledge
11 New Fetter Lane
London EC4P 4EE

Routledge is an imprint of the Taylor & Francis Group.

10 9 8 7 6 5 4 3 2

Library of Congress Cataloging-in-Publication Data
Feagin, Joe R.
   White racism / Joe R. Feagin, Hernán Vera, Pinar Batur.—2nd ed.
      p.   cm.
   Includes bibliographical references and index.
   ISBN 0-415-92814-1 (hb) — ISBN 0-415-92461-8 (pb)
   1. Racism—United States.   2. United States—Race relations.   I. Vera, Hernán,
1937–   II. Batur, Pinar.   III. Title.

E185.615.F39 2000
305.8'00973—dc21

00-025873

Contents

Acknowledgments

We are indebted to many people who have read various drafts of this manuscript, including Noel Cazenave, Rodney Coates, Rhonda Levine, Julie Netzer, Nikitah Imani, Debra Van Ausdale, Tiffany Hogan, Joane Nagel, Connie Williams, Holly Hanson, Jessie Daniels, Mohammad A. Chaichian, Loren Christenson, Joseph Jones, Nicolas Vera, William L. Smith, Juan Perea, Lynn Weber Cannon, James Button, and Felix Berardo. We are greatly indebted to Clairece Booher Feagin, Noah Sawyer, and Karyn McKinney for research or copyediting assistance. We also thank those who gave of their time for our interviews, individually or in focus groups, in several cities across the country. We are grateful as well to our students (especially Susana McCollom, Debra Van Ausdale, Holly Hanson, Tiffany Hogan, Julie Netzer, Peggy Moore, Mark Dulong, Katherine Dube, Kim Lersch, John Talmadge, Brian Fox, E. J. Brown, and Kay Roussos), who conducted most of the interviews cited in or undergirding the arguments in Chapters 7 and 8. In addition, our graduate students have provided critical ears for many of the arguments in this book, and discussions with them have clarified and sharpened many once obscure points. We are indebted to the staff at the University of Florida library for helping us in various ways, including access to Mead Data Central's Lexis/Nexis database. And we especially appreciate the strong support from Ilene Kalish, Heidi Freund, and Jayne Fargnoli, our editors at Routledge.

Preface

One of the great ironies of U.S. history is the way in which freedom and liberty were developed for white Americans on the backs of African Americans and other Americans of color. For example, the first part of the Capitol building in Washington, DC, which has long housed the deliberations of a white-dominated U.S. Congress, was built by enslaved African Americans, whose white owners were paid for that labor. Those who actually did the work on this great symbol of democracy were not paid, nor have their descendants been compensated for this theft of labor. This history is even more ironic, for it was enslaved African Americans who put the statue of *Freedom* at the top of the Capitol dome in the 1860s. This statue was of a Native American woman warrior dressed in a flowing robe and helmet. Those who cast the statue, loaded its pieces onto wagons, assembled it, and hoisted it to the top of the Capitol building were African American workers who did not possess the freedom they were helping to celebrate. And the indigenous American peoples represented in this statue to freedom were in the process of being eliminated or subordinated as well.[1]

Not only has the story of the construction of the Capitol and its statue of freedom been forgotten by almost all Americans, but the implications and consequences of this long-term racial oppression of African and Native Americans are also largely denied or brushed aside today by most white Americans. U.S. society and its basic institutions and daily-life rhythms are still riddled with the elements and practices of white racism, a systemic reality with deep roots in the past and major consequences for all Americans in the present. It is this continuing reality that we address in this book.

This second edition of *White Racism* incorporates a range of new material on racist events and incidents across the United States in its eight chapters. In addition, we have added a few new concepts and have reworked or honed some of the original concepts about individual and institutionalized racism in the United States.

Thus in Chapter 1 we now begin with recent civil rights protests over the Confederate battle flag in some of the southern states. In this chapter, among other things, we have updated data on hate crimes, sharpened our discussion of the so-called "binary paradigm" for U.S. racial relations, discussed the issue of a "color-blind" U.S. Constitution, and fine-tuned our discussion of the rituals of racism. In Chapter 2 we have added a discussion of the Rutgers University case as well as a new conclusion, which briefly integrates some ideas of African American theorists Stokely Carmichael and W. E. B. Du Bois. In Chapter 3 we have updated the Denny's and Shoney's restaurant cases with recent details; added a discussion of other problems, such as pizza shops not delivering to black communities; and reworked somewhat the conclusion on collective consumption and racism. For Chapter 4 we have added to the original discussion of racist murders the case of the lynching death of James Byrd, Jr., in Jasper, Texas, an incident that supports the added concept of macro-aggression. We have also included in this reworked chapter some discussion of other supremacist cases, such as those of Timothy McVeigh and Benjamin Nathaniel Smith, and have added new material on antiracist strategies and community action.

In Chapter 5 we have added other major cases of police profiling, brutality, and killings to the archetypal Rodney King case, which precipitated the most serious urban uprising in the United States in the last century. We also discuss the recent killing of Amadou Diallo and the vicious attack on Abner Louima by New York police officers, as well as the huge Rampart division scandal in the Los Angeles police department. This ongoing scandal, which involved police violence and fabricating evidence, has led the courts to free numerous wrongly imprisoned people of color. Here we have also incorporated other material on racial profiling and honed our theory of racism in regard to social costs and societal waste. In Chapter 6 we expand our previous discussion of racism in the halls of power by including a major corporate racism case, that of Texaco. Here we also examine the long-term discrimination against black farmers by the U.S. Department of Agriculture's Farm Service Agency and show how racism is an integral part of both corporate and government policy. We also enhance our previous discussion of the denial of racism and the reality of continuing white privilege. In Chapter 7 we have polished and expanded our original idea of the sincere fictions of the white self, added some new material on aspects of the white "soul," and discussed how "merit" testing can be viewed as white people's affirmative action. In the concluding Chapter 8 we draw on the various cases to polish and reframe our ideas on the taking of individual and collective action against racism—on antiracism as both social movement and personal stance—thereby giving more importance to antiracist struggles of ordinary people. We begin the chapter with the South African struggle against racism, which intends in part to accent the linkages of U.S. racism to the global scene. Increasingly, U.S. varieties of white racism are being exported by U.S. tourists, government officials, corporate operatives, and media outlets across the globe. In this way U.S. racism becomes a central part of the world racist order.

1

The Waste of White Racism

Introduction

On the Martin Luther King holiday, January 17, 2000, some 46,000 protesters, black and non-black, marched in downtown Columbia, South Carolina, protesting the flying of the Confederate battle flag atop the South Carolina state house. Since the days of the 1960s Civil Rights Movement, no crowd this large had gathered to protest what has become one of the nation's major symbols of white privilege. The march was a loud cry against racism. On this occasion, it had only been a week since 6,000 white supporters of the Confederate battle flag had demonstrated in front of the state house in celebration of the symbol, which they claimed to be part of their southern heritage.

The white demonstrators argued that the battle flag symbolized for them the southerners' courage to secede from the union. They were proud because South Carolina is the only state to still fly the battle flag on its state house. Moreover, as of mid-2000, South Carolina is also the only state in the country without official recognition of Martin

Luther King Day. One black state employee, who took a discretionary day off to march along with her eight-year-old daughter, said "my little girl has to see that flag every day on her way home from school. But now she can see that her people is stronger than any flag." Indeed, the voice came loud and strong from 46,000 marchers, and the voice was calling for an end to all elements of white racism.[1]

In the United States "white" racism is a centuries-old system intentionally designed to exclude Americans of color from full participation in the economy, polity, and society. Here we place the word "white" in quotation marks to problematize the term. Those called "whites" in the United States and across the globe are really not white in skin color but rather are some shade of brown, tan, pink, or mixture thereof. These truer-to-life skin colors, however, are not generally associated with the qualities—such as purity, innocence, and privilege—to which "white" skin is often linked. "White" people do not really exist in the flesh; they are a social construction. In the rest of this book we will generally leave off the quote marks for this word so as not to make the text cumbersome, but the reader should keep the quote marks in mind whenever this word is used in our text or elsewhere.

Today, racial prejudices and ideologies still undergird and rationalize widespread white discrimination against people of color. We realize that this view of a racialized and white-dominated America is not popular among most white analysts and commentators in the twenty-first century. More popular is the belief that African Americans and other people of color have made great progress, so much so that white racism is no longer a major barrier in most of their lives. Indeed, few whites are aware of how important racism is to their own feelings, beliefs, thinking, and actions.

When we presented the outline of this book to the editors of another major New York publisher, they rejected it and complained that our book did not deal with black racism. From the perspective we take in this book, black racism does not exist. We conceptualize racism in *structural* and *institutional* as well as individual terms. From its first use by Magnus Hirschfeld as a term to describe European ideas and actions against people conceptualized as biologically infe-rior in Europe in the 1930s, the concept of "racism" has meant much more than personal prejudices and scattered episodes of individual discrimination.[2] In its fullest definition, racism is a *system* of oppres-sion of African Americans and other people of color by white Euro-peans and white Americans. There is no black racism because there is no centuries-old system of racialized subordination and discrimina-tion designed by African Americans that excludes white Americans from full participation in the rights, privileges, and benefits of this society. Black racism would require not only a widely accepted racist ideology directed at whites but also the power to systematically exclude whites from opportunities and rewards in major economic, cultural, and political institutions. While there are black Americans and other Americans of color with antiwhite prejudices and sporadic instances of people of color discriminating against whites, these are *not central to the core operations of U.S. society.*

What is often referred to as "black racism" consists of judgments made about whites by some black leaders or other commentators of color to the effect that "no white people can be trusted" or "the white man is the devil." But these critical ideas or negative prejudices are *not* the equivalent of modern white racism. The latter involves not just individual thoughts but also widely socialized ideologies and omnipresent practices based on entrenched beliefs of white superior-ity. The prejudices and myths used to justify antiblack actions are not invented by individual perpetrators, nor are they based only on per-sonal experience. For centuries now, these widespread ways of feel-ing, thinking, and acting have been deeply embedded in a white-centered society—in its culture, major institutions, and every-day rhythms of life.

Antiblack feelings, ideas, and actions are widely developed and dis-seminated by parents, peers, the media, and the educational system. They have been passed along from generation to generation now for more than three centuries. Whites can avail themselves of this racial-ized thinking as needed. Racial categories form part of this Eurocen-tric culture of off-the-shelf taxonomies that classify and organize certain features of the social world into a coherent whole. In this sense, racial categories form part of the social blueprint that whites, as well as other people, use to orient their actions. The broad availability of racist categories, prejudices, and myths helps to explain, to an important extent, how many new immigrants to the United States soon adopt negative images of African Americans (and often of themselves). Many immigrants from Europe and other parts of the globe hold antiblack prejudices and stereotypes even *before* they set foot in this country. These beliefs and myths are imbibed from U.S. movies, television programs, and publications, which are now viewed in nearly every country around the globe. The U.S. version of modern white racism is more than a national phenomenon, for it now encircles the globe.

This book probes the nature of certain cases that many have thought to be examples of white racism. Looking at these cases, we examine sets and series of events that show what many white Americans believe and feel and how they sometimes act in regard to African American men, women, and children. We look at who these whites are and make a distinction between active participants in racialized actions, those who are acolytes, and those who are but passive participants. We examine some of the causes of white racism and probe deeply its nuances. As we will see, racialized actions by whites are not always motivated by racial hatred. Fear, ignorance, a sense of personal vulnerability, the desire to carry out the orders of others, and jealousy can propel whites to engage in or passively acquiesce in such practices. As we saw in the opening of this chapter, many whites passively consent to racial rituals such as the flying of the Confederate battle flag that symbolizes racial oppression to black Americans.

In this book we examine a wide range of misconceptions and myths about African Americans and about whites themselves—what we call "sincere fictions." Usually unfeigned, whites' negative beliefs about and images of African Americans and other Americans of color still provide the make-believe, but no less effective, foundation for white dominance and supremacy. We will show that the sincere fictions of whites encompass more than negative images of the out-group; they also involve images of oneself and one's own group. The key to understanding white racism is to be found not only in what whites think of African Americans and other people of color but also in *what whites think of themselves*. It is on these fictions that white privilege is constructed as a taken-for-granted base of U.S. society.

We focus mainly on the practices of white racism as it targets and exploits African Americans because that racism is an archetype for other subsequent patterns of white treatment of people of color. Our discussion is on white racism, which targets not only African Americans but also Latino, Asian, and Native Americans, as well as other Americans of color. These latter groups are often framed and exploited within the ideological and action framework that whites have developed over four hundred years of oppressing African Americans at the center of white society.

In paying this central and detailed attention to white racism as it is directed against African Americans, we are not adopting a so-called "binary white/black paradigm," a confused term sometimes used by analysts critical of an emphasis on issues of white and black Americans in the United States. We clearly recognize the oppression that whites have routinely imposed on Americans of color other than African Americans. However, the usual critiques of the binary black/white paradigm fail to note that the reality implied in the terms "black" and "white" here is much more than an abstracted scholarly paradigm. The underlying structural reality is the nearly four-hundred-year-old system of *white-on-black oppression.* This structural framework is the *oldest* system of racist oppression developed systematically by white Europeans for a non-European group that was central to the *internal* operation of their new society—the enslaved Africans, who from the mid-1600s onward were important to the labor needs within the new colonies of North America. The foundation for nearly four hundred years of subsequent incorporation and oppression of other non-European groups by whites was set in place in the 1600s in the importation, subordination, and exploitation of African slaves and in the subsequent elaboration and rationalization of that oppressive system.[3]

The oppression and exploitation of the Africans was contemporary with, if not predated by, the archetypal model of genocide that white Europeans developed in the process of stealing land from the indigenous populations of the Americas. In the early centuries of conquest and colonization Native Americans had their lands taken from them by chicanery and force. Most Native Americans were not incorporated into the white economy and society but instead were killed off in genocidal actions, driven westward beyond the boundaries of white interests, or restricted to segregated enclaves called reservations.

African Americans became a *central part* of the new Euro-American communities. Their lives were soon governed by a legally protected system of oppression reaching across all societal institutions. The white economy, polity, society, values, and religion, and even the white self, were constructed and reconstructed with the enslaved African Americans—and after emancipation those legally segregated—as a central point of reference. In North America a racist ideology was developed in hundreds of books and thousands of articles defending white superiority and African inferiority. This ideology has dominated white thought from the seventeenth century to the twenty-first century. White racism and the black struggle against it have shaped the character not only of the founding documents of the United States, such as the Declaration of Independence and the U.S. Constitution, but also of a huge body of law and much social practice over the intervening centuries. From the 1600s to the present, a majority of white Americans have held a range of antiblack prejudices and images, which are webbed into a full-fledged racist ideology and which have played a dynamic role in implementing an extensive and institutionally buttressed set of discriminatory practices against African Americans and other peoples.

Over the intervening centuries since 1619 other non-European groups, such as Latinos and Asian Americans, have—to a substantial extent—been brought into this preexisting ideological and structural matrix of white-on-black oppression. We need to underscore the point that once this archetypal system of white-on-black oppression was put in place, other non-European groups that entered into the society later were oppressed and positioned *by whites* within the preexisting racist framework. Many of the problems with white racism faced by other groups of color stem from essentially the same source. It is within this antiblack framework that certain other groups have been assimilated, constructed, and oppressed. Subsequent non-European immigrants such as the Chinese and Japanese immigrants of the nineteenth and early twentieth centuries or Mexican and Central American immigrants since the early 1900s have also been defined by many whites as somehow subhuman, noncitizens without rights, or second-class citizens. Immigrant groups not of European background have found themselves defined and treated by whites more like African Americans than like Euro-American whites. Constructed and incorporated in a centuries-old racist framework, they have become "Chinks," "Japs," "Gooks," and "greasers." Eventually, some in these nonblack groups have been able to improve their status within the white-dominated society, but only because whites have come to see them as "better" in cultural or visual-racial terms than African Americans. Even so, "better" has never meant full social, economic, and political equality with Euro-Americans.

All types of white-on-others racism are important, and there is a great need to eradicate them all. Yet we believe that they cannot be adequately understood until we understand deeply the character and history of white racism as it has targeted African Americans. What is crucial to understand is racism's aim in creating and maintaining white privilege.

Traditional discussions often treat racism as a zero-sum game of power and resources, a view that assumes a scarcity of critical societal resources for which all groups inevitably contend. We depart from this narrow perspective to argue that white racism legitimates the squandering and dissipation of an important *surplus* of societal resources and human talents. On reflection, many whites can recognize some of the waste of black talent and resources brought about by discriminatory barriers, but few realize how great and painful this loss is for African Americans and their communities. Even fewer whites perhaps realize the huge amount of energy and talent that whites themselves have dissipated in the construction of antiblack attitudes and ideologies and in their participation in the system of racist discrimination. Even fewer still realize that living with white racism facilitates both direct and indirect participation in the erosion of possibilities for equality and social justice for all. In this book we explore the impact of omnipresent white racism on all Americans by emphasizing the dissipation of the energies and talents of racism's victims as well as of the discriminators themselves.

Clearly, however, the costs of racism are *far greater* for the oppressed than for the oppressors. Our argument about the costly character of racism recognizes that black and other targets of racist oppression pay a *direct, heavy, and immediately painful* price for racism, while white discriminators and onlookers usually pay a *more indirect and seldom recognized* price.

We believe that U.S. society in general is paying a heavy price in material, psychological, and moral terms for the persistence of white racism. We demonstrate in this book that white racism is a system of institutionalized human waste that this society cannot afford. We depart from much mainstream research on racial relations to focus on specific events in particular places and on those whites whose actions have a negative impact on people of color. If white racism is so wasteful, why does it still persist? The answer lies in the fact that the system of racial subordination, exploitation, and privilege is taken for granted and woven into every major institution in this society. The racism we accent in this book began as a system to provide a source of chained labor for European American slave masters in the North American colonies. Ever since, most whites—some more than others—have benefited in a variety of ways from this racist system.

Moreover, racial stereotypes and prejudices are useful for whites in explaining why certain people of color do not have as much or do as well as whites across multiple areas of the society. Racist notions of genetic or cultural inferiority help explain why there are great inequalities in a society with egalitarian ideals. Racist notions have brought ill-gotten resources and benefits to many white Americans, yet few whites realize the heavy price that they, their families, and their communities have paid and will pay for this institutionalized racism. White Americans have paid greatly in the form of their ignorance and fears, in human contributions and achievements sacrificed, in the failure to create a just and egalitarian society, in the resistance and lashing out of the oppressed, and in the fundamental ideals and egalitarian morality thus betrayed. In our view U.S. society certainly cannot afford white racism in the long run, for it may well destroy this society as we know it sometime in this century.

Focusing on the massive character of the social waste that is so basic to this nation should be useful for initiating a reinvigorated debate on the solutions for white racism. In this book we are very much concerned with solutions for the archetypical white-on-black racism. We are under no illusion that a lessening or elimination of racist thought and practice will be easy. In the past, many have tried to lessen or eradicate white racism, and these attempts have often been limited in effect or have been outright failures. Historically, conservative solutions for racial discrimination deny there is a structural problem and focus on reforming the victims or their cultural values. Liberal solutions tend to tackle symptoms or deal with truncated aspects of the problem of racism with modest reforms or civil rights laws and regulations that are usually weakly enforced. Both the conservative and liberal agendas stress education of the oppressed, thereby taking much of the blame for racial inequalities off of white Americans and of white society.

Clearly, much more profound and aggressive action is needed to eradicate white racism and create an egalitarian, multicultural society. Our analysis is not just about the negative character of white racism and its impact on black, white, and other Americans but also about the ideas and values on which effective solutions must be based. A key question is, "On whose terms are we going to live together, if we are to live in harmony?"

In later chapters we examine strategies and realities of antiracism by an array of Americans, both those who are the targets of oppression and those among whites who are their allies. As we see it, it is not enough to show how racism works without also showing how this age-old system of oppression can be eradicated. At this point in U.S. history, the majority of whites do not want to live according to the egalitarian terms and practices necessary for full social justice and harmony. Reaching the goal of a truly democratic, nonracist society will require the thoroughgoing education or re-education of the majority of white Americans not only in regard to U.S. racial-ethnic history but also in regard to the massive costs of white racism for the black and other victims of racism—and for whites themselves, their children, and the society as a whole. To achieve this nonracist society a reform of white ways of thinking and feeling is not enough. Both racist practices and the institutionalized conditions they create or reinforce must be dissolved and eradicated at their roots.

Racist practices can be eradicated in part by massive efforts to demythologize the structures of our society. Debates about modest remedial programs such as affirmative action may be necessary and useful, but they provide little practical hope for Americans interested in bringing about "liberty and justice for all." The greater challenge is to generate, maintain, and pass to the next generation the strategies of antiracism, which include practical plans for the eradication of racism and the ability to dream a better society.[4] We have much to gain by claiming equality, freedom, and social justice, and thus asserting our common humanity in one human race. We envisage as well much multiracial organization to bring these goals.

Denying the Reality of White Racism

Until civil rights laws were passed during the Lyndon Johnson administration in the 1960s, most African Americans faced blatant discrimination that was legally prescribed or permitted. Few had the resources to vigorously oppose it, and the legal system offered little support. The civil rights revolution of the 1950s and 1960s upset the way equality and democracy had been conceived and practiced by expanding the rights of African Americans and other Americans of color. In the years following this revolution, as state-enforced segregation was demolished, many felt optimistic about the future. Black people began moving into many formerly forbidden areas of U.S. society, and whites began to encounter a greater black presence in historically white public facilities, workplaces, businesses, churches, schools, and neighborhoods.

However, the civil rights revolution came to a standstill in the 1980s, and many African Americans now believe that the country and its government are moving backward in the quest for racial justice.[5] Presidential use of the White House as a "bully pulpit" for conservative political agendas during the Reagan and Bush years of the 1980s and early 1990s was particularly devastating to racial relations. Federal civil rights enforcement programs were weakened significantly in this period. The political denial of white racism made its way into intellectual circles and the mass media, where the concept of the "declining significance of race" became fashionable. Since the mid-1970s many influential commentators and authors have argued or implied that white racism is no longer a serious, entrenched national problem and that African Americans must take total responsibility for their own individual and community problems.

A majority of white Americans in all social classes, including jurists, scholars, and commentators, now appear to believe that serious racism is declining significantly in the United States, that black Americans have made great and continuing civil rights progress in recent decades, and that blacks should thus be more or less content with that progress. Whites see intentional and widespread discrimination in most institutional arenas as a thing of the past. In particular, many whites seem to believe that the black middle class in particular no longer faces significant discrimination and is thriving economically—indeed, more so than the white middle class. Whites typically view problems of the black "underclass" as the central issue for black America and believe that class's condition has little to do with discrimination. Thus the white notion that any black person who works hard enough can succeed is reflected in white reactions to such mass media programs as the *Cosby Show*, as described by researchers Sut Jhally and Justin Lewis. Many whites felt the famous television series, which portrayed a successful black upper-middle-class family and became the highest-rated sitcom on national television during the 1980s, showed a "world where race no longer matters." Jhally and Lewis noted that this view of the show enabled whites to "combine an impeccably liberal attitude toward race with a deep-rooted suspicion of black people."[6]

Furthermore, since the 1980s a number of issues not previously related to race have come to be "interpreted through a framework of racial meanings, often through the use of coded language, symbols and images."[7] For example, this racialization of new topics can be seen in the defection of those Democrats who left their party to vote for Ronald Reagan and George Bush in the 1980s presidential campaigns. For many white workers, according to one analysis, "Blacks constitute the explanation for [the white workers'] vulnerability and for almost everything that has gone wrong in their lives." One white worker is quoted in one study as saying that "blacks get advantages, Hispanics get advantages, Orientals get advantages. Everybody but the white male race gets advantages now."[8] Sociologist Michael Omi has noted that these sentiments are manipulated by conservative groups and have thus provided a basis "for a conservative reappraisal of the nature of discrimination and state policies designed to promote equality."[9]

Paradoxically, in this post–Civil–Rights–Movement era the denial of white racism takes the form of the deracialization of a number of other issues—such as affirmative action in such areas as college admissions and state contracts—by recasting them in terms of "merit" or the "need for color blindness." Toni Morrison has described this escapism eloquently: "Evasion has fostered another, substitute language in which the issues are encoded, foreclosing open debate. . . . It is further complicated by the fact that the habit of ignoring race is understood to be a graceful, even generous, liberal gesture. To notice is to recognize an already discredited difference. . . . According to this logic, every well bred instinct argues *against noticing* and forecloses adult discourse."[10]

In this evasive environment affirmative action programs have been targets for conservatives who did not want them in the first place. A key weapon in the attacks on affirmative action is "the myth that the Constitution requires a color-blind approach to all but a very narrowly excepted class of race-based problems."[11] The white male framers, of course, never intended the Constitution to be color-blind. Their intent, as one can tell from their debates and the final document, was to create a very color-conscious Constitution. African Americans were intentionally excluded from citizenship, and their enslavement was directly facilitated and buttressed by numerous provisions inserted in that Constitution. Thus, the Constitution regarded African Americans as but "three fifths" of a person when it came to counting people for representation—that is, congressional representation in the form of white representatives.[12]

There is a blatant hypocrisy in the color-blind argument, hypocrisy that the late Justice Thurgood Marshall once noted well: "For it must be remembered that, during most of the past two hundred years, the Constitution as interpreted by this court did not prohibit the most ingenious and pervasive forms of discrimination against the Negro. Now when a State acts to remedy the effects of that legacy of discrimination, I cannot believe that this same Constitution stands as a barrier."[13] The Constitution and most of its white interpreters have always been color cognizant.

The Reality of Racism

The substantial white consensus on the decline of racism is not based on empirical evidence. On the contrary, research shows that black men and women still face extensive racial discrimination in all arenas of daily life. A brief overview of the current racial scene is appropriate at this point to set the frame for our analysis in subsequent chapters. Recent in-depth studies have documented continuing antiblack discrimination, ranging from blatant acts reminiscent of the legal segregation period to subtle and covert forms that have flourished under the conditions of desegregation. The belief in the declining significance of race cannot be reconciled with the empirical reality of racial discrimination. Great anger over white racism can be found today in every socioeconomic group of black Americans, from millionaires to clerks and day laborers.[14]

White supremacy groups have been at the forefront of attackers of African Americans. Membership in the Ku Klux Klan, the largest white supremacy group for most of the twentieth century, reached five million in the 1920s. After a period of decline, Klan membership began to grow again in the 1970s, and in the early 1990s the number of white Americans in various Klan factions was estimated at about ten thousand. Newspaper reports have documented Klan violence against minorities and have described paramilitary training camps designed to prepare Klan members for "race war." From the 1970s to the present, the Klan and other white supremacy groups have been involved in hundreds of antiblack and anti-Jewish attacks; several members of such groups have been convicted of murdering or assaulting black people.[15] Other white supremacy groups, such as the White Aryan Resistance (WAR), headed by white supremacist Tom Metzger, and the World Church of the Creator, led by Matthew F. Hale (see Chapter 4), have emerged in recent years. Hundreds of hate groups are active in the early twenty-first century, ranging from Skinheads to a variety of neo-Nazi and other white supremacy organizations. White supremacy groups in the United States have been estimated to have at least thirty thousand hard-core members, with perhaps another two hundred thousand active sympathizers, not including the million or more people who read the hundreds of racist Internet websites.[16]

During the 1980s and 1990s hundreds of acts of vandalism and intimidation were directed at black Americans and other Americans of color. A notorious incident occurred in 1986 in the Howard Beach area of New York City, when three black men were beaten and chased by white youths. One of the men died when he was chased into the path of a car. A few days later five thousand people, black and white, marched through Howard Beach to protest the attack.[17] In some years in the 1990s there were more than two dozen hate-motivated murders of Americans of color by white killers in the United States. Many other hate killings undoubtedly went unreported. In one incident, two white men went on a rampage in a Washington, DC suburb. They were looking for black pedestrians to attack. They ended their night by tearing the clothes off a black woman and calling her "nigger."[18] In another case two white men were convicted in south Florida of the kidnapping, robbery, and attempted murder of a black stock-brokerage clerk who was vacationing in Tampa. The black man was set ablaze by the whites, who left a note saying, "One less nigger, more to go."[19] Indeed, there were 8,049 bias-motivated (hate) crimes reported to the federal government in 1997. In these cases, 59 percent of the victims of these crimes were attacked because of racial reasons, and black Americans accounted for 39 percent of the targets of this hatred.[20]

Yet hate crimes targeting African Americans represent only the tip of the racist iceberg. Black people also continue to face discrimination in the workplace, in business, in colleges, in public accommodations, and in historically white neighborhoods. Millions of cases of discrimination occur each year. More than half of the black respondents in a one ABC News survey agreed that black workers generally faced discrimination when seeking skilled jobs; 61 percent gave a similar reply regarding managerial jobs.[21] The racial discrimination lawsuit against Texaco (see Chapter 6) provided painful examples of the many problems faced by black managers and employees. A 1991 Urban Institute report presented a study in which white and black applicants with similar qualifications were sent to the same employers to apply for jobs; a significant proportion of the black applicants suffered discrimination in the hiring process.[22] Even if a black applicant is hired, discriminatory barriers are likely to impair career progress. Racial discrimination continues to handicap African Americans today in all major institutional arenas of our society.[23]

The effects of employment and other economic discrimination have been documented by Andrew Hacker, who is one of the few white social scientists to examine declining-significance-of-race arguments in a book published by a major commercial press. Hacker presents data showing persisting and major economic inequalities between black and white Americans: For example, black workers still make on the average much less than white workers and face discrimination in many areas of employment.[24] Other data underscore Hacker's conclusions. Consider unemployment, a social plague that few Americans today attribute solely to lack of individual effort. Unemployment robs people not only of income but also of self-respect and personal and family happiness. Since the 1940s the black unemployment rate has consistently been about twice the white unemployment rate and this continues to be the case in the year 2000 after a decade-long economic boom. In recent recessions black workers have lost jobs at twice the rate of white workers. The black underemployment rate, which includes those working part time and those making poverty wages, is even higher than the unemployment rate. Some estimate that at least one-fifth of all black workers are today unemployed or underemployed.[25]

Persisting racial inequality can also be seen in the continuing wide gaps in black and white family income and wealth. Today the median income of black families is about 58 percent of that of white families. Blacks are almost three times as likely to live in poverty as are whites, and the median net worth of black families is less than 10 percent of that of white families.[26] These data underscore the long-term advantages of being white in this society. Young white Americans sometimes argue that they have not personally held slaves or discriminated against black people and therefore should not have to pay the price of remedies for racial discrimination. However, this argument fails to take into account the many ways in which young whites have benefited from their forebears' access to land, decent-paying jobs, and wealth at a time when most African Americans were excluded from those things. Two decades of very modest government remedial programs like affirmative action have not offset several hundred years of white enrichment and advantage. Although the economic benefits of white privilege have gone in disproportionately large amounts to the employer and middle classes, all white groups derive at least some psychological benefit from having a group below them, from the feeling of superiority that is especially important for whites who are not doing well economically.

Sociologist Sidney Willhelm has pointed out that black workers, often concentrated in racially stratified low-wage jobs, have been abandoned as capitalists have turned to automation to restructure corporations and increase profits. In his view the U.S. economy no longer needs large numbers of black workers for full-time jobs, and this abandonment of much black labor has created major costs for both black and white communities.[27] As black workers become less necessary "in an automated society, they turn to crime with greater frequency in order to obtain the material needs of life; they confront a white America increasingly determined to meet crime with state violence."[28] Much of the crime committed by poor black men can be seen as individualized revolt against unemployment, substandard housing, and the other by-products of economic discrimination. Whites, especially those in the upper economic classes, have helped create the high cost of such crime by perpetuating the wasteful system of racial exploitation. This connection between crime and unemployment or underemployment is by no means limited to black Americans, for in recent decades increasing crime rates have affected most racial and ethnic communities in the United States. Moreover, U.S. history is replete with instances of members of racial and ethnic groups, including white immigrants such as the Irish and the Italians, turning to crime when racial-ethnic discrimination or the workings of the capitalist economy prevented them from securing decent-paying jobs.

A New Concept: Racism as Societal Waste

White racism can be viewed as the *socially organized set of practices, attitudes, and ideas that deny African Americans and other people of color the privileges, dignity, opportunities, freedoms, and rewards that this nation offers to white Americans.* The concept of white racism designates discriminatory practices and actions as well as the attitudes and ideologies that motivate these negative actions. Racist acts have ranged from overt extermination and murder to subtle gestures of social exclusion to passive acquiescence in the racist acts of others. Typically, racist acts and practices are institutionalized; they are embedded in and shaped by social contexts. These practices have sometimes been defined as illegal under U.S. law. This is the case for certain types of blatant employment, educational, and housing discrimination that fall under the 1964 and 1968 Civil Rights acts.

However, as we will see in the chapters that follow, a significant number of white actions that deny black Americans their full human dignity or restrict black opportunities for advancement have not been defined as illegal. Indeed, some of these practices may be so embedded in the way U.S. institutions operate, or may be so subtle or covert, that it may be difficult for a white-controlled legal system to deal effectively with them. (For example, to this day many Hollywood moviemakers include, with few white protests, negative stereotypes of African Americans, Latinos, and Asian Americans in their profitable products.) Moreover, antiblack practices, whether legal or not, have prevented far too many black women, men, and children from developing to their full potential and have kept their families, churches, and employers, as well as the larger society, from enjoying black contributions and achievements that can only be imagined. It is also important to note that in the United States racist ideas, practices, and institutions are often in flux; they are not static but change and mutate over time.

Viewed in broad terms, white racist practices represent socially sanctioned ways of dissipating much human talent and energy. Our thinking about the extreme wastefulness of racism is influenced by some ideas of Georges Bataille, who in *The Accursed Share* developed Karl Marx's social surplus product concept by proposing that human societies ordinarily generate more energy and human resources than are necessary for sustaining life at a minimal level. The excess energy can be used for positive personal growth or to enhance the social system, or it can be wasted: "It must be spent, willingly or not, gloriously or catastrophically."[29] In his thought-provoking analysis Bataille argues that many social institutions and practices dissipate excess human energy by design and that, because of their propensity to waste and destroy, human beings often forego major achievements and societal advances.[30] Historically, human beings have engaged in various strategies to use up this excess human energy. The construction of huge projects such as castles, pyramids, and cathedrals and the super-luxurious lifestyle of the upper classes are examples of such dissipation of human lives, talents, and energies. From the sixteenth century to the early twentieth century the imperialistic expansion of European nations seeking wealth and exploitable labor brought much human and ecological destruction to indigenous societies around the globe. War is the foremost example of the catastrophic and multiple destruction of human beings, and the many brutal wars of the "civilized" twentieth century show the proportions that the squandering of human lives and energy can attain. The Nazi-generated Holocaust of the 1930s and 1940s is yet another illustration of devastating human waste and has close parallels to U.S. racism.

Much wasteful dissipation of human talent and energy persists in the contemporary world, although a system of energy and resource dissipation is not a functional prerequisite for a society. Some societies have had the wisdom to avoid much human waste and destruction. For example, some contemporary European countries have invested their excess wealth and energy in impressive social-welfare systems and thus have less poverty, crime, and human suffering than the United States. What constitutes rational action or useless waste in a particular time and place is, of course, culturally and socially determined. A central thesis of this book is that Americans should see white racism for what it actually is: a tremendously wasteful set of practices, legitimated by deeply embedded myths, that deprives its victims, its perpetrators, and U.S. society as a whole of much valuable human talent and energy and many social, economic, and political resources.

The Rituals of Racism

Social practices that dissipate human resources and energies are often *ritualized,* that is, they are routine and recurring actions distinguished by symbols that pervade and guide their performance. Recent social science research has paid little attention to the ritual nature of racist events, although general observers have occasionally noted the ceremonial and formalized character of U.S. racial relations. Note, for example, the following comment made by Lillian Smith, a white southerner, during the era of legal segregation: "For we [whites] used those lynchings as a symbolic rite to keep alive in men's minds the idea of white supremacy, and we set up a system of avoidance rites that destroyed not bodies but the spirit of men."[31] We find the imagery of rites and rituals useful in analyzing racism in U.S. society. The concrete events and actions of white racism frequently have a ritual nature. Racist rites typically involve victims of color, several categories of white participants (*officiants, acolytes,* and *passive observers*), a range of acts (gestures, words, avoidance, physical attacks), an assortment of instruments (workplace appraisal forms, burning crosses, police batons), and an array of myths (stereotypes about Americans of color) that legitimate racist acts in perpetrators' minds.

Officiants are the central participants in racist rites. They perform principal actions, make key decisions, and articulate the critical epithets and other racist words. In contemporary racism the officiants may act individually or in groups. They may act openly and for themselves, or they may hide behind others who front for them. White supremacists who burn a cross may be acting for themselves (see Chapter 2), while white restaurant managers who discriminate against black customers (see Chapter 3) may be *acolytes* willingly or unwillingly carrying out the agendas of their employers. Members of the white clientele in a restaurant or store may become *passive participants* as they watch and understand the meaning of racially hostile acts.

By the use of physical, psychological, or symbolic force racist rituals deprive their targets of fundamental human rights and destroy talents, energy, and lives. The millions of people of color in the United States who have been and continue to be sacrificed to the mythological needs of white superiority are in certain ways like the sacrificial victims in the religious rites of some ancient societies: alien others who may be compelled to forfeit their lives or well-being in the name of compelling dominant-group interests. The targets of racism vary in their ability to redress their abuse. Those who are poor (see Chapter 4) generally do not have the power and resources to counter discrimination that are available to middle-class victims (see the case of the Secret Service agents in Chapter 3).

Racist rites are acted out at propitious times and places. As we will see many times in later chapters, racial myths—which take the form of prejudices, stereotypes, everyday racial fictions, and broader ideologies—are key components of racist rites. In Chapter 2 we examine a spate of cross-burnings in Dubuque, Iowa, in which the white officiants' intentions were both to symbolize antiblack emotions and to alert other whites to what the officiants perceived as threats to whites' jobs and lives. Racist rituals such as these are usually formalized and full of well-known symbols. The century-old cross-burning ceremony is often undertaken under cover of darkness and in ghost-like dress. Although such acts may appear to be private or limited to one or two individuals, most are understandable only as *social* practices and thus may be defined as rituals. Racialized rituals broadcast to the entire community the racial mythologies held by many in the dominant white group. Through such rituals unspoken understandings about white people and black people are maintained and propagated to present and future generations of Americans in all racial and ethnic groups. The impunity usually awarded to such acts sends a message to all that U.S. society and its government condone racist rites. Moreover, and perhaps most importantly, racist rituals signify just who whites *are.*

Officiants in racialized actions, such as cross-burnings, police brutality, or employment discrimination against African Americans, frequently have the support of acolytes. Their actions may also be witnessed by passive participants, whose failure to intervene allows discrimination to persist. For example, organized white supremacists such as Klan members are often officiants in racist rites, functioning as the equivalent of high priests. Yet many other whites subscribe to white supremacist literature or more or less silently sympathize with some aspects of white supremacist racial mythology. Studies of supremacist publications have found discussions that differentiate several groups of whites: white male officiants who engage in aggressive racist actions, white male and female acolytes who provide support, and passive white sympathizers who do not participate in designated racist actions but who share with officiates and acolytes certain myths that portray African Americans as less competent and less human than whites.[32]

The United States has a lengthy history of extraordinarily brutal and wasteful racial rituals. One example is the ritualized lynching of African Americans. From the 1860s to the 1990s thousands of black Americans were lynched by groups of whites. Between 50 and 161 lynchings of black men and women were recorded every year from 1889 to 1916. The number dropped to 10–24 a year in the 1930s and 1–6 a year from 1938 to the 1950s, and occasional lynchings have occurred since the 1950s. At least half of all lynchings of black Americans were never recorded, and many were carried out with the participation of police authorities.[33] Some lynchings were part of large-scale community attacks: For example, in 1908 crowds of whites moved through the black area of Springfield, Illinois, burned black-owned buildings, flogged fifty black people, and lynched two, chanting as they went, "Lincoln freed you; we'll show you your place."[34]

Lynchings have often involved the dismemberment of the victim's body and the ritualized distribution of its parts to white participants as mementos. Trudier Harris has noted that the brutal "lynching and burning rituals reflect a belief, on the part of whites, in their racial superiority."[35] Such rituals also reflect white notions about punishing black challenges to white authority and white commitment to barring blacks from white status and privilege. Many lynchings were precipitated because black men were not deferential to whites or because they allegedly touched or simply looked at white women. Other lynchings were unrelated to the real or alleged behavior of the black victims but were simply intended to show local black residents that they must "know their place."[36] Although physical lynchings as such have mostly (but not completely; see Chapter 4) disappeared from U.S. society, economic, political, psychological, and symbolic lynchings of African Americans have persisted in large numbers to the present day.

Some racist rituals are not as publicly visible or bloody as lynchings, but they still do much damage. In places of employment, for example, a white supervisor may act as a racist officiant in denying an earned promotion or deserved salary raise to a black employee or other employee of color. Those whites who help the perpetrator implement or rationalize this workplace discrimination act as acolytes. And the fellow employees who for fear of their jobs maintain a code of silence are acting as passive participants. Similarly, in the classroom those white teachers who deliver antiquated stereotypes and racist images in their class presentations and discussions act as officiants, while the students who actively parrot these racist notions act as acolytes. Those members of the class who are uneasy but remain silent can be seen as passive participants. In such settings, moreover, students of color often must learn about their own inferiority; they are subjected to a type of symbolic violence that is part of this racist ritual.

Racial Discrimination and Racial Mythology

One active part of racism, discrimination, has rarely been defined in the social science literature. For example, in *An American Dilemma* Gunnar Myrdal noted widespread discrimination in U.S. society but never delimited it. Subsequent researchers of black-white relations have usually not provided a specific definition.[37] Researchers who have ventured on more precise delineations in recent years have emphasized group power and institutionalized factors: For instance, Thomas Pettigrew has suggested that discrimination is "an institutional process of exclusion against an outgroup."[38] Joe R. Feagin and Clairece B. Feagin have defined discrimination as "practices carried out by members of dominant groups which have a differential and negative impact on members of subordinate groups."[39] The crucial point of these definitions is that the ability to carry out significant and repeated discriminatory acts flows from the power one group has over another. In addition, both individual and collective discrimination can occur in an array of locations—in public accommodations, schools and colleges, workplaces, and neighborhoods.

Discriminatory practices are supported by ideological constructions taken on faith. Racial myths are part of the mind-set that helps whites interpret their experience and that influences behavior, alters emotions, and shapes what whites see and do not see.[40] The cognitive notions and stereotypes of contemporary racism, which include myths of the dangerous black man, the lazy black person, the black woman's fondness for welfare, and black inferiority and incompetence, make as little empirical sense as the hostile fictions that underlay the Nazi Holocaust. However, such antiblack fictions are sincerely held by many whites (see Chapter 7).

The persistence of antiblack discrimination indicates how deeply myths of racial difference and inequality have become embedded in white thinking. Such myths often influence the important decisions that whites make, from selecting a spouse to choosing a residential neighborhood.[41] Yet white views of blacks are often not based on significant personal experience with African Americans. In contrast, black views of whites are much more likely to be grounded in personal experience because most blacks have had substantial experience with whites by the time they are a few years old. In her classic analysis, *Killers of the Dream,* Lillian Smith noted that prejudiced thinking and antiblack practices become "ceremonial," that they "slip from the conscious mind deep into the muscles."[42] These attitudes and propensities are learned at such an early point in a white child's development that they become routinized and unconscious. Smith also pointed out the insidiousness of racial learning in early childhood: "The mother who taught me tenderness . . . taught me the bleak rituals of keeping Negroes in their place."[43]

The stereotyped portrayals of African Americans and the unrealistically sanguine views of contemporary racial relations often presented in the mainstream media, such as local TV news programs, help perpetuate the racist myths held by ordinary white Americans. Leonard Berkowitz, among many others, has argued that the mass media play an important role in reinforcing antisocial images and behavior.[44] The U.S. media are overwhelmingly white-oriented and white-controlled. White control of powerful institutions—from the mass media to cor porate workplaces to universities to police departments—signals white dominance to all members of society.

At the individual level, much antiblack discrimination is perpetrated by whites who are not overtly aware of their ingrained prejudices and negative emotions. A white supervisor in the workplace may refuse to hire a black applicant because of the belief that white workers or customers are uncomfortable with people unlike themselves (see Chapter 3). Even in predominantly white colleges and universities, black students and faculty members are frequently victims of white prejudices, many of which seem buried deep in white consciousness (see Chapter 2). Whites do not need to be aware of their racial motivations to inflict harm on blacks.

The paradoxical phenomenon of whites who claim not to be racist while they perpetrate racially harmful acts can be explained in part by the fact that "racism" has come to be held in such opprobrium that few whites are willing to accept "racist" as a personal trait. This marks a change from the past. At an earlier time in U.S. history, even white powerholders paraded their racism as a sign of honor. Employers and politicians publicly joined the Klan in the 1920s and 1930s. Today the powerful may hide or deny their racist attitudes out of fear of disgrace, but racist acts have not ceased. The layers of euphemisms and code words that often cover racist acts today can make it difficult to demonstrate that such acts are in fact intentionally discriminatory.

Racism and the White Self

Racism is a fundamental part of U.S. culture and is spread throughout the social fabric. It reaches into the lives of all, whether they are white, black, or other Americans. Because virtually all white men, women, and children participate in a white-racist culture, most harbor racist images or views of others. At the extreme end of the spectrum are white perpetrators of physically violent racist acts: These whites share with other whites some common antiblack attitudes, but one distinguishing feature is their fixation on blacks. Obsessive racists may use their racial prejudices to resolve deep psychological problems. Many white supremacists seem to fit into this category. At the opposite end of the spectrum, the least obsessive racists may hold traditional antiblack prejudices simply to conform to their social environments.

Racism, as we noted earlier, encompasses more than the way whites view the black "others." It also involves the way whites view themselves as a result of participating in a culturally and structurally racist society. Prejudice, a term that ordinarily refers to negative views of others, can also apply to inflated and unrealistic views of oneself or one's own group. Prejudices and related discriminatory practices reflect an internal representation of oneself as well as of those held in contempt or hated as the "other." In the process of developing this self-definition, whites have created a set of "sincere fictions"—personal and group constructions that reproduce societal myths at the individual and group level. In these fictions whites portray themselves as "not racist," as "good people," even as they think and act in racially antagonistic ways as officiants, acolytes, or passive participants. It is common for a white person to say, "I am not a racist," often, and ironically, in conjunction with negative comments about people of color. The sincere fictions embedded in white personalities and white society are about both the black other and the white self. Long ago Frederick Douglass termed the white fictions about the black other "an old dodge," "for wherever men oppress their fellows, wherever they enslave them, they will endeavor to find the needed apology for such enslavement and oppression in the character of the people oppressed and enslaved."[45]

Among the important fictions about the white self is an internalized conception of "whiteness" that is often deep and hidden in the individual psyche. As Ruth Frankenberg found in interviews with white women, whiteness is "difficult for white people to name. . . . Those who are securely housed within its borders usually do not examine it."[46] Frankenberg also notes that the dimensions of whiteness include not only ways of thinking about the white self but also "ways of understanding history."[47]

Several historians have researched how the collective fiction of whiteness and its component image of white superiority came to be socially constructed over several centuries of U.S. development. For example, David Roediger and Theodore Allen have shown how nineteenth-century European immigrants, who initially defined themselves as Irish, German, or Italian, came over a few decades to view themselves as "white Americans."[48] Allen has provided evidence that the white ruling class response to agrarian and labor unrest among white immigrants in the eighteenth and nineteenth centuries included an increased emphasis on racial solidarity for an invented "white race." Early on, racial privileges were intentionally provided for propertyless white workers to encourage their alliance with the white elites, which had direct and indirect economic interests in the enslavement of African Americans. Particularly striking was the way in which poor Irish immigrants to the United States in the 1830–1890 period, who had been the victims of racialized oppression at the hands of the English in Ireland, became "white" and thus vigorously antiblack in their views and propensities. Among the Irish the psychological movement from a likely sympathy for the plight of black Americans to virulent white racism was intentionally fostered by employers, the press, Protestant and Catholic religious leaders, and Democratic Party organizations such as Tammany Hall.[49]

In his brilliant classic *Black Reconstruction,* W. E. B. Du Bois long ago demonstrated how white workers accepted lower than necessary monetary wages in return for a "sort of public and psychological wage. They were given deference . . . because they were white. They were admitted freely with all classes of white people to public functions, public parks, and the best schools."[50] He adds that this public and psychological wage had little effect on white workers' economic conditions but a "great effect upon their personal treatment and the deference shown them."[51] White workers have paid a heavy price for their "white selves." Since the nineteenth century, racist attitudes among white workers have prevented them from seeing clearly their own class exploitation and from organizing effectively with workers of color. As a result, they have suffered lower wages and poorer working conditions than their European counterparts, who have generally been better organized and more aware of the reality of the exploitative capitalism that is the real source of workers' economic problems. In the South and the North white workers have typically been unable to see the class interest they have in common with black workers and have therefore accepted "stunted lives for themselves and for those more oppressed than themselves."[52]

The Emotions of Racism

The social and personal construction of whiteness entails more than antiblack stereotypes and conceptions of whiteness. White racial attitudes usually involve *feelings* and *emotions* that lie near the core of the white self. Antiblack actions may have a venomous aspect, a visceral hate dimension. Joel Kovel calls this the "madness" of white racism.[53] Du Bois argued in *Dusk of Dawn* that the "color bar" is created not only by ignorance and ill will but also by more powerful motives, by "unconscious acts and irrational reactions unpierced by reason."[54] Experimental psychologist Gordon H. Bower conducted experiments on how mood-states like anger affect imaginative fantasies and social perceptions. Angry subjects tended to tell hostile stories, find fault with others, and generate angry associates. Bower found that people attend to, and learn more about, events that match their current emotional state.[55] Whites' underlying emotional states can shape and sharpen their discriminatory behavior. We do not need a special vocabulary of emotions to refer to antiblack feelings and practices; the regular vocabulary of emotions is adequate. Practices that negatively affect black Americans are carried out by whites who express a range of emotions toward their victims, from indifference to fear to anger. Adult emotions are often shaped by childhood experiences. Joan Karp has suggested that racial stereotyping and prejudice may be rooted in nonracial pain and distress experienced by whites as they grew up. People of color, and also Jewish Americans, often become socially convenient scapegoats for unreflective whites who fail to understand the true sources of their pain.[56] In a pathbreaking analysis Kovel has argued that whites reject blackness and black bodies because they project their own fears, rooted in childhood, into the dark otherness of the black person. In the socialization process, whites learn, consciously or unconsciously, that blackness symbolizes dirt, excrement, danger, ignorance, or the unknown. Antiblack impulses may be heavily shaped by the world of the unconscious.[57]

Racism in thought and practice destroys the feelings of solidarity that people normally feel toward each other. A target of discrimination is no longer seen as "one of us." The other becomes less than human, a nonperson. White racism transforms the black self, the other-outsider, into something less than the white self and reduces the black individual's humanity. Black individuals become "they" or "you people." Black men, women, and children become hated objects instead of subjects. White racism involves a massive breakdown of empathy, the human capacity to experience the feelings of members of an outgroup viewed as different. Racial hostility impedes the capacity to realize that "it could have been me."

Case Studies

The chapters that follow examine contemporary events with a racial dimension, public as well as private, in order to probe the character of white thinking and action in regard to people of color, particularly African Americans. Events classified as public are those that have attracted media and public attention: for example, the use of the image of a black man, convicted rapist William Horton, to exploit whites' fear of crime in George Bush's 1988 presidential campaign. Private events are those that have received little or no media or other public attention. They may involve actions by one white person or by a group of whites in private settings such as restaurants, hotels, and workplaces. The racial motivation of white discriminators in some of these events seems obvious; in other incidents the motivation of the white perpetrators is shrouded in subtly coded images and messages.

The absence of public attention does not make the private events of racial discrimination any less important for understanding the anger black men and women today have over persisting racism. Indeed, public racist events may begin as private events, which escalate to involve larger communities and the mass media.

The events analyzed in Chapters 2–6 demonstrate how contemporary white racism, despite its benefits for white victimizers, constitutes an entrenched system of extraordinarily wasteful individual and collective actions. The cases we have selected involve recent incidents in towns such as Olivet, Michigan, and in cities from New York to Boston to Dubuque to Portland to Los Angeles to Jasper. These narratives, most of which are broad-ranging accounts of what happened to black and white people in particular U.S. cities, typically present sequences of events. The black victims range from poor and working-class urbanites to members of the black middle class. The white perpetrators also come from all social classes. Our case studies reveal both collective action and social structures.

Narratives of events are particularly instructive because they reveal the ways in which actions create and reflect structures both in and through time: that is, the racialization of events can be viewed at one point in time or as a process over a period of time. Modern racism is very much a process, with one set of racist rituals often having an impact on the next to occur. Our narratives expose social phenomena as "temporally ordered, sequential, unfolding, and open-ended 'stories' fraught with conjunctures and contingency."[58] Most of these events could have followed a different path if certain factors were slightly or substantially different or if certain people had acted in different ways. The actions in these accounts may unfold in a linear and expected fashion or may be irregular and idiosyncratic.[59]

Chapter 7 draws on in-depth interviews conducted with well-educated white Americans in several regions of the United States to provide an exploratory and provisional examination of white thinking about racial matters. There we provide a rare look at whites' complicated ideas and feelings on racial issues and offer some interpretations. In this process we analyze important images such as criminality and violence, welfare and laziness, interracial sex and marriage, and "reverse" discrimination, and we examine the cognitive and emotional dimensions of everyday white attitudes. In Chapter 8 we examine the broader implications of our case studies and interviews for antiracist solutions to the persisting problem of white racism.

Conclusion

The mythology of white racism is, at its core, part of a rationalization of the destruction of human talents, energies, and resources. From the individual point of view, ideological racism is one way that whites legitimate the mistreatment of people of color and defend their self-conceptions as actors and observers in antiblack dramas. From the institutional point of view, racism is the social organization of the wasteful expenditure of energy aimed at sacrificing the human talent, potential, and energy of targeted racial groups such as African Americans. It is important to explore not only the character of the problem of white racism but also solutions to that problem. We noted in the opening of this chapter that a successful antiracist struggle will involve a critical examination of the many sincere fictions undergirding racist action. A dramatic change in individual, group, and societal ways of seeing requires a change in white thinking about the history and reality of racism. Many whites oppose a thoroughgoing destruction of racism because of the zero-sum idea that whites will only lose in the process. This fiction has supported much racial discrimination, but it is inaccurate and destructive. We propose a refocusing of our social vision to closely scrutinize the human propensity to waste excess energy and resources. This change will require a radical reordering of our thinking and, even more importantly, a radical restructuring of our interracial ethics and interpersonal connectedness.

Those who press for antiracist strategies are constantly confronted by criticisms that they are utopian or uninformed about human nature. Those who continue with racist discourse allege that they in contrast are armed with a more "realistic" view of the U.S. past, present, and future and assert the permanence of racial inequality. However, this continuing conservative discourse often denies the existence of racism and its savagery and denounces antiracist positions as paranoia. In such a hostile context, conceiving of, and taking, antiracist action is a challenge to institutionalized racism and is thus a constant struggle, whether in a street march or in a classroom. As we see it, antiracist strategies require an eradication of the separation of knowledge and theory from action. Antiracist strategies demand alternative ways of knowing, conceptualizing, and protesting. The challenge of developing critical knowledge to be used against racism is not just about self-actualization but is essential for those Americans who can collectively redefine themselves in antiracist terms to generate practices and actions that will transform the institutions of white racism. As the 46,000 people marching in South Carolina against the Confederate flag demonstrate, collective participation is an integral aspect of antiracist action to define not only what we Americans are but also what we strive to be.

We propose that all Americans, but especially white Americans, search for more positive and productive ways of using this society's excess energy and resources. A better utilization of resources currently being wasted by racism will improve the lives of all Americans. Much pessimism has been recently expressed about the possibility of major change in U.S. racial relations, and we understand well why this is the case. Yet we do not share this pessimism. In our lifetimes we have seen major changes in U.S. racial relations, even though many of these changes were forced on whites by civil rights protest movements. These changes have benefited not only African Americans and other people of color but also white Americans. This nation has changed in the past in the direction of greater racial equality, and *it can do so again.*

On May 2, 1992, after three centuries of white rule in South Africa, Nelson Mandela addressed a crowd celebrating the end of apartheid: "This is one of the most important moments in the life of our country. I stand here before you filled with deep pride and joy—pride in the ordinary, humble people of this country. You have shown such a calm, patient determination to claim this country as your own, and now the joy that we can loudly proclaim from the rooftops—Free at last! Free at last!"[60] In his speech Mandela made three important points. First, he notes that, working together, ordinary people can challenge and change oppressive racist regimes. Second, the antiracist ideas linked to antiracist confrontation connect ordinary people from "rooftop to rooftop," as well as leaders from Martin Luther King, Jr., in the United States to Nelson Mandela in South Africa. A third point was his call for the possibility of confronting white racism now, the call to be "free at last" in South Africa and in the United States.

White racism is one of the most difficult problems facing the United States and the most consequential for the nation's future. White racism has a devastating effect on the social and political structure of the United States. White racism has marked the last four centuries with shame and has perpetuated its oppressive legacy into the twenty-first century. The problem of the "color line" is no longer the problem of the twentieth century, as W. E. B. Du Bois once noted, but is now a burden into the twenty-first century. When will white-on-black and other racial oppression come to an end? When can we all stand on the rooftops to proclaim our humanity, our dignity, and our rights?

Racism in Practice:
Case Studies

In the mid-1990s Rutgers University's president Francis Lawrence reportedly referred to black Americans as "a disadvantaged population that does not have the genetic, hereditary background" to be able to score equally with white Americans on the Scholastic Aptitude Test, which is often used as a college admissions device.[1] When his speech was publicized, protesting black students sat down at midcourt to interrupt a Rutgers University basketball game. Their protest was joined by students at other campuses, including the University of Texas (Arlington) and Vassar College. Lawrence later retracted his statement, arguing that "the ideas that intelligence levels differ based on ethnicity and that minorities are genetically inferior are monstrously perverse, demonstrably false and completely unacceptable" and apologized "from the bottom of my heart." Lawrence argued that he could not explain his making a "remark that said precisely the opposite of my deeply held beliefs."[2] In these cases one may find what W. E. B. Du Bois called "unconscious acts and irrational reactions unpierced by reason."[3]

This chapter focuses on two significant cases of white-black interaction in the Midwest that illustrate among other things the depth, complexity, and irrationality of white racism. The first involves cross-burnings and other antiblack activity in Dubuque, Iowa—the reaction of some whites to a proposal to recruit black families to improve the diversity of the city's population. The Dubuque case illustrates our argument that white racism, including violent racist acts, can take place anywhere in the United States, even in a nearly all-white midwestern city with no history of plantation slavery or extensive legal segregation.[4] The second case study looks at antiblack attitudes and actions at a liberal arts college founded by white abolitionists in the mid-nineteenth century. This case illustrates how whites with apparently little exposure to African Americans can harbor ingrained antiblack beliefs and can act suddenly in punishing ways. We examine the role of stereotyping and rumor, the dramatic character of black student reaction to white racism, and the mass media's role in the ritual enactment of racialized events. As Kovel points out, regardless of the level of interaction between blacks and whites, and regardless of reason and educated consciousness, whites project the dark otherness to blacks, which destroys any feeling of solidarity and the capacity to achieve empathy and reflectivity.

These cases take place in two different worlds, one black and one white. A striking aspect of the contrast between these worlds is the source of each group's knowledge of the other: Black views of whites are primarily grounded in concrete everyday experience with many whites, while most whites' views of blacks come from the mass media, parents, relatives, and other traditional sources of stereotypical knowledge rather than from direct experience. Both cases show white men, women, and children living in a spatial and psychological "bubble," separated for the most part from the world of African Americans, with the mass media providing their primary window to the black world. These case studies confirm our thesis that racism is the socially organized waste of human energy, talent, and resources, and they dramatically reveal the irrationality in the "bubble."

Racism in the Farmbelt: The Dubuque Case

During the 1980s and 1990s cross-burnings in a number of U.S. communities conjured up images of a racial past that most white Americans had considered long dead, a violent past in which a powerful Ku Klux Klan left a trail of brutality directed against the nation's black citizens. Who would want to resurrect such despicable symbols and acts, and why? Do these recent events indicate that the tradition of antiblack hostility and violence never died? For the United States as a nation, the answers to these questions are very important.

The Events

Built in the 1830s on the Mississippi River, Dubuque, a city with numerous church spires and a population of about 58,000 people in 1990, has seldom been in the national spotlight. The city was chartered in 1841, when its population numbered 2,987, including 72 African Americans.[5] Today the city has a tiny black population of 331; black Dubuquers constitute less than 1 percent of the total population.[6] In recent decades several of the city's major employers have been connected to the agricultural industry. Although the region's troubled agricultural sector suffered substantial job layoffs in the early 1980s, by the early 1990s its economy had recovered. New jobs were being created in the service sector, although they were usually not equivalent in pay to the jobs lost. Still, Dubuque was weathering the national economic recession better than most cities.[7]

In 1991 some of the city's whites engaged in racist attacks on black residents. Crosses were burned, and black residents were the targets of hate messages and other verbal and physical harassment. Even though cross-burnings were not new for Dubuque,[8] the city's white leaders expressed surprise, for most did not view their city as having racial problems like those in larger cities or the South.[9]

The trigger for the unexpected antiblack explosion in Dubuque was a city council recruitment plan. In the spring of 1991 the Dubuque Human Rights Commission unanimously approved a plan proposed by the local Constructive Integration Task Force. Titled "We Want to Change," the plan was designed to attract about twenty black families annually for a total of one hundred families by the mid-1990s. The plan was in part a response to the burning in October 1989 of one local black family's garage, in which a cross and "KKK lives" graffiti were found. Perhaps reflecting the national concern about multiculturalism, the task force members felt the city should make a symbolic gesture of recruiting black families to overcome Dubuque's lack of diversity. Private employers were to execute the plan and lure black workers to jobs in the city. Initially, some city money was to be used to subsidize the newcomers' mortgages and rents, but this part of the plan was dropped after some whites protested. A modest version of the plan was submitted to the city council. One white council member, Donald Deich, voted against the plan because he reportedly saw it as benefiting only "a select minority," not those truly in need. The watered-down version of the task force plan that was passed by the city council specified private job recruitment only where job vacancies existed.[10]

Reaction to the modest city council plan came swiftly. Aggressive white responses included a dozen cross-burnings and bricks thrown through the windows of black homes. Cross-burnings also occurred in other Iowa cities, including Des Moines, Waterloo, Jefferson, and Iowa City. The meanings of the cross-burnings for white and black Dubuquers were dramatically different. The white men arrested for the Dubuque incidents saw the crosses as symbols of the white community's alarm at the job losses that the perpetrators assumed would result from the recruitment plan. However, the only black school principal in the city, who had seen a cross burned across from his predominantly white school, commented: "My dad used to often tell us about when he was a boy, how the crosses would be burned up on the hills and how they could stand out late at night and watch it, watch the Ku Klux Klan people. . . . I'm living in 1991, and I'm seeing the same thing." He added that the cross-burnings gave him the sense of being "personally violated." Another black resident explained that for African Americans the burning of crosses symbolizes exclusion and "death."[11]

In Dubuque, as in other cities, the burning crosses signaled a community's fear: white residents' fear of losing their jobs, black residents' fear for their lives. African Americans' historical experiences with the burning cross symbol explain the depth of their personal fear, but how is one to interpret the fear of whites, a fear so strong that it led them to send fellow black Dubuquers a message of death?

In addition to the smoldering crosses and racialized vandalism, hate letters and racist graffiti were directed at local black residents and white supporters of the recruitment plan. The dozen black students at overwhelmingly white Dubuque Senior High School (which had 1,471 white students) were racially harassed; police officers patrolled the halls to deter white violence. The high school principal reported that white students were thinking in zero-sum terms: They felt "their parents would lose their jobs and homes to minorities."[12]

Dubuque's racist incidents quickly became more than a local problem. Representatives of national white supremacy organizations descended on the city to exploit its interracial tensions. The long-standing agenda of these organizations includes stirring up local black-white conflict; some of their leaders even envision an open war that will polarize the entire nation into racial camps. Thom Robb of Arkansas, national director of the Knights of the Ku Klux Klan and a Christian Identity (another supremacy group) minister, held a white unity meeting in Dubuque that about two hundred whites attended. An even larger segment of the white community supported at least some white supremacy views. A white labor leader commented, "You hear people saying that the Klan sounds kind of reasonable, and that's scary." The Klan leader's rhetoric apparently had the desired effect of persuading whites who were not normally Klan supporters to adopt aggressive, "throw the blacks out" sentiments.[13] The city's mayor, James Brady, noted that in earlier years he had "heard local union members brag that they had no black people in their union and never would have them as members."[14] Although local unions were initially opposed to black recruitment, they agreed to endorse the plan after the deletion of a job-security provision that disregarded union seniority regulations.

A Mississippi attorney, Richard Barrett, leader of the neo-Nazi Nationalist Movement, also came to Dubuque to exploit tensions. The day before the national holiday on the birthday of Martin Luther King, Jr., Barrett held a public meeting that was attended by about fifty people, among whom were young white men wearing T-shirts that bore the initials NAAWP, the acronym for David Duke's National Association for the Advancement of White People. Barrett's message that "Kingism means loser take all" was a clear articulation of racial relations as a contest in which whites only lose as blacks advance. He proposed that "Kingism" be destroyed and replaced with his white "Americanism."[15] Bringing whites' half-conscious fears of African Americans into public view, the white supremacists rationalized the explosion of opposition to an increase of black residents in Dubuque as a war against black encroachment on the "white way of life."

How widespread was local support for antiblack views and actions? The evidence suggests that antiblack sentiments were fairly common. For example, the local *Telegraph Herald* carried a number of hostile and ill-informed letters opposed to the recruitment of, or even the presence of, black families.[16] The paper also ran a recurring advertisement opposing the plan. A *Des Moines Register* poll suggested that, throughout Iowa, more whites opposed the plan than supported it. Half of the Iowans responding to the poll believed the plan to be a bad idea; only a third favored it.[17] More than two thousand whites in Dubuque signed a petition against the recruitment plan circulated by a local business leader, who was quoted as saying that "to wholesale integrate this town because 'by God we're going to integrate' is not fair."[18] Code words such as *quota* have often been used by conservative political leaders, including high officials like former president George Bush (see Chapter 6), as an effective political device to generate opposition to programs for black advancement. In Dubuque local opposition to remedial programs reflected similar debates on the national scene.

A Question of Jobs?

One of the most prevalent white objections to black recruitment was phrased in terms of the threat to white jobs. This racialized thinking had a distinct social class dimension, for it was white blue-collar workers' jobs that were supposedly threatened. Major employers seemed supportive of the plan, perhaps welcoming job competition. The original plan's specific declaration that it was not a program of preferential employment but recruitment for new or unfilled positions across the entire spectrum of employment, including professional jobs, did not alleviate "the unnecessary fear of employees that they will lose their present job to people of color."[19] An unemployed firefighter complained, "I can't get a job and now I want someone else to come in and compete against me?"[20] Speaking even more forcefully, a white auto mechanic told a *New York Times* reporter that it was bad enough to have to compete with a white man for a job, then added: "But a black guy? It would mean you lost a job to someone that everybody knows is lower than you."[21] Such comments underscore an important function of white racial attitudes: Black workers often serve as a gauge of where the status floor is. Some white workers feel better, no matter how poorly they are doing, if they are doing better than black workers.

Economists often attribute attacks on black workers and their families in cities like Dubuque to severe unemployment problems.[22] Yet at the time Dubuque's employment situation was more complex than this simple explanation suggests. Large-scale layoffs by major employers in the late 1970s and early 1980s created high unemployment rates for a time. However, during the two-year period before the outbreak of antiblack hostility and cross-burnings, the Dubuque unemployment rate had dropped to 6 percent, a figure lower than that for the nation as a whole. Rather than reacting to present-day unemployment, white workers may have been concerned that they were not doing as well as they had a few years before. Most jobs lost earlier were better-paid, skilled jobs, and many laid-off workers had to leave the city or move into less-skilled service jobs. Competing for these generally lower-wage jobs and frustrated over loss of status, many whites targeted black individuals and families as scapegoats. In the United States working-class and middle-class whites often seek a racial explanation for local economic problems; they are less likely to condemn the corporate executives responsible for most capital flight and urban deindustrialization. Indeed, most white workers have yet to question seriously the capitalist system and its corporate elite. Understanding modern racism requires an understanding of this fictional black threat to jobs and how it is constructed in the white mind. Racialized images may be fictional, but their consequences are nonetheless real.

The proposed number of black families to be invited to the city was extremely small. Even if all stages of the plan had gone into effect over the projected period of several years, the total number of black individuals invited would have been some 300–400 people in 100 or so families. This influx might have brought the total number of black men, women, and children in Dubuque to 700, or about 1 black person for every 83 white inhabitants, hardly the flood envisioned by many local whites. In addition, task force supporters of the plan explicitly took the position that they wanted to draw black professionals to the city. Indeed, one recent black entrant was a badly needed medical doctor. Regardless of how widely the myth was believed, no significant job threat existed. In addition, implementation of the recruitment plan would probably have created some jobs for whites in businesses (for example, health care and real estate) serving the new residents.

Many white Americans, from presidents to average citizens, have accepted the view that race is declining in significance in the United States. A white counselor at a local high school who was a member of the task force that drafted the plan commented that some local residents she talked with wondered how there could be "a race problem when we don't even have minorities."[23] The events in Dubuque invalidated assumptions that black population concentrations or interracial interaction are necessary prerequisites for significant racist thoughts or actions. The eruption of infectious white racism in a nearly all-white heartland city with no history of extensive legal segregation confirms that this problem is neither confined to the Deep South nor a creature of the distant past.

The national context of events in Dubuque is important because the period from 1980 through the 1990s was an era of persisting white attacks on African Americans and of white insensitivity to the realities and pain of racism. During the 1980s then president Ronald Reagan spoke of "welfare queens" (a racist code meant to delegitimate the welfare system) and opposed most new civil rights laws and expanded enforcement efforts. Reagan cabinet member Terrell Bell, a moderate Republican, complained that middle-level white aides in the Reagan White House told racist jokes; referred to Dr. Martin Luther King, Jr., as "Martin Lucifer Coon"; spoke of Arabs as "sand niggers"; and called Title IX the "lesbian's bill of rights."[24] Most members of the administration, some of whom (including then Attorney General Edwin Meese) labeled Bell "Comrade Bell," had little commitment to the enforcement of civil rights laws. Dubuque's National Association for the Advancement of Colored People (NAACP) chapter president summarized the impact of the national context on Dubuque: "Reagan made it okay to hate again."[25] This trend continued when, in 1988, presidential candidate George Bush made use of a racially stereotypical series of advertisements in his campaign (see Chapter 6). After his election Bush, too, opposed an aggressive expansion of civil rights enforcement and only grudgingly signed a civil rights bill that had overwhelming congressional support.

Local White Attitudes and Beliefs

Most whites in Dubuque and in Iowa would undoubtedly support "liberty and justice for all" in the abstract. On the surface most local residents appear to support racial tolerance. Some 88 percent of the (mostly white) respondents to a Dubuque-area opinion survey were favorable to "racial and ethnic diversity"; 86 percent felt that "positive attitudes" on racial issues were important.[26] However, as opinions expressed in the statewide *Des Moines Register* poll mentioned earlier indicate, support for the implementation of racial diversity was not so strong among Iowans. Half of those who responded to the poll believed the Dubuque recruitment plan to be a bad idea.

Stereotypes about blacks, openly expressed by numerous whites in Dubuque, revealed whites' general lack of understanding of black people. The white mayor of Dubuque, James Brady, stated on an ABC television program that he knew whites who thought all successful blacks were athletes. Some local whites expressed ignorance about African Americans in letters to the newspaper.[27] Images of black people as criminals and "welfare cheats," which some whites revealed in media interviews, suggested deep fears and contributed to whites' hostile reactions to the diversification of the city. Some whites cited the negative images of black men on television and in movies. One white resident writing to the *Telegraph Herald* explained that local whites were "frightened and for a good cause. . . . We want to keep our town just like it is, a great place to raise a family, not frightened enough to stay in at night and close our windows." Another writer imagined that the plan would precipitate a flood: "Five families a year will bring in 25 more families of friends or cousins, and the latter will not be educated, housed and with jobs."[28]

For a city whose population included such a small proportion of black residents, the range of antiblack myths that surfaced seems substantial. One local rumor warned that armed gangs were coming to Dubuque from Chicago, and in the language of racism "gang" can become code for "any group of young black men."[29] Several young white Dubuque men interviewed by a *Toronto Star* reporter about their support for the white supremacist movement spoke in stereotyped terms of blacks threatening the purses of older women, of black male advances to white women, and of black vandalism. A territorial view of the United States as a *white* country that should not include people of color seemed indisputable to some, including a construction worker: "I love my country. And they're taking control of it little by little." Echoing this white nationalism, a laid-off worker said: "Every time a white person stands up for his rights, it's called racism."[30] A local white supremacist and member of the NAAWP who reportedly had a criminal record himself told a *Time* magazine reporter: "Blacks have higher crime rates, welfare rates, and birthrates. Why should we change our life-styles to give blacks preferential treatment?"[31] An older white resident complained, "They come in fast enough now. Why bring in more trouble?"[32]

Although only small numbers of whites engaged in racial violence, the behavior of other whites revealed a supportive or indifferent attitude toward such acts. Fellow workers reportedly congratulated and applauded some of the young men who burned crosses when they returned to work after short jail terms. Local judges gave relatively lenient sentences to several cross-burners. In addition, the federal Department of Justice delayed enforcing national civil rights laws there until the spring of 1992, when one young white man was finally indicted for violating the civil rights of a black Dubuque woman in a cross-burning incident. The federal government soon secured convictions of six whites in connection with the cross-burnings. Among these were William and Daniel McDermott, two local men who were reportedly activists on behalf of white supremacy causes. They were convicted of burning a cross and violating black Dubuquers' civil rights. A modest measure of justice had finally been secured for the city's black community.[33]

White Isolation

As we noted earlier, Dubuque's population and institutions are overwhelmingly white. Although never officially segregationist, Dubuque has long been known as unfriendly to new black families. In the 1940s and 1950s white police officers, using a tactic then common in certain midwestern cities, told black travelers who ventured off the train at the local station not to stay. This practice gave Dubuque a negative image among potential black immigrants in some southern communities. Then, as today, the benefits to whites of discouraging blacks from residing in the city seem to have been more ideological and psychological than material. During the 1940s and 1950s there were no more than five black families in the city, who, as one white observer put it, "all put their heads down when they were stared at."[34]

In the early 1990s, with fewer than four hundred black residents, Dubuque was one of the whitest cities in the nation. The police force and fire department were all white. Virtually no blacks held positions of power in any major institution—no black teachers, politicians, or corporate leaders, and only one black school principal. As in many cities, a majority of whites in Dubuque seem to live in an isolated bubble more or less segregated from regular contact with African Americans. Mayor Brady described the city as a place where "people can go all their lives without seeing a black person."[35] The head of the city's Human Rights Commission, a Nigerian-born newcomer, remarked that whites in Dubuque had little chance to associate with people of different cultures: "The real reason for these problems is deep down racism."[36] When Dubuque's black principal, the only black educator in the public schools, was offered a job in 1991, he was told that no white barber in the city would know how to cut his hair. The principal told *Time* magazine, "This is a white person's town. On my first day at school, a kid asked me whether I was Bill Cosby."[37]

Everyday Black Experience

Although local whites and many in the white media tended to see the recent racial violence in Dubuque as unprecedented, there were ample warning signals that some whites in the city were hostile to African Americans. The social waste that is racism had long been evident to the black citizenry. After the recent incidents, black residents began to speak about earlier harassment, cross-burnings, and other hate crimes. One black woman, who had come to Dubuque earlier, discussed an incident that occurred when her two granddaughters were walking to a store to buy ice cream. A group of white men, attempting to spit at the children, called out, "Niggers get out." She added, "You're afraid to walk in the streets because you're harassed."

Street safety is a major issue for many whites, yet street harassment faced every day by African Americans receives little attention. This grandmother went on to point out the moral dilemma that whites' antiblack propensities pose: "The ones that I have the hardest problem with are the ones that go to church every Sunday and then won't sit on the pew beside you."[38]

Black residents also talked about the recurring *pain* they experienced when whites made racial remarks in their presence with no apparent regard for their feelings. The black principal recalled some whites openly "telling nigger jokes" at a local hotel.[39] The pain engendered by racist jokes and comments can be severe and long-lasting. The local NAACP president told a *Toronto Star* reporter that her twenty-one-year-old daughter refused to reside in Dubuque and spoke of the lasting scars her thirteen-year-old son bore: "He was just a little boy. He went with his dad to take the car in for repair. . . . And a couple of mechanics came out and my boy heard one of them say, 'That's that nigger's car.'"[40]

Reactions in the Media

Because of its scale, the racism expressed in Dubuque attracted state and national media attention. A white city council member who supported the black recruitment plan worried that media coverage of the cross-burnings and white supremacy gatherings was "fanning the flame." In his view the "glare of the national press is going to encourage people to take sides and become more polarized."[41] Some outsiders were calling Dubuque the "Selma of the North," and the Des Moines Register ran a front-page headline referring to Iowa's "new racist image." Most major national newspapers and several national television programs ran stories on events in the city. National coverage was generally negative regarding cross-burnings and supremacist rallies, but it failed to explore the implications of these events for the problem of white racism in the nation.

Some reporters of the conservative press took up the side of the antiblack Dubuquers. They played down the racist incidents as the work of a few extremists, an approach that was sometimes taken in the liberal media as well. Stating that Dubuque was no more racist than the rest of the state, a *National Review* article blamed the disturbances on a numerically insignificant "fringe element" of "young bloods." The writer argued that "bigotry is hardly rampant" in the city and that Iowa's mass media had exaggerated racism in Dubuque. The writer also took liberal national newspapers to task for "tiptoeing" around the black crime issues in assessing Dubuque's racial crisis. Suggesting that one reason for white opposition to the recruitment plan was fear of increased crime, the *National Review* reporter tried to make the case that white fear was realistic by citing data on black overrepresentation in crime in other Iowa cities.[42] However, most of the crime in Iowa and in Dubuque is committed by whites, yet white newcomers were not the target of overt protests.

A City Responds to Racism

Some local whites did protest the violent expressions of racism in Dubuque. One counter rally held by whites protesting cross-burnings and the Klan rally drew hundreds of people. Girl Scouts, with the aid of some businesses, passed out thousands of black and white ribbons to local residents as a sign of commitment to better relations between racial groups in the city. Sermons in local churches accented tolerance. Billboards sponsored by whites concerned about bettering conditions asked, "Why Do We Hate?" Some whites wrote letters of apology to black victims of violent acts. Three hundred local businesses ran an ad in the local newspaper supporting the black recruitment plan. The local school system expanded multicultural education.[43]

Yet these actions seem too modest to reach to the depths of racism. Antiblack actions in Dubuque, as in other American cities, have revealed a significant breakdown in many whites' capacity to empathize with the feelings and interests of members of the black outgroup. We have found no evidence in published reports of the Dubuque incidents that whites collectively have made large-scale efforts to deal aggressively with the persistence of everyday racism since the more violent expressions of racism subsided.

Interpreting Rituals of Racism

The antiblack actions of whites are often repetitive and formalized. Burning a cross is a ceremony that needs the propitious darkness of the night, some technical knowledge, certain materials, and, in some cases, ritual costumes. Whites spitting at black children or adults and yelling "niggers, get out" are using traditional words and engaging in ritualized actions that have been performed many times before. Whites who refuse to share a pew with blacks in church, those who tell or laugh at "nigger jokes," and those who refuse service or provide service of inferior quality to black customers are engaging in the ritualized behavior of racism.

Such acts are rituals because no matter how private they appear, when enacted inside a church, a mechanic's shop, a high school corridor, or in the dark of night, they are preeminently traditional and social affairs. Such actions define socially acceptable practices and socially relevant knowledge for the community, including its youth. Whites acquire tacit understandings about black and white people and about racist attitudes and actions through these rituals.[44] The French social theorist Emile Durkheim referred to the degree to which people have a common life filled with rituals as "moral density." Yet it is clear that racist rituals are divisive as well as integrating. While such rituals may bind together whites in a celebration of a socially invented "whiteness," they alienate blacks from the common life shared by the dominant white community. In this sense, the racist rituals provide an "immoral density" ultimately destructive of the broader social fabric of a community.

Apparently the class composition of extreme white supremacist groups has varied over the course of Dubuque's history, as have the targets of racial and ethnic hostility. During the 1920s, Ku Klux Klan members came from the white working and middle classes and also from the business community. The Klan's targets then were usually

Catholic Americans, especially German Catholics. In recent years the majority of Dubuque's extreme white supremacists have been drawn from the white working class.[45] Prejudiced individuals in the business and middle-class segments of the white community who expressed opposition to the black recruitment plan appear to have chosen less extreme acts, such as circulating or signing a petition.

Most of the active participants in Dubuque's racial crisis were white men. Those yelling "nigger" and those lighting up the crosses functioned as "officiants" in the rites, but active officiants require, indeed even recruit, a large number of acolytes and passive participants. Those who sign petitions or who passively observe aggressive racist acts without protest are as much a part of the racialized rituals as those who officiate.

These rituals can have a significant impact on a community's children. Only a few of Dubuque's white children and teenagers officiated in the cross-burnings or engaged in overt racial harassment at school. Yet regardless of the degree of their disapproval of the racist actions or their empathy with the victims, most white youth, like most of their elders, did not speak out. Such passivity is a first step in learning to ally oneself with white victimizers against black victims. Remaining passive during one incident may make it harder to actively oppose racism in the future.

Across the United States millions of whites become passive participants in white racism as they witness antiblack violence by way of the media. They have been socialized to remain more or less impassive in the face of police and Klan abuse of these black "others." The fact that antiblack violence seldom provokes an eruption of white citizen solidarity to eradicate such actions is evidence of the national proportions of the breakdown in human empathy across the arbitrary color line.

As we have noted previously, the process of denying humanity to a person of color betrays the moral principles of equality and justice on which this nation is theoretically founded. Making African Americans habitual objects of white abuse is a brutal dissipation of human talent and energy. Such abuse modifies the moral status of the person who accomplishes it: The discriminator is affected by the discrimination.[46]

Those who exclude and segregate, torture, burn crosses, and otherwise intimidate or deny legitimate rewards to fellow human beings may realize some material or psychological benefits. They may feel racially superior. But they assume a position directly counter to the American ideology of "liberty and justice for all." That position is tolerated, even privileged, by the complementary role played by passive white participants.

White observers may be tempted to view violent racist acts as the work of marginal elements. This common response allows many white individuals to distance themselves from societal racism. However, the ritual character of recurring antiblack acts indicates that they have become a traditional part of white communities and of the larger white society. Individuals who engage in cross-burning, one of the most painful and threatening of all white actions to black citizens, can remain *in good standing* at their workplaces, in their churches, and in their families. The American Civil Liberties Union (ACLU) has defended as legitimate speech the right to engage in some cross-burnings; the U.S. Supreme Court has ruled that such acts are protected by the First Amendment. The court granted impunity to one white teenager, who had burned a cross on a black family's lawn, by knocking down a St. Paul, Minnesota, law banning such hate crimes.[47]

Fear has been cited as a driving force behind racist violence like that in Dubuque. Who or what did many whites fear? The objects of this white fear appear to be stereotyped images and the unknown. White workers tend to direct their anxiety over personal or social problems, such as unemployment, recession, or crime, toward society's subordinate racial or ethnic groups; far less often they focus their concern on the actual sources of their discomfort. Some studies, for example, have found that many white workers who are laid off because of plant closings believe that their employers could not make a profit primarily because the latter were required to hire workers of color, and thus these white workers blame the job losses on blacks, Asians, or Latinos. Yet there is usually no empirical evidence for this white notion.[48]

By definition capitalism is a system of great inequality. Ordinary workers have less power, receive less income, and own less wealth than do managers and employers. Conceivably, Americans could defend this class inequality by arguing that "people who receive higher rewards deserve them by virtue of their noble birth."[49] Yet most do not. Americans tend to believe that class position is based on merit. Similarly, whites could attribute their more privileged position vis-à-vis blacks to the fact that they were born white. However, most white Americans do not accept this explanation for racial inequality. Instead, whites have developed defenses of inequality that hide stark racial realities behind a language of "equal opportunity": "Since blacks already have equal opportunity, their lack of prosperity relative to whites is the result of poor values or a weak cultural heritage." Whites who hold such a view tend to believe that black Americans are much less hardworking, more inclined to welfare, and more likely to be criminal or violent than are whites. These white rationalizations of privilege provide, Immanuel Wallerstein has suggested, "the only acceptable legitimation of the reality of large-scale collective inequalities."[50]

Still, white workers have much to gain from a recognition that their racial fictions and rationalizations blind them to the economic realities of social class. White workers' anger against African, Latino, or Asian Americans might better be directed against the powerful *white* actors and institutions directly responsible for their troubling economic conditions. White workers who blame or attack subordinate Americans of color as scapegoats for these conditions either do not understand how modern capitalism works or do not know how to protest capitalist-led restructuring and deindustrialization. The white economic elites who are usually responsible for capital and job flight are seldom critically analyzed in mainstream media or scholarly analyses of economic changes. U.S. workers have no widely available conceptual framework, such as the class analysis found in Europe's socialist media, to explain the restructuring and other vagaries of U.S. capitalism. In contrast, the racist ideology is readily available for white workers to use in explaining their economic and social problems. Indeed, as we noted in Chapter 1, the corporate elite has on occasion encouraged suffering white workers to adopt antiblack interpretations of such problems. The psychological comfort that white workers experience because some black workers are lower on the ladder may be real, but it serves employer interests by keeping the workforce divided—thereby weakening union activity and keeping wages down for all workers.

Progressive change in Dubuque is not synonymous with losses for whites. On the contrary, lifting the heavy curtain of racism would empower whites as well as blacks. Whites could use the time, energy, and resources they now waste on racist actions and emotions to confront their economic and political problems. The price that whites of all classes pay for racist attitudes and incidents has rarely received comment or analysis. Many whites in Dubuque expended great energy debating the modest recruitment plan. Political, court, and police officials spent energy and resources dealing with the racial upheaval. Those who burned crosses or yelled "nigger" might have had a cathartic experience, but what might they have achieved had they devoted the same time and energy to self- or societal improvement? What would the lives of all citizens in Dubuque be like if there were less racial fear and hatred?

How have Dubuque's racial problems affected the city's future? Will industry seek this pristine white town? Will local companies want to risk a boycott of products by blacks and sympathetic whites? Indeed, one meatpacking executive told *Newsweek* reporters that some shoppers in other cities had already boycotted products labeled "Dubuque." Concern over the city's negative image and the implications of that image for the business climate has influenced Dubuque businesspeople to create a new Council for Diversity, although some local observers have viewed this Council as an attempt to displace the original Constructive Integration Task Force plan just as it was about to be implemented. Significantly, the new council's goals do not include racial "integration."[51]

Events like those in Dubuque may seem ephemeral: a few months of burning crosses, some street demonstrations, a petition drive, several heated city council meetings, and modest attempts at multiculturalism in the schools. After a few months the dramatic events passed, and the media moved on to other stories. But Dubuque's black community still has great cause for concern about racist thought and action. In 1993, more than a year after the last cross-burnings, black Dubuquers held a demonstration at the county courthouse protesting white police harassment and brutality. The demonstrators were also distressed that the police department still had no officers of color.[52] The burden of white racism for black Dubuquers is still heavy in all arenas of their daily lives. Each racist act moves the city—and this nation—backward and makes clear how much remains to be done on America's equality agenda.

The Olivet College Case

Our second case takes us to another unlikely place for racial conflict, the town of Olivet in the industrial state of Michigan. Olivet is home to only 1,604 people, very few of whom are black. The location of the racial incidents we recount in this section is an institution of higher education: Olivet College, which was founded by a white abolitionist, John Shipherd, in the mid-nineteenth century and began its history with a very liberal racial image. Unfortunately, antiblack incidents have become common at historically white colleges since the early 1980s. There is something tragic and ironic about outbursts of overt racism in such places because antiblack actions are commonly attributed to thoughtless bigotry and ignorance, traits that higher education is meant to eradicate. The media image of the white racist is usually not that of a well-educated person but rather of a poorly educated person. Indeed, such stereotyping makes it easier for better-educated whites to distance themselves from the reality of everyday racism. The Olivet case demonstrates that it is quite possible for whites in places of higher education to engage in racial thought and racist action.

Spring is normally a quiet time in Olivet, which is located among Michigan's cornfields. In the spring of 1992 the college of seven hundred had approximately fifty-five black students. Racial trouble apparently began brewing when some white male students openly objected to black male students dating white women. Then, on the first day of

April 1992, a white female reported that she had been assaulted by several black students. A police investigation produced no arrest warrants because police and college officials reportedly questioned her story. Nonetheless, the account of the alleged assault circulated around the campus, and that evening some trash cans were torched, presumably by white students, near black student leaders' dormitory rooms. Soon a series of racial incidents erupted, including a fight between approximately thirty or forty white and ten to twenty black students.[53]

The Main Events

One major incident, which took place after the torching of the trash cans, involved a white female student and three black students. Somewhat different versions of the incident have been reported in the news media, but the essential facts seem to be these: A white female reported that she was sitting in a dorm room with a white male friend of her (white) boyfriend. Four other students, three of whom were black, came to her door to discuss various matters. One of the black students had come to ask about a paper the white woman was typing for him. The white student at the door, a friend of the woman's boyfriend, asked her about the white man already in the room. After some discussion about the typing commitment, the black students departed.[54]

Later, according to press accounts, the female student, very upset, telephoned her friends to report receiving a threatening phone call. White fraternity members who were present when she called also talked on the phone with her about the threatening call and her fears. According to one of the fraternity men, she claimed the black students were responsible for the phone threats. A dozen or so of the white fraternity men went to the dormitory where they confronted two of the black students who had come to the woman's room earlier. The white students directed racial epithets at the black students, according to the report of a black student leader. The black students responded with some insults. More people gathered, someone threw a punch, and an interracial fight ensued.[55] Two of those present were injured seriously enough to need medical attention. As one injured black student was helped away, some whites reportedly yelled, "Run, niggers, run."[56]

Over the next few days many black students became worried that they might be attacked on the campus. Some white students and anonymous callers reportedly directed more verbal taunts and threats at the black students, and some whites, probably outsiders, distributed Ku Klux Klan material on campus.[57] (Some nearby towns are said to have active Klan groups.) Rumors spread that outsiders were coming to the campus to make trouble. Reportedly, many white and black students who were roommates or had studied together ceased speaking to each other.[58] Most black students left the campus not long after the dormitory fight, before the end of the spring term. Two weeks after the incidents *only four* of the fifty-five black students remained on campus.[59]

Several days after the fight in the dormitory, the departure of a few white and most black students forced Olivet's president to cancel classes for two days—in effect a long weekend—for students to "cool off." The president offered students the option of completing their course work from home. A number of black students and their parents came to the president's office to complain about his slow response to the incidents, in particular that he had not moved quickly enough to improve campus security for the black students.[60] New security guards soon patrolled the campus. The administration brought in conflict resolution experts to talk with students, and the president announced the hiring of the first black faculty member. Two students, one white and one black, were suspended for participation in the dormitory fight; another white student was put on probation and banned from campus activities for his actions.[61]

Racial incidents on predominantly white college campuses reflect the failure of white administrators and faculty to effectively counter antiblack attitudes and practices over a long period of time. Olivet's administrators were apparently no different from most. According to some reports, for several years the college's administration had ignored alumni and student warnings that black students were upset about campus conditions. One alumni spokesperson quoted in the *Chicago Tribune* said, "I told them . . . you all are very behind in every issue surrounding minority students. I warned them, if this continues you will lose all your black students." She added that she had laughed when she heard the Olivet president claim he did not know the black students were unhappy. The college's whiteness was obvious in a number of areas. At the time of the incidents the college had no black professors or administrators; only 1 of the 130 employees was black— the minority recruitment officer. In this regard Olivet College was no different from many other mostly white colleges across the nation. Ironically, before the dorm incident the college had established a core curriculum, to be implemented the *next* school year, that required all students to study multicultural issues.[62]

Black Student Experiences

Some of Olivet's black students commented publicly on their negative experiences. One black student who was present at the fight reported hearing comments such as, "We're sick of these niggers. We're going to get them." When he entered the dorm during the fight, he said white female students grabbed him, saying, "Nigger, you better not touch my boyfriend."[63] He added that he had heard these comments even at the edge of the white crowd. The same student also commented: "Many students you thought were your friends, roommates, teammates [were] calling you all types of names—coon, spearchucker, nigger. . . . Were the first three years a facade, a fake, and finally everybody showed how they really felt?"[64] Other black students spoke of receiving death threats. One reported some whites told him, "Nigger, you're dead! Nigger, meet us in the town square. We're burning crosses tonight."[65] The experiences of Olivet's black students are reminiscent of the antiblack hostility exhibited by some whites in Dubuque.

Reflecting on the various events, a black student leader commented: "Right now we're in the midst of a civil war on this campus. . . . I feel as though I have to make a stand here."[66] One of the black students who remained at the college following the incidents commented on the name-calling and on feeling unwanted: "None of us feel we can trust white people anymore."[67] A student who returned home told a reporter, "I think the blacks you see here are the last you will see here in a long while."[68] A parent of one black student even described the campus climate as "Mississippi in the 1950s."[69] This comment parallels one heard following Dubuque's cross-burnings—that the city was the "Selma of the North." Clearly, the problems of white racism are not limited to one region of the United States. In recent decades openly racist attacks on African Americans have been reported at least as often in the North and West as in the South.

White Student Interpretations

When National Public Radio contacted a white fraternity at Olivet about the incident, no one would speak on the record, but one member did wonder out loud why blacks would want to come to Olivet since, as he saw it, most were from Detroit and did not fit into this heavily white community.[70] This view of the racial identity of places is fundamental to white racism in the nation at large. As we saw in Dubuque and will see again in later chapters, the racial geography of place is deeply embedded in the consciousness and self-conceptions of many whites and blacks. Indeed, this is one reason black men walking or jogging in historically white residential areas often face harassment by local police, who view them as out of place there, even though they are residents.

When interviewed, some white fraternity members denied that they were the cause of the racial problem on campus. The president of one fraternity said the racist epithets had come from other whites in the crowd that gathered during the fight. Speaking on ABC News, he said: "I don't know of anybody here that's ever used, quote-unquote, the word *nigger*, coming from anybody in this house."[71] This may have been the case, but it is difficult to believe in light of the epithets expressed openly at Olivet and in interviews that we and our students conducted with white students on predominantly white college campuses (see Chapter 7). The same student later argued that the black students in the dorm struggle had yelled back slurs such as "honky." He also defended his own racial tolerance, noting that he had gotten mail from whites off campus calling him a "nigger lover" because he had made conciliatory comments to the media. He told a *Washington Post* reporter that he was "appalled at the U.S. for the overall ignorance" about race and disturbed about racial hatred. He added: "I didn't see it on this campus, but it's there."[72] It is curious that a campus leader did not "see" the racial hostility at his college. Such ignorance suggests how oblivious whites can be to the racism around them and how little whites reflect on the racism that is embedded in everyday life.

Olivet's racial conflict broke many interracial relationships and friendships. One white fraternity member at the fight commented about a black woman who had been his friend; he added, "We would high-five each other and study for tests. . . . I don't know whether she's hating me or what."[73] Some white students feared that outsiders were using the campus to promote the ends of white supremacy. One white fraternity member told a *Chicago Tribune* reporter, "I went home a few days myself. I was scared when I heard the KKK was coming on campus." He added that he felt the black protests would eventually benefit the college because they revealed the presence of a racial problem on campus.[74]

Mixing Whites with Blacks in a Rural Setting

Olivet College mixes white students, most of whom are from rural and suburban Michigan and have had little contact with blacks, with a small group of black students, many of whom are from the city of Detroit. Olivet's white students knew little about the black civil rights struggle. Most had no prior experience with black protests. Some clearly recognized their insensitivity and isolation. One white student reflected on the fact that her cohort of white students had never faced a racial conflict like this: "I didn't know what to say to the blacks I know."[75] Like the fraternity president quoted earlier, this young woman indicated in her newspaper interview that she was not sensitive to racism on campus until it exploded in major public events.

The town of Olivet is more white than the college and is more congenial for white than black students. Some white storeowners and other residents expressed disbelief that racial conflict could take place at the college. Some reacted negatively to the black students who left town because they felt threatened by white extremists. Laughing, one white storekeeper said the black concerns were groundless: "You tell me it's safer in Detroit than it is in Olivet!"[76] Town officials were interviewed by a number of reporters about the presence of the Klan or other hate groups in the area. Even though Klan groups are said to be active in nearby areas, townspeople denied that any existed in Olivet.[77]

The Mass Media

Olivet's racial conflict received national media attention, thereby providing numerous passive observers for the racialized events. At one point both the Federal Bureau of Investigation (FBI) and the Michigan Department of Civil Rights were said to be looking into the campus situation. Olivet town officials set up their own public relations committee to deal with the town's increasingly negative image. White students at Olivet complained that they wished the reporters would leave so that campus life could resume its usual pace. One student told a United Press International (UPI) reporter, "People like you just keep on showing. It should have died down by now. Most of the troublemakers who caused it have left."[78] This white student apparently was referring to the black students who had left. The idea of black "troublemakers" stirring up racial conflict is an old one in this society. During the civil rights crises in the South in the 1950s and 1960s, diehard segregationists regularly blamed their troubles on "outside agitators." For decades the mayors of cities across the nation have made similar statements about the causes of riots in their cities.[79] The focus on outside agitators is a way of deflecting blame from the white attitudes and actions at the heart of much racial conflict.

Some public interpreters played down the racism in the Olivet College events. Like the *National Review* journalist cited in the case of Dubuque, a white columnist for the *Washington Times* commented to the Cable News Network (CNN): "I think that we shouldn't make too much of this particular, this instance. . . . It was just an angry situation that flared into being called a racial incident." He added that describing the events as racist is unfair because racism was not "at the root of it at all."[80] Other media interpretations used the notion that everyone was equally at fault for living in separate worlds. Tom Foreman, an ABC News reporter, commented that in the view of some critics the events at Olivet College showed that simply mixing black and white students "does not overcome prejudice built up in many years of living apart."[81] Such comments remove blame from the central problem of institutionalized white racism. In the case of public racial conflict many whites appear to have a strong need to look for explanations other than white thought, actions, and institutions.

The international mass media paid attention to Olivet. In Great Britain a writer for *The Economist* commented: "The site was not the deep South, nor the city ghettos of the north; it was Olivet, a town in the cornfields of southern Michigan. There, on the campus of a small and previously tolerant college, blacks and whites turned on each other." The news report continued with the argument that interracial conflicts like those at Olivet are "rare; but they serve to show how racial fears still lurk near the surface of American life, occasionally flaring up, and stubbornly refuse to go away. . . . Yet the precise nature of the 'race question,' and how it may be addressed, remains as vague as ever."[82] This international commentary echoed the U.S. media's view of the events at Olivet as rare or occasional episodes and asserted the alleged difficulty of understanding the U.S. racial problem. Yet the "race question" at Olivet is clearly rooted in racist attitudes and actions that were obvious to the black students, if not to the white students and administrators. Emphasizing the difficulty of understanding racial problems and conflicts is a convenient way for whites to evade responsibility for eradicating racism.

Interpreting the Events

The outbreak of racist action at Olivet was not unusual. Many colleges and universities in the United States have experienced similar incidents. In 1992 the Michigan Department of Civil Rights investigated a racially motivated fight at the University of Detroit and the distribution of racist hate literature at Hope College.[83] A day after the interracial fight at Olivet, a brawl broke out between black and white students at Valparaiso University in Indiana.[84] Shortly after that, Harvard Law School students conducted a sit-in to protest the absence of blacks and women from the faculty. For a brief time Olivet College had become part of the national media discussion on racial matters, and events there may have stimulated or legitimated similar antiblack incidents on other college campuses.

One issue of the *Chronicle of Higher Education* devoted the front page of its "Students" section to an article on antiracist protests at several college campuses. The report rambled through a series of explanations for unrest that was viewed as surprising in light of college efforts to create multicultural curricula. The writer suggested that the cause of the unrest was "rising expectations" among minority college students. Other explanations were offered: the movie *Malcolm X,* the state of the economy, and the election of Bill Clinton, who had "fired students up."[85] Significantly, white racism was not mentioned as a possible cause of the protests. Multiculturalism in college curricula and college cultures has usually come in doses too small and too late to substantially reduce racist barriers and thus to prevent protests by black students against conditions at the nation's historically white colleges and universities.

Black journalists usually have had no difficulty understanding the causes of the "race problem." Olivet College is, as Isabel Wilkerson of the *New York Times* explained, "a kind of everycampus," and the conflict there is "a painful rebuke of the country's early and naive assumptions about solving the matter of race."[86] Wilkerson, a Pulitzer prize winner, stressed that the Olivet case shows that merely mixing students is desegregation but not integration. The remedial steps taken by white political and educational officials in response to historical racism have mostly involved a mingling of black and white bodies. Black students are brought into white institutions without significant efforts to change the racist attitudes of whites or the white-dominated culture of the colleges and universities.

At Olivet College, as in Dubuque, Iowa, bigoted whites engaged in racial rituals. When white students yell "nigger," they use traditional sacramental words from racist rites that have been repeated across the nation. This name-calling entails more than the hurling of a few hostile words; for many whites, the epithet "nigger" conjures up fearful or comic images of dehumanized black Americans. For most African Americans, in contrast, the epithet likely conjures up images of antiblack discrimination and violence. White students who engaged in harassment by phone or in person or who broke off friendships because of race participated in the routinized behavior of modern racism. Racial rituals, whether acted out in private or public, are first and foremost social events because they reflect the socially derived knowledge and understandings linked to the historical practice of racism. We noted earlier the tendency for many whites to view blatant or violent racism as carried out by marginal elements of the white community. The main problem for black students at Olivet, however, came from other white students, from what some would view as the "best and brightest" of the nation's white youth.

White bystanders at Olivet—those administrators, teachers, and students who did little to eradicate campus racism before, during, or immediately after the events of the spring of 1992 or who passively watched as active officiants of the racist rituals yelled "nigger" or engaged in other racial harassment—were participants even though they did not engage in direct victimization. Millions of whites witnessing Olivet's events through the mass media also passively took the normative position that antiblack actions should be more or less tolerated. As we noted in the Dubuque case, this response, or lack of response, is a measure of the breakdown in human empathy across racial lines. The acquiescence of passive participants is essential for the perpetuation of white racism on both the local and societal levels. The black students were not the only victims of racism on the Olivet campus. Most whites paid a price for the antiblack events. Some wasted energy and time in racist actions. Others wasted energy and time dealing with the impact of those actions. By seeing black students as very different, by denying them their humanity, these whites denied themselves the same humanity.

Because of the events in the spring of 1992, Olivet expanded its efforts to recruit new administrators. In the fall of that year, Gretchen Kreuter, a historian, became the interim president of the college and announced her commitment to making the college a place where multiculturalism really works. Multicultural courses were added to the curriculum. Kreuter also supported expanded security and more facilities for black students. In a speech to students she signaled a strong new commitment to equality and cultural diversity.[87] But racial tensions at Olivet have persisted. In April 1993 a contested referee's call at a campus basketball game triggered a new outbreak of racial rumors that spread across the campus. In summer 1993, the college's new president, Michael S. Bassis, former provost at Antioch College, took office. He announced that he would "reinvent" Olivet College by forcing the campus community to confront the basic question that confronts all U.S. institutions of higher learning: "How do you best prepare students to live in a radically changing world?" During Bassis's tenure—he left in 1998—the school's population of students of color doubled to 34 percent of its current 934 students. Moreover, in December of 1999, Frederico Talley became the first black president of Olivet College. Under his leadership, the college has adopted a plan requiring students to engage in community services, take diversity classes, and keep portfolios of their community experiences in order to earn their college degrees. By the early twenty-first century the college seemed to be moving back toward its antiracist roots.[88]

Conclusion

The Dubuque and Olivet cases reveal racism in places that had no history of legal segregation. What then reinforces "unconscious acts and irrational reactions unpierced by reason" that reveal the irrationality of white racism?[89] Some liberal whites in both places felt that the community would benefit from diversity. The city of Dubuque announced plans to shed its lily-white image with a modest plan. Olivet College was beginning to educate its students for life in a multicultural society. In both settings the outbreak of virulent racism was surprising to many white observers inside and outside the towns. Yet the outbreaks could have been predicted if whites had not ignored early warning signals.

In both places the white perpetrators of racism carried out their acts with impunity or minimal punishment. Racist acts—the cross-burnings, racist epithets, and distribution of hate literature—may not have been common in these places until the recent events, but such acts have a long history as the tools and weapons of racist victimization in the United States. In both places the number of actual perpetrators was small compared with the much larger number of passive white observers. The racist actions in the two cases were not restricted to a fringe white supremacy element. In Dubuque the most extreme actions, such as cross-burnings, were carried out by a few individuals, some of whom served modest jail sentences. But the black recruitment plan provoked a variety of negative reactions, including signing petitions and articulating antiblack images, from numerous whites in various social classes.

Racist incidents raise basic moral issues by bringing into question the American equality creed. Even the mass media, for a brief time, paid some attention to the morality of the events. The moral status of the places and many of their inhabitants was discussed publicly during and after the incidents, in part because the unjust victimization of blacks took place with the acquiescence of a large number of whites. It is also important to note that in both places some perpetrators of overt racism were apparently reintegrated into their community as citizens in good standing. The suffering inflicted on the black individuals and families was as wasteful as it was useless. It could not have advanced the personal fortunes of those whites who inflicted it or those who tolerated it. Moreover, the considerable time and energy expended by white discriminators and bystanders in Dubuque and Olivet certainly did not advance the long-term interests of U.S. society.

In addition, the Olivet case shows how pervasive and serious the problem of white racism is. A college education does not necessarily liberate students from racist attitudes and actions; well-educated whites can be as racist as those who are poorly educated. Drawing on several sources, we estimate that about *half* the leaders of major white supremacy organizations in the United States have a college education. One prominent white leader has a Ph.D. in physics from the University of Colorado and was for a time a professor at a university in Oregon. In the mid-1990s he was head of the National Alliance, which disseminates huge amounts of racist literature. Clearly, over the last few decades the operative desegregation and multicultural strategies in higher education have not touched the depths of white racism. Simply mixing young black and white Americans together has not been a sufficient solution, and the routine operation of higher education has not created many antiracist white Americans.

In a famous 1966 speech civil rights leader Stokely Carmichael (Kwame Ture) said that in this society, "if one was black, one was automatically inferior, inhuman, and therefore fit for slavery. . . . We are oppressed because we are black, and in order to get out of that oppression, one must feel the group power that one has. Not the individual power which this country then sets [as] the criteria under which a man may come into it. That is what is called in this country as integration. You do what I tell you to do and then we will let you sit at the table with us."[90]

The challenge today in educational and other U.S. institutions remains the same as in 1966: How can we sit at the American table as equals? As we see it, this equality cannot depend on one group inviting another group to sit at "its" table. The decision to sit at the table together should be generated out of real interracial cooperation and coalition. Both blacks and whites would then feel that they have power and that unification adds to the power of black and white people. This cooperation and coalition can be extended to all Americans, not just to blacks and whites. Moreover, this cooperation is only possible when all groups face the reality of white racism and engage in communication about antiracist strategies. Successful coalitions against racism, as we will see in the last chapter, require a meeting of the minds. Carmichael argued that integrating and co-opting individuals one-way into existing institutions will ultimately result in making them less powerful, as long as there is the foundational reality of institutional racism. He also argued that "building a relationship based on humanity, when the country is the way it is," is impossible. Changing the foundation can begin with interracial coalitions, as was just starting to be tried in Dubuque.

3

Ghosts of Segregation: Discrimination in Restaurants

On February 1, 1960, four African American college students sat down at a Woolworth lunch counter in Greensboro, North Carolina. Although black patrons could purchase items in other areas of the store, they were not served at the food counter. In a later interview one white employee said that she would have served the black students, but her managers would not allow her to do so. The next day, as word got around, more than two dozen black students occupied the counter, doing schoolwork when they were refused service. As their numbers grew over the next few days, a few whites joined the students, but most whites heckled them. Whites across the nation verbally assaulted the student demonstrators for transgressing the color line. The protest spread to the rest of Greensboro's lunch counters, all of which were quickly closed. The spontaneous actions of these black students protesting racial discrimination in public accommodations marked the beginning of the modern sit-in movement.[1]

The Reverend Martin Luther King, Jr., told the black student leaders "not to forget that the struggle was justice versus injustice, not black versus white."[2] The efforts of black customers to be treated fairly in white-owned restaurants are but one example in the long history of African Americans' struggle to overcome injustice. The sit-ins were not just about gaining access to food counters. The rituals of racism at lunch counters or family restaurants, as well as in other public accommodations, proclaim a message of exclusion from the national society that few other acts of discrimination can deliver with as much force. For black Americans today, encounters with discrimination in public accommodations summon up this collective memory of past degradation. For black and white Americans, discrimination of this type is yet another marker of the racialized geography of American towns and cities.

Eating out is often a meaningful social event and is a frequent activity for many families. The restaurant industry is one with which many Americans, white and black, have repeated contact. Yet even though African Americans spend a quarter of their food budgets eating away from home, some segments of the restaurant industry, including some "family restaurants," still discriminate against black customers.

The idea of the family-restaurant chain originated in the United States and then spread around the globe. Conrad P. Kottack has noted the behavioral uniformity one finds at such restaurants: People "know how to behave, what to expect, what they will eat, and what they will pay."[3] The racial uniformity imposed by whites at public eating places like lunch counters, the forerunners of fast-food and family restaurants, was obvious during the days of legal segregation. It was not by chance that these public eating places were selected by civil rights activists in the 1960s as major targets for desegregation. This chapter examines the continuing reports of racial discrimination in America's family restaurants, first in employment and then against black customers.

Discrimination in Employment

The restaurant industry is the largest employer of service workers, white and black, in the United States. This institutional arena is filled with opportunities for whites with racist inclinations to victimize blacks. In some cases it is white customers who create problems for black employees, but most publicized complaints in recent years have been against management. Restaurants across the nation have been charged with discrimination against black employees.

Although black workers make up one-tenth of all those employed in the United States, they constitute 13 percent of those in food service jobs. Sixteen percent of kitchen workers and 19 percent of cooks are black, compared with only 5 percent of waiters and waitresses and less than 3 percent of bartenders. Black workers are more likely to be in the back of a restaurant than in the front. The food service industry hires more black employees than all other major industries, but few are to be found in the ranks of the industry's management or as owners of franchises.[4] In the District of Columbia in 1993 the lack of black workers in customer contact jobs precipitated organized protests that brought increased opportunities for black workers. The district's 1,500 restaurants employed 30,000 workers, but a 1993 survey found that many of the district's best restaurants employed no black servers or bartenders. Black workers were buspersons or kitchen workers. As a result of the protests, numerous restaurants improved the representation of workers of color in their better-paying jobs.[5]

Few black entrepreneurs have been able to secure franchises in major family-restaurant chains. Black entrepreneurs have also had difficulty obtaining bank loans to start restaurants, either on their own or as part of a franchise arrangement. One black businessperson in Los Angeles recently noted that when a black person deals with banks, "a definite barrier [is] set up." In 1992 this man started a Denny's franchise in Watts, a black community in Los Angeles. Until then, no one had succeeded in obtaining money for a new full-service restaurant in the area since the major 1965 Watts riot. In the early 1990s this was the only Denny's owned by an African American.[6]

Shoney's, Inc., and Charges of Employment Discrimination

Headquartered in Nashville, Tennessee, the Shoney's family restaurant chain is one of the largest in the United States. In 1993 it included 1,800 restaurants (under several names) with 30,000 employees in thirty-six states. During the 1980s a number of individual lawsuits were filed against Shoney's charging employment discrimination, and the federal Equal Employment Opportunity Commission (EEOC) reportedly received hundreds of discrimination complaints involving the firm's hiring practices. In 1989 the chain's national image was damaged when a number of black job applicants along with black employees and former employees, with the aid of NAACP Legal Defense Fund attorneys, filed a class-action job discrimination suit against the company. This case involved the largest number of employees and employment locations of any class-action suit in the history of such workplace litigation.[7]

The suit charged that Shoney's had "turned away black applicants and relegated the few it hired to kitchen chores."[8] Black employees stated that they were assigned the least desirable hours. Some white supervisors reported that they were fired or threatened with demotion if they refused to obey instructions to restrict black employment in the company. A former assistant manager reported that she was told to darken the "O" in the Shoney's logo on job application forms to indicate that an applicant was black.[9]

According to some reports antiblack attitudes and policies had been common in the company from its beginning. Depositions from job applicants, employees, and managers at all levels of the company implicated numerous restaurant managers, supervisors, and executives in discrimination in hiring, firing, and promotions. A number of executives have described the racial views of Raymond L. Danner, Shoney's cofounder and chair of its board. Former chief executive officer (CEO) Dave Wachtel said Danner's negative views of African Americans were widely known and that Danner had even said that he would match donations by his executives to the Ku Klux Klan.[10] A former personnel director stated, "Danner would say that no one would want to eat at a restaurant where 'a bunch of niggers' were working." A vice president said that Danner believed that "Blacks were not qualified to run a store" and that "Blacks should not be employed in any position where they would be seen by customers."[11] Danner was also charged with instructing his managers to fire black employees when they became too numerous and with using racial slurs when talking about his black employees.[12] During lawsuit depositions, Danner himself admitted to having used the "nigger" epithet and also that he had discussed one store's "possible problem area" being the presence of "too many black employees" relative to the "racial mix" in the store's geographical area.[13] In an important investigative report in *The Nation* Steve Watkins noted that Danner had once put into a letter his personal concern over too many black workers at one of his southern restaurants.[14]

These reported views of blacks were not just those of the company's founder. Watkins also reported that the views of some restaurant managers at Shoney's reflected the perspective attributed to Danner. Among the numerous racist code words reportedly used by some managers were "Arnold Schwarzenigger" for a muscular black man, "re-nigging" for rehiring blacks in a restaurant, and "nigger stores" for those in black communities.[15] It seems likely that the opinions attributed to Danner and some of his associates are not unique. The view that white customers dislike black servers, or at least too many black servers, has been found among other whites in the restaurant industry. Black cooks in the kitchen may be acceptable, but blacks in customer contact positions sometimes are not.[16]

Prior to the class-action suit, less than 2 percent of the managerial and supervisory positions were filled by black employees. Only one of the sixty-eight division directors, and not one of the top executives, was black. The majority of black employees were in positions that did not involve regular contact with customers.[17] The chain's position that the restaurants needed only a small number of black workers, even in the low-wage positions, brings to mind Sidney Willhelm's argument that much black labor is no longer needed by a U.S. economy that is restructuring to take advantage of low-wage immigrants and workers overseas (see Chapter 1).

Henry and Billie Elliott, the white supervisors of a Captain D's restaurant in Florida, part of the Shoney's chain, said that they were dismissed for refusing to terminate black workers and put whites in their place. The Elliotts filed suit to recover lost wages. They and their attorney, Tommy Warren, compiled two hundred boxes of company records that reportedly reveal racial discrimination in the Shoney's empire. Eventually the Elliotts, who had taken jobs driving school buses, won their private legal struggle and received a substantial monetary settlement.[18] The Elliotts' experience signals a very important aspect of contemporary racial relations—that whites too can be victims if they stand against what they feel to be unfair racial discrimination.

Lawsuits Bring Changes at Shoney's

The lawsuits and related publicity had a major impact on the corporation. White corporate executives usually do worry about the images of their companies, and a steady drumbeat of bad publicity can force them to take action whatever their own personal inclinations may be. This fact is especially true for an industry where an image presented in the media can affect everyday business. Shoney's executives made an agreement with the Southern Christian Leadership Conference (SCLC) to hire and promote more black workers and to increase opportunities for blacks to secure business franchises. By the end of 1992 the firm had reportedly spent more than $120 million in black communities as a result of its agreement with the SCLC. Moreover, SCLC soon signed another agreement with Shoney's new head, Taylor Henry, Jr., who commented that he had "never seen any other covenant of this type in our industry." This second agreement committed the corporation to spending $60 million over several years to help black entrepreneurs buy land for business franchises and to establish black-owned businesses to supply Shoney's restaurants.[19]

By 1992 Shoney's had also increased its number of black employees, including managers and executives, significantly. Some black applicants were hired at Shoney's Nashville, Tennessee, headquarters. A woman hired as vice president of corporate and community relations became the first black senior executive. A half dozen others were subsequently employed at the home office. Shoney's had begun to change its image and was making one of the most aggressive moves to hire minorities in the restaurant industry. The firm substantially increased its business with black suppliers.[20] Disagreement within the firm arose, however, over the aggressive implementation of the remedial and affirmative action plans. In December 1992 Leonard Roberts, the chair and chief executive hired to deal with the charges of racism and affirmative action, resigned his position. Three other top managers working on the remedial plans were fired. According to some sources, Roberts was forced to resign because of his aggressive approach to affirmative action, although company representatives denied this charge. Roberts was replaced with Taylor Henry, Jr., late in 1992.[21]

In November 1992, the restaurant chain's executives agreed to settle the major class-action lawsuit out of court. This action did not require that the firm's executives admit to discrimination, and they were also able to avoid the negative publicity of a major court trial. Shoney's agreed to pay $105 million between 1993 and 2000 to the many former and present black employees who had charged the company with discrimination and to some white employees who were fired for protesting what they saw as discriminatory company actions. Although this amount was far less than the $350 million in back pay and $180 million in punitive and compensatory damages that the litigants had originally sought, it was the largest settlement ever in a job discrimination case. The firm also agreed to hire more black local managers and regional directors.[22] Taylor Henry, Jr., stated that the lawsuit had focused the company's "priorities on doing what is right. We are a changed company, and we regret any mistakes we made in the past."[23] After the settlements, Danner resigned from the board, charging that the firm had not dealt with him fairly.

The $105 million Shoney's settlement was discussed in the media as an indicator of the high cost of persisting racial discrimination. In a February 1993 column titled "Paying the Price of Racism," writer Clarence Page made this point and noted that the Shoney's case, among others, shows "how racism is alive and well in America" even in a society with "sweeping anti-discrimination laws."[24] In a restaurant industry publication one writer spoke candidly of "recent discrimination scandals involving the Denny's and Shoney's chains." The writer continued with a lengthy discussion of the "disturbing and costly problems" of racial discrimination "still dogging the restaurant industry."[25]

Remedial responses to reported discrimination such as those made at Shoney's are particularly important because of the difficulty individual victims have in dealing with government enforcement agencies. Employment discrimination in the United States is a major problem for African American workers in all income groups, but as a rule antidiscrimination laws are weakly enforced, and government-aided remedies usually come slowly if at all. The 1964 Civil Rights Act and later amendments officially prohibit racial discrimination in employment; the EEOC was created to enforce the act by investigating complaints, seeking conciliation, and filing suits to end discrimination. For a time, the federal courts and the EEOC played a major role in reducing racial barriers, but, under the conservative Reagan and Bush administrations in the 1980s and early 1990s, the number of broad, institutionally focused investigations of discrimination conducted by the agency declined sharply.[26] As reported by the EEOC, black complaints of job discrimination grew from 112,000 in 1990 to 124,000 in 1992, and the pace of resolving complaints was usually slow. As a result, many black victims of discrimination turned to the NAACP for help. The chair of Howard University's Afro-American Studies Department noted: "Folks are turning to them [local NAACP chapters] on the assumption they have the manpower to handle the problems they are talking about, but many branches are just discussion groups."[27] The NAACP's small legal staff has become overwhelmed; this organization cannot replace governmental agencies whose mandates include the eradication of discrimination in employment across the nation.

During their terms Presidents Ronald Reagan and George Bush appointed several conservative justices to the U.S. Supreme Court, which in the years since has handed down a number of restrictive decisions that made it more difficult for workers to bring and win discrimination suits.[28] As a result of the court backtracking on antidiscrimination enforcement, it became more difficult for the victims of employment discrimination to win in court. As we noted in Chapter 1, an Urban Institute research study that sent matched white and black applicants to the same employers found that a significant proportion of the black applicants suffered discrimination in the hiring process. In addition, the overwhelming majority of black respondents in one national survey felt that if an equally qualified black and white were competing for the same job, the black applicant would be likely to suffer racial discrimination.[29]

Family Restaurants and Black Customers

The problems African Americans face at family restaurants extend beyond employment to a variety of customer service issues. Indeed, the degrading racial images used by some restaurant chains have caused black customer boycotts and protests. For example, in the late 1970s some critics targeted the Sambo's family restaurant chain, a California-based firm with one thousand locations across the nation, because of the stereotypical "Little Black Sambo" story its name suggested and because some restaurants used that story's cartoon-type character as a logo. Complaints were filed against the firm with the Rhode Island Commission on Human Rights, which ruled that the name made black customers feel unwelcome and ordered the name of Sambo's restaurants in that state to be changed. Subsequently, Sambo's restaurants in a number of states changed their name to Sam's or A Place Like Sam's, although the company denied that these changes were made because of charges of racism. Soon the chain was losing millions of dollars and had closed half of its restaurants, and by the mid-1980s all of its restaurants were closed or sold.[30] The name controversy and declining black patronage were likely contributors to the chain's demise. Here again black families were major victims of symbolic violence, but they were not the only ones to pay a price. The cost of racial insensitivity was also substantial for the whites involved.

The Denny's family restaurant chain has faced numerous charges of racial discrimination against black customers. In the mid-1990s this firm had nearly 1,500 restaurants across the nation. About 70 percent were company owned; the rest were mostly white-owned franchises. In the early 1990s Denny's reportedly faced more than 4,300 complaints of racial discrimination by black customers. One report from Denny's management noted that among the restaurants under the company's umbrella the Denny's chain had the fewest patrons who were not white.[31] A lawyer for one group of black plaintiffs who filed a class-action suit against Denny's noted the direct historical connection between the student sit-ins of the 1960s and the discrimination recently reported at Denny's restaurants: "It evokes the memory of segregated lunch counters in the Deep South in the 1950s. And it's appalling to see this kind of 'Jim Crow' discrimination occurring in a California restaurant in the 1990s."[32]

In 1993 one U.S. Department of Justice lawsuit against the company was resolved by a consent decree in which Denny's acknowledged no discrimination but agreed to conduct sensitivity training for all employees and to place notices in each restaurant indicating that patrons of all racial and ethnic groups would receive good service. The suit had alleged that the firm had a "pattern . . . of discrimination" that included such practices as requiring black customers, and not white customers, to prepay for their orders, demanding special identification, and excluding black patrons.[33] In various interviews about the charges of racial discrimination at Denny's, corporate officials denied that there was a company policy of discrimination but did admit that some Denny's restaurants had been the scene of "isolated" or "individual" instances of racial discrimination from time to time.[34] In response to the many complaints of discrimination, Jerome J. Richardson, the company's CEO, took an aggressive approach to remedying Denny's racial problems. Richardson met with Benjamin Chavis, the NAACP executive director, to discuss a "fair-share" agreement. Typically, such agreements are privately negotiated and oblige firms to take positive action to address civil rights and equal opportunity concerns. Fair-share agreements between civil rights organizations and businesses have sometimes been effective in channeling investments into communities of color. One NAACP analysis of forty fair-share agreements made by U.S. firms found that the companies had invested no less than $47 billion in minority employment, service companies, and franchises.[35]

Richardson made a broad agreement with the NAACP that included aggressive recruitment, more franchises, and more use of service and support firms owned by people of color, including insurance and law firms. The agreement also included outside monitoring of the fairness of service at Denny's restaurants.[36] Denny's parent company agreed to invest $1 billion in black- and other minority-owned franchises and restaurant support firms and to place workers of color in 325 new management jobs in its restaurants by the year 2000.[37] The company agreed to substantially increase its purchasing from supply firms owned by people of color in this same period.[38] Television ads asserting the company's new image ran in forty-one cities.[39] Impressed by the extent of Richardson's actions, Chavis commented, "In my 30 years in the civil rights movement, I've never seen the commitments made by this CEO today."[40] Richardson said the agreement was "tangible evidence" of the company's intention to end discrimination in its operations.[41] In addition to the NAACP agreement, some company executives and other representatives made highly visible appearances at NAACP and Urban League conventions, and newspapers reported that the company planned to arrange meetings with community groups.[42]

Significantly, however, the company's official position was that it had *not* fostered racial discrimination in its operations in the past or the present. While it is common for employers to refuse to admit past guilt when reaching a settlement, Denny's explicit denial had negative implications for the general public, both black and nonblack. Such a denial reduces the amount of media coverage and public discussion of the reality of discrimination in business settings. In addition, the settlements imply that the problem of antiblack discrimination is not basic to the U.S. economy by suggesting that a few short-range programs will solve whatever racism remains.

A California Class-Action Lawsuit

About the same time that Denny's executives agreed to the aforementioned consent decree with the Department of Justice, a class-action suit against Denny's was filed in a California federal court. Thirty-two black plaintiffs alleged that they had faced discrimination at Denny's restaurants,[43] charging that white personnel at Denny's restaurants had discriminated against them in a number of ways.[44] They decided to pursue their case even though the consent decree had dealt with some of the general racial complaints against the firm.

The class-action suit focused on alleged incidents of discrimination in several California cities. Several incidents cited in the lawsuit involved prepayment for meals or special cover charges not applied to white patrons. A middle-class black couple had been required to prepay for their meals in a San Diego Denny's. The white manager of a San Jose Denny's had refused to seat a group of eighteen black high school and college students—who entered the restaurant after attending a symposium on what college life was like for black students—unless they paid a cover charge and prepaid their meals. Reportedly, white students sitting nearby had not been required to prepay. The black students decided to leave, and the incident made the local news.[45] One of the young people said that the incident made him "embarrassed. I was mad that it was happening." Reflecting on the lawsuit, his father added, "We are not concerned with money. We just want to be able to go to a restaurant and order a meal like everyone else."[46]

Another incident cited in the lawsuit involved a free birthday meal. Seeking a pleasant family outing, a black couple had taken their children to a Denny's restaurant to celebrate their daughter's birthday, but the restaurant refused to honor the girl's baptismal certificate as proof and denied her the birthday meal. At a news conference on the events at the restaurant the mother stated, "I felt violated, humiliated and embarrassed, so we didn't eat there. I can't adequately describe the pain that you feel to see this happen to your child."[47] The daughter also reported great embarrassment: "They acted like we were begging for a meal. Everyone was angry after that and it wrecked my birthday night."[48] The goal of these complainants is clear: to be treated fairly and equally. The cost of the humiliation for the black targets is also evident in their words: pain, frustration, and embarrassment.

The documents provided to the court indicated a range of racial problems. In an affidavit attached to the class-action suit, one Denny's employee documented "repeated instances of racial prejudice" in which employees treated black customers badly or differently from white customers. *Blackout* was used as a code word for too many black customers in a Denny's at one time; managers were expected to prevent these so-called blackouts.[49] In a statement for the media, a Denny's manager in California said his superiors had taught him "to avoid blackouts by requiring black customers to pay for their meals in advance or simply close the restaurant for a few hours." He added that when he objected to such action, his supervisor told him they would have to get another manager.[50]

These events reveal certain important aspects of white thought about black Americans in everyday situations. The code word *blackout* for too many black customers in a store may have originated as an attempt at humor, but the term has significance beyond racist joking. Like the electric blackout for which it is likely named, it represents a loss of proper functioning. White feelings and fears about African Americans can prevent whites from functioning in normal human ways. Concern over the presence of too many blacks relative to the number of whites is common among white Americans in many social settings. The racial geography we noted earlier has its own territorial imperative. Whites are often uncomfortable if the proportion of blacks in a given group—a residential neighborhood, for example—exceeds a modest percentage, perhaps 5–10 percent. One Detroit survey in the 1970s found that the proportion of white respondents who said they would be unwilling to move into a hypothetical neighborhood with black families increased as the black proportion increased. If the neighborhood were 8 percent black, just over one-quarter said that they would be unwilling to move in. But if the neighborhood were 36 percent black, three-quarters of the whites expressed an unwillingness to live there.[51] It is probably still true that a majority of whites would refuse to move into a substantially black community if they were faced with that possibility.

Indeed, many whites are uncomfortable with the presence of *any* black people in what they view as white territory, such as historically white restaurants. Why are so many whites uneasy in the presence of black people? One answer may be that these whites reject black people because they project certain fears onto the dark otherness. We noted in Chapter 1 the work of Joel Kovel and others who suggest that these antiblack fears and impulses are irrational and that they are rooted in the world of the unconscious. For some whites "blackouts" may symbolize dirt, danger, even the unknown—symbols rooted deeply in the white unconscious. Such reactions mark a breakdown in understanding across the color line.

Because of the consent decree Denny's made with the Department of Justice, the firm's lawyers argued that the California class-action lawsuit should be set aside. However, lawyers for the black plaintiffs countered that the many charges of discrimination at Denny's restaurants across the United States provided ample reason to continue the private lawsuit.[52] Referring to Denny's persisting discrimination after the decree, a lawyer for the Washington Lawyers' Committee for Civil Rights and Urban Affairs contended that the U.S. Department of Justice should hold Denny's "in contempt of court for violating the terms of the consent decree."[53]

A Politicized Incident

On April 1, 1993, Dan Rather opened the *CBS Evening News* with a statement about black Secret Service agents. As a company executive remembered it, Rather said, "They put their lives on the line every day, but they can't get served at Denny's."[54] The six black Secret Service agents had received what they viewed as discriminatory service at a Denny's restaurant in Annapolis, Maryland. They waited for about an hour while fifteen white agents, as well as white customers who entered the restaurant after they did, received speedy and repeated service. The agents made several attempts to get their waitress to serve them and then sought the manager, who did not come out immediately. Both the black and the white agents were in the same section of the restaurant, and all were dressed the same way.[55] This account suggests that any African American, regardless of economic status, can be the victim of discrimination in public accommodations.

One of the black agents later remarked, "I was somewhat invisible that day."[56] He explained that he and the other black agents, like many black Americans, were reluctant to seek redress: "It was very difficult for us to come forth with this information. The question that went through our minds was, 'If not us, who? If not now, when?' And we answered that if we are about social responsibility as well as the Secret Service, we had to step forth."[57] These Secret Service agents felt a responsibility to confront discrimination on behalf of the black community. Denny's officials said that the problem that day was not discrimination but a backup in the kitchen. The manager was fired, but only for not reporting the incident. This well-publicized incident encouraged other black customers of Denny's to complain openly. Within a few months the agents' lawyers had received 250 reports of racial discrimination in service at a number of Denny's restaurants.[58]

The discrimination charges involving Denny's received widespread national attention. Newspapers and television news shows carried editorials condemning the poor treatment of the agents. At the Annapolis restaurant civil rights organizations held a protest demonstration reminiscent of the 1960s lunch counter protests. Even the White House responded. President Bill Clinton's communications director stated that the president "is strongly against discriminatory practices against anyone. Discrimination against black Secret Service agents would be a very serious problem."[59]

Both the California class-action suit and another class-action suit brought on behalf of the black Secret Service agents were eventually resolved by a consent decree in which the company agreed to pay damages of $46 million to the victims of discrimination as well as $9 million in lawyers' fees.[60] In its report on the court settlement *Business Week* noted that the parent company of Denny's had "apologized for apparent racism" in some of its operations.[61] The head of the company, Jerome Richardson, stated that the firm settled in part to show that Denny's wants black customers: "We deeply regret these individuals feel they were not treated fairly at Denny's. We invite any customers who have perceived discrimination at Denny's to give us another opportunity to serve them."[62] He also indicated that some employees had been terminated because of the discrimination lawsuits.

In a news conference regarding the settlement Assistant Attorney General Deval Patrick stated that the Denny's decree was one type of solution for illegal discrimination in public accommodations: "There will be a high price to pay for unlawful indignities, and the Justice Department will exact that price whenever the law is violated."[63] Patrick indicated that the decree required Denny's to hire an independent monitor to watch over its implementation, the first time such a monitoring requirement had been agreed upon. He noted that in addition to the payment of monetary awards, the settlement required Denny's to advertise nationally that patrons from all racial and ethnic groups were welcome and "to conduct random testing to determine whether black patrons continue to be treated differently, because this testing helps to uncover this particular subtle form of racism."[64] This major U.S. Department of Justice involvement in racial discrimination lawsuits in the early Clinton administration was a clear break from the policies of the previous Reagan and Bush administrations and a hopeful indicator of renewed federal efforts to enforce existing civil rights laws in the area of public accommodations.

The events had a major impact on Denny's executives and company policy over the long haul. In 1999 Denny's corporate parent, Advantica Restaurant Group, produced a documentary entitled "The

Denny's Turnaround" and purchased time on local television stations in Washington and New York to broadcast their new image. Denny's new chief executive now argued "as this country grows in the next 15 years, the racial composition of the country will change dramatically."[65] Along with this statement came statistics showing that in 1993 just one of the Denny's franchises was owned by a black person, but only six years later, blacks and other people of color owned 36 percent of the Denny's franchises. In 1992 no Advantica contract supplier was owned by a person of color, but by 1999 the company did 18 percent of its business with such businesses. According to the company, nearly half its 50,000 person workforce was black, along with one-third of its management team. The twelve-member board of directors had four black and Latino members. A quarter of executives' salaries was now tied to meeting diversity goals, encouraging them to find nontraditional suppliers and franchise buyers. The policy Denny's advertised was now "if you discriminate, you're fired." Still, Denny's stores continue to be sued by customers reporting continued discrimination in table service at particular restaurants.[66]

Problems at Other Restaurants

Shoney's and Denny's are of course not unique. Other family and fast-food restaurants have faced charges of racial and ethnic discrimination. Some are small and local and receive little media attention. A bar in Champaign, Illinois, that refused to admit black customers until compelled to do so by the Department of Justice is but one example.[67] Most incidents that have received national media coverage have involved restaurant chains. In the late 1980s, after a number of complaints from potential patrons who represented a number of racial and ethnic groups, the California Department of Alcoholic Beverage Control ruled that the Red Onion chain had discriminated against patrons of color as part of company policy. The firm denied the charge of discrimination, but in the late 1980s it agreed to pay more than $200,000 to twenty-nine people of color who charged they had been unfairly denied entry.[68]

In January 1993 another major chain, the International House of Pancakes (IHOP), with more than five hundred restaurants nationwide, agreed to pay $185,000 in settlement of a discrimination lawsuit.[69] The lawsuit charged that the white manager of an IHOP in Milwaukee refused entrance to a group of black college students when the restaurant locked its doors to several groups of black youth in December 1991. The fifteen black plaintiffs, who had just attended a party hosted by Howard University alumni, reported that the IHOP manager and staff told them the twenty-four-hour restaurant was closed, although white customers were being admitted.[70]

In 1998 it took a federal judge's order for a Domino's Pizza franchise to accept orders for deliveries to American Beach, Florida, where all but four of the seventy-five residents are black. In court the restaurant owners had argued that security concerns, not racism, forced them to limit deliveries to the town with mostly black residents. The judge pointed out in his decision that no proof of security risks had been established.[71] Many white-owned delivery companies assume that predominantly black areas are dangerous without checking the empirical realities.

Executives at family-restaurant chains, like those at other major businesses, have reportedly viewed racial and multicultural issues as diversions from their major business goals. Consequently, as some industry analysts have noted, racial and ethnic matters have often been approached in a superficial or too-bureaucratic manner. Company officials may address such issues on paper, but until they are confronted with a crisis most take little significant action. A *Business Week* report concluded that top officials at Denny's, as well as those at other large firms, "depend too heavily on policy statements instead of active monitoring and training to avoid discrimination complaints."[72] According to the head of Denny's Franchisee Advisory Council, until the late 1980s only ten to twenty minutes of the month-long training provided to franchisees involved learning about problems of discrimination.[73] One analyst of corporate responses to interracial problems has noted that written policies are not the same thing as "the way people really behave." He added that corporate cultures "reflect the behaviors and values that are rewarded."[74]

For a time, the national publicity of the Denny's and Shoney's lawsuits forced the restaurant industry to pay more attention to persisting problems of racial and ethnic discrimination. These two companies and other major chains began to require more racial and ethnic sensitivity training for their employees. It remains to be seen, however, how long this emphasis on multicultural training will last.

Conclusion

Why is the family restaurant sometimes a site of racist rituals? Is there something especially significant about such places for white Americans? At first glance contacts between white diners and black employees or diners appear to be fleeting, making restaurants unlikely settings for interracial friction. Yet there is more to consider. The preparation and sharing of food have long had socioreligious meaning. Since biblical times, Jews, Christians, and Moslems have celebrated some of their most important religious traditions around a table. The ceremony of sharing food is one of the powerful symbols of communal solidarity in these and other religious traditions.[75]

The collective consumption of food, from harvest festivals to national celebrations like Thanksgiving or Independence Day, can symbolize a common destiny—the "we" feelings that theoretically bind families, groups, and the nation together. But the meaning of the symbols can be problematic. As Native Americans have pointed out, while the Pilgrims offered thanks for what was given, they also took away land and the "life, liberty and the pursuit of happiness" from those who helped them settle and survive after they arrived. Furthermore, since the time of slavery it has been acceptable among most whites for black workers to plant and harvest the food and to cook and serve the food, but not to share the food with whites at the table. As we saw in this chapter's opening, the right to sit and eat at the same commercial counter was gained by African Americans as part of a nationwide struggle for civil rights.

Not surprisingly, then, these racist rituals are still carried out by some whites in the food service industry. They victimize black workers and customers by perpetuating racial hatred, discrimination, and segregation. In addition, these racist rituals are symbolic, serving to remind both whites and blacks that racist ideas are alive in white hearts and minds, which still claim America as a land centered in whites. Moreover, while the costs of this discrimination are directly borne by black customers and workers, other costs are paid by the society as a whole. Paul Claudel has written about European social stratification in eating arrangements, which he calls "an eternal class struggle" in food fashions. In Europe the nicer restaurants represent very clear and privileged markers of social class differences. Food fashions reflect and reinforce social class differences "that nothing can compensate for."[76]

In the United States, food fashions represent class and racial divides. For example, in an effort to improve their image among black customers, the Denny's restaurant in the predominantly black Watts-Willowbrook section of Los Angeles serves soul food, and those in the Southwest include food items like burritos and green chilies.[77] This does not represent an attempt to move away from the hamburger or hot dog but reveals an understanding of the relationship between profits and customers of color. As a Denny's executive pointed out, "if you're not in touch with the tastes of minorities, or in a position to reach them through ads, you're going to miss an incredible opportunity."[78] Thus the food industry is not confronting the rituals of racism so much as responding to the loss of customers and falling rates of profit.

Still, the reactions of Shoney's and Denny's top executives to the racial discrimination lawsuits are encouraging. While it took a number of lawsuits to bring major changes, it is clear that among the major cases of white racism examined in this book, perhaps the most substantive remedial actions have been taken in the cases of Shoney's and Denny's restaurants. Some newspaper reports and editorials celebrated the resolution of the lawsuits with strong headlines such as this one in the *Chicago Sun Times*: "Denny's Pact Combats Racism."[79] We agree with these editorials and with civil rights observers who have been complimentary to Denny's and Shoney's for compensating the black plaintiffs in response to the discrimination lawsuits, for bringing greater racial diversity through their employment and purchasing policies, and for working to eliminate future discrimination in their operations. Yet some observers have taken a watchful attitude toward these ongoing corporate changes, hoping for continuing improvements but aware that *retrogression* is possible. Some civil rights advocates with whom we have spoken have expressed concern that the major remedies taken as a result of the many charges of discrimination and several lawsuits have been linked to consent decrees in which the companies publicly deny that there is discrimination in their operations. This public denial by influential corporate officials of what seems obvious to many Americans, especially African Americans, contributes to the impression common among white Americans that racism is no longer a serious problem in the United States.

The many attempts to exclude or restrict African American access to family restaurants strike a blow at America's fundamental values of equality and democracy. Many white Americans regard the family as their distinctive province, perhaps in part because many whites believe that African Americans have weak families and poor family values. For many black and white Americans the word "family," whether in "family values" or "family restaurant," has become a code word for "white." As a result, most black customers who enter family restaurants across the nation do so with caution or the expectation that they will be unwelcome or unwanted. The 1964 Civil Rights Act officially banned discrimination in all places of public accommodation. However, several decades later this nation is *not close* to eradicating racial discrimination in its restaurants or many other types of public accommodation.

It was not by chance that the desegregation of lunch counters was among the first events of the Civil Rights Movement to gain national attention. The symbolic value of food and food-sharing dramatized the physical and moral divide that white racism introduced in our national conscience. In 1960 the Student Nonviolent Coordinating Committee's statement of purpose underlined that "by appealing to conscience and standing on the moral nature of human existence, nonviolence [protest] nurtures the atmosphere in which reconciliation and justice become actual possibilities. . . . Justice for all overthrows injustice. The redemptive community supersedes systems of gross social immorality."[80] The actions of those who sat in at the lunch counters, who demonstrated in front of Shoney's and Denny's, or who gave their time and effort to sue discriminating restaurants and other public facilities are critical to making advances against the racist system of the United States. By standing up these Americans not only have advocated for a society in which all people are treated equally but also have taught how that equality might be achieved. The voices heard from the black students in the first sit-ins in Greensboro are still rising to confront white racism across the United States.

4

Racism and Murder: The Cases of Boston, Portland, and Jasper

White racism is an open secret in America, and most white people sense its presence at some level but fail to acknowledge its effects on people of color or their role in it.[1] In everyday life the majority of whites engage in a routine of acknowledgment, pretense, and denial. Today many whites play an "I am not a racist" game. This game is important today because of the generally negative view of overt racism in public discussions. Gordon Allport has noted that "cruelty is not a favored human trait. Even the top Nazi officials who were tried after World War II pretended that they knew nothing about the inhuman practices in the concentration camps."[2] Patricia J. Williams has noted the "incantation of innocence and guilt" now common among white Americans. Analyzing the 1986 attack on three black men by whites in New York's all-white Howard Beach community, Williams observed a "pernicious game of victim responsibility" in which white violence against blacks is legitimized by the presumed evil of the innocent black victims.[3] Whites' inability or unwillingness to take responsibility for their racist actions is a critical aspect of racism today.

This chapter examines cases of racial victimization with violent dimensions. The first analysis reviews Charles Stuart's story of his wife's murder by a black attacker in Boston's Mission Hill area and asks why Stuart's account was so easily believed by the Boston police department, local politicians, and local and national mass media commentators, even though it was clear from the beginning that his story was probably a hoax. The second case concerns the brutal murder of a black man by a group of modern American Nazis, called Skinheads, who killed the man apparently because they regarded him as inferior. These Portland, Oregon, Skinheads had been indoctrinated in part by organizers from the white supremacy organization White Aryan Resistance (WAR). The analysis looks at how Tom Metzger, one of the leaders of WAR, became a political candidate in California and persuaded a number of whites to vote for him. It also examines organized resistance to racism, in particular the Southern Poverty Law Center's attempt to obtain a judicial remedy for this case of racist action. The third case is about a modern lynching—the vicious and brutal dragging death of a black man, James Byrd, Jr., in Jasper, Texas. Given these blatantly racist incidents, we will examine the growing influence of white supremacist groups in U.S. cities, towns, and suburbs.

The Carol Stuart Murder in Boston: White Fear of Black Men

Murderous Events

Boston, the cradle of American liberty, was the scene of an unusual murder case that reveals much about how racism operates in society and how the game of white pretense and denial is played out. On the evening of October 23, 1989, Carol DiMaiti Stuart, a young white professional and expectant mother, was shot in the head while driving with her husband through the Mission Hill area of central Boston. Her wounded husband, Charles Stuart, reported over his car phone to a police dispatcher that he and his wife had been shot by a black man. According to Stuart's story the black attacker broke into the couple's car as they were going home after a class at a nearby hospital. The "heart-rending details" reported in the *Boston Globe* made the story seem worse than the commonplace crime many Bostonians were accustomed to: "A frantic call for help from a bleeding Charles Stuart over his car telephone to a coolheaded State Police dispatcher; the emergency Caesarean delivery of a seven-month baby boy from the dying Carol Stuart and the infant's death 17 days later; a lyrical last love letter from the hospital-confined husband is read aloud at his wife's funeral."[4]

The response of the Boston police was quick and massive; numerous black men were stopped in the vicinity of the murder as more than one hundred police officers made a vigorous effort to find the murderer. Police Superintendent Joseph Saia defended the broad scope of the search, stating: "You have a complete disregard for human life in this case. If he'd kill a pregnant woman, he'd kill anyone."[5] Boston's liberal mayor, Raymond Flynn, who had pledged to end Boston's racial conflict in an inaugural speech, was among the white politicians who expressed outrage at the black assailant; Flynn pressed the police department to call out all available detectives. Other white officials went so far as to press for the reinstatement of the state's death penalty law.[6] This get-tough-on-black-criminals approach had been at the heart of the 1988 Bush-Dukakis presidential campaign, and many Boston politicians had aligned themselves with this age-old white approach to urban crime. The governor, mayor, and other local politicians even went to Carol Stuart's funeral, further politicizing the events. The reaction of white police and politicians helped support Stuart's story and buttress the general white image of black men as dangerous. Local whites expressed anger at the black community. An acquaintance of the Stuarts told a reporter the events had made the city "a war zone."[7]

Mission Hill is one of the most integrated areas of Boston; just under half the residents are white, about one-fifth are black, and one-third are Latino. Mission Hill is considered one of the safest areas in

Boston.[8] For several days after the murder police officers combed the area, searching for a suspect Stuart described in great detail, a black male "with a wispy beard, about 5 feet 10 inches tall . . . wearing a black jogging suit with red stripes and driving gloves with the knuckles cut-out."[9] Soon the police arrested William Bennett, a black man with a criminal record whom the recuperating Stuart identified as the murderer in a police lineup. The police reported that a relative of Bennett had heard him say that he shot the Stuarts. Police sources leaked the story that Bennett was the prime suspect. Later, when the true story became public, the police were criticized for these leaks.[10] The white-controlled media in the northeast and across the nation quickly fell for the story and "apotheosized the couple as starry-eyed lovers out of Camelot cut down by an urban savage."[11]

Revealing the Hoax

Stuart's story gradually unraveled, and his lies became clear. Claiming he was an unwitting participant, Charles's brother Matthew Stuart later confessed to the police that Charles had asked for his aid in the murder, which was part of an insurance scam. Matthew had gone to the site of the shooting and picked up Carol's purse and the gun, which he and a friend disposed of. Two months before the murder Charles had asked another friend, David MacLean, for his assistance in the killing, but MacLean did not report this to the police.[12] On January 4, 1990, the day after his brother Matthew's confession, Charles Stuart committed suicide, but the note he left did not confess to murder.

Even after Matthew's confession that Charles was the architect of a murder, the police were slow to examine Charles Stuart's car.[13] It was now clear that Stuart had plotted to kill his wife, shot himself, and made up the story of a black male attacker. Yet local white officials had taken two and a half months to begin to question what one journalist called the "forest of lies" in Charles Stuart's story.[14]

Given the admissions of Matthew Stuart and another man, the grand jury investigating the murder exonerated William Bennett, but not everyone accepted this as the end of the black man's culpability.

As late as August 1991, the president of the Boston Police Detectives Benevolent Society stated that the police had not eliminated William Bennett as a possible suspect.[15] Matthew Stuart's guilty plea to conspiracy to commit insurance fraud and to obstruction of justice eventually resulted in a three- to five-year prison sentence. He was not prosecuted for his role in the murder, even though he admitted participating in a practice run the day before and disposing of the weapon.[16] In addition, some of Matthew's acquaintances reportedly knew of his involvement but failed to notify police. A number of whites had kept the Stuart brothers' secret even while black men were being harassed for the crime.[17]

The mass media finally began to give attention to the hoax in January 1990. A report on ABC's *Nightline* opened with the question, "Is this story a study in the effects of racism?"[18] A television movie, "Good Night, Sweet Wife: A Murder in Boston," shown in September 1990, retold the Stuart murder case for a national audience. Interestingly, the producers chose to film in Chicago because they regarded the story as too incendiary to film in Boston. The next year Joe Sharkey published the book *Deadly Greed*, detailing the story of Carol Stuart's murder. The cover of the book reads: "What would make a young husband kill his pregnant wife? DEADLY AMBITION. What would make him think he could blame a black man for the crime? DEADLY ARROGANCE. What would make the police and the media believe his story and shake a city to its core? DEADLY RACISM."[19] The movie and the book were widely discussed, and the nation was finally confronted with the truth about the racial hoax.

In the years prior to the Stuart murder, Boston had reportedly been "one of the safest metropolitan areas in America," especially for whites.[20] Yet the local media began what Sharkey called "a steady drumbeat of crime news."[21] A newspaper circulation war accounted in part for the exaggerated attention given to local crimes. After the murder the local press's appetite for covering the story seemed insatiable. Journalists sought to outdo each other in their portrayal of an all-American couple victimized by a horrendous crime. The power of the mass media to construct and legitimate racial relations stories from a white perspective is clear. In contrast, black leaders' early reactions were much more critical of Stuart's story. Had those leaders been able to influence police or media investigations, the investigations would likely have been more skeptical and cautious.

Later, Mayor Flynn and other white politicians defended the police response as completely appropriate because at the time the police did not know Stuart's story was a hoax.[22] Some white analysts also tried to excuse what later was determined to be police malpractice. An ABC *Nightline* correspondent reasoned that on the street whites justifiably feared black men because black men account for two-thirds of violent crime arrests in Boston, where blacks are only a quarter of the population.[23] But if local crime statistics were to be considered, the rate of blacks targeting whites for murder would be the most relevant statistic. In the nation as a whole, less than one-fifth of all violent assaults on whites are committed by blacks, and almost 90 percent of the murderers of whites are *white*. The white politicians and white correspondents were actually saying that in their opinion it is reasonable for whites to fear black men because some black men commit violent crimes against whites. Yet they do *not* suggest that irrational fears of all white men on the street would be justifiable simply because many white men in Boston commit violent crimes.

Later on, U.S. Attorney Wayne A. Budd released a report explaining that the Boston police had secured information linking Bennett to the murder by pressuring witnesses to provide false statements to the police and grand jury.[24] The police were so eager to solve the murder that they constructed a case grounded in white assumptions about the racial character of the crime. Later on, the Boston Police Department would admit that certain officers had violated the law several times in connection with the Stuart case.[25] Despite these findings, however, Budd and the Massachusetts attorney general decided not to press charges against the police department because their investigations had "failed to find sufficient evidence to guarantee a conviction against the officers."[26] Prosecutors are required by federal law to prove that officers who violate the civil rights of a suspect do so intentionally.

Black community leaders were critical of the police response to the murder even before Charles Stuart's hoax was revealed. They had long objected to discrimination in local police services, a common complaint in black communities across the nation. Recent murders of black victims in central Boston had not received nearly as much police attention as did the Stuart murder, which involved white victims from suburbia. The president of the Boston chapter of the NAACP commented, "We can have a 14-year-old [black] boy shot and killed, a mother on a playground shot and killed, and that doesn't spur people to move. We've got to look at our values in this society. If people don't value black lives, fine, but the cancer continues to spread."[27]

Gradually, the scope of the police harassment of black men in the Stuart investigation became evident. A black resident of the Mission Hill area told ABC's *Nightline*: "It's just been a lot of police, you know, harassing a lot of people, thinking that we're the bad guys." Another black resident commented: "A white cop came to me and he asked me, 'Where's the nigger with the trigger?'"[28] Some residents spoke of the police as "storm troopers." Anger in the black community increased when some blacks interviewed by the police reported they had been coerced into false statements; anger increased again when the hoax was revealed.[29]

Later, in a gesture of guilt, some whites established a foundation in Carol DiMaiti Stuart's name to provide college scholarships to disadvantaged youth in the Mission Hill area. This attempt to improve Boston racial relations may have signaled a loss of innocence among some whites about the character of racism in their city.[30]

The murder and the way it was portrayed in the media had lasting effects on the Mission Hill area and on Boston. Two years after the murder, area merchants reported their business was still down, and many whites in other parts of the city seemed reluctant to venture into Mission Hill. In 1991, after the events of the Stuart case had become clear to all who read the newspapers, a poll of 814 registered voters by the *Boston Globe* revealed that nearly half believed racial relations in the city were *worse* than eight years before.[31]

Interpreting the Boston Events

In the aftermath of the murder and hoax, many whites in Boston and across the nation *denied* that racism was a major factor in police and public reactions. One presumably white caller to a local talk show commented: "Bigotry on both sides has jumped on this case, and has used it to further reinforce their bigotry." The talk show host replied by criticizing local politicians for exploiting the incident and commented that "both black and white people used it to further their racist attitudes."[32] Blaming blacks and whites equally for bigotry or discrimination is a common white reaction to charges of white racism: "Everybody is prejudiced." This racial parallelism attempts to absolve whites as a group of responsibility. While both whites and blacks can indeed be prejudiced, few blacks have the power and opportunity to implement their prejudices in repeated antiwhite discrimination. In contrast, many whites, including business executives, politicians, educators, landlords, and police chiefs, have the power to implement their prejudices in repeated antiblack discrimination. Indeed, in Boston racial stereotypes held by mainstream whites, not those held by whites in fringe groups such as the Klan, caused the major inconsistencies in Stuart's murder story to be overlooked and the antiblack actions by the police to be tolerated.

Interestingly, a white customer in a bar in Revere, Massachusetts, the area near Boston where Charles Stuart was raised, commented to a reporter: "Don't discount the way people think here; racism is a fact, good or bad. We divide people up into groups, and you will notice no blacks live in Revere."[33] Stuart leaned on and exploited this climate of racism in his attempt to deceive the police and the public. His hoax depended on the common white belief in black criminality, and it worked. It is likely that a majority of whites today view young black males in most everyday situations as potentially dangerous.[34] It is significant that this image of black criminality is gendered, for black women are typically not part of the stereotype. (A counterpart black female stereotype is that of the "welfare queen.") Indeed, the stereotype includes the notion that the black male criminal is especially threatening to white women, a factor that made Stuart's story even more credible. This imagery will appear again in cases examined in later chapters.

The white tendency to view people of African descent as deviant and threatening is centuries old. Since perhaps the 1400s, Europeans have projected their ignorance and fears onto the blackness of Africans, creating in the other a distorted image of themselves. By the eighteenth century Europeans had come to see Africans as symbols of deviant behavior, including sexuality. By the nineteenth century, African and African American mores and physique had come to represent the antithesis of European mores and beauty. In the European literature of the time, Africans were stereotyped as more intellectually and sexually primitive than Europeans.[35]

These anti-African images were imported by the colonies, where images born in European ignorance were used to justify the subjugation of Africans bought and sold as slaves. Negative images of African Americans were accepted by the framers of the Declaration of Independence and the U.S. Constitution. Prominent European Americans in the early history of this nation were slaveholders, including the southerners George Washington, James Madison, and Thomas Jefferson. In an early draft of the Declaration of Independence, Jefferson attacked slavery but was careful to blame it on England's King George. However, because of slaveowners' opposition, Jefferson's antislavery language was omitted from the final version of that founding document. Despite his indictment of slavery, Jefferson himself was a major slaveowner with very racist ideas. Writing in *Notes on Virginia*, Jefferson argued that what he saw as the ugly color, offensive odor, and ugly hair of African American slaves indicated their physical inferiority and that their alleged inability to create was a sign of mental inferiority.[36]

Strong antiblack images have persisted in various forms over the intervening centuries. In an analysis of the South in the 1930s, John Dollard commented on the white southerner's obsession with the allegedly oversexed black man, who was viewed as a special danger to white women.[37] As we noted in Chapter 1, in the century after the end of slavery there were thousands of lynchings of allegedly "uppity" black men in the south, many of whom were accused of raping or simply looking at white women. Today, images similar to those used to justify slavery and lynching are still present in many white minds and are used to excuse the abuse of black men, as in the Boston case. As Charles Stuart demonstrated, black men have much to fear from the white stereotyping of black men.

The Stuart case also reveals the personal and structural racism that exists in police and judicial institutions. Charles Stuart counted on the strong presumption among powerful whites that a white businessperson would be telling the truth in his account of a black male attacking a white woman, even though his story was full of obvious inconsistencies. The unnecessary stopping and frisking of black men who are doing nothing suspicious has been a racist police ritual in many U.S. cities. The harassment and coercion of black men in Mission Hill after the Stuart murder tarnished the reputations of several government agencies, including the local police department. After the murder the failure of state and local agencies to prosecute the admitted malpractice in police investigations also hints at a racial bias in U.S. judicial institutions.

Parallel Cases

The intentional use of negative images of African Americans to deflect police and public suspicion from a crime by a white man is not unique to Boston. On April 27, 1992, a white man, Jesse Anderson, was arrested in Milwaukee, Wisconsin, for killing his wife. Initially, Anderson reported that two young black males (again note the gendered racist image) had stabbed him and his wife in a local restaurant's parking area. Like Charles Stuart, this man said that his wife was attacked first. He also said the young black men had dropped their weapon and a baseball cap. Responding more quickly to the contradictions in the white man's story than the Boston police had, the Milwaukee police soon found that Anderson had bought the cap, that he was seriously in debt, and that he had contacted an insurance firm to check on his wife's insurance before her murder.[38]

Nonetheless, the initial police treatment of the case was strongly criticized by local black leaders, who pointed out that the Milwaukee police were stopping and checking black men in connection with the case even when the evidence that Anderson had committed the crime was already substantial. University of Wisconsin-Milwaukee professor Walter Farrell, Jr., argued that "Milwaukee owes the black community an apology for jumping to conclusions based on Mr. Anderson's story." Milwaukee alderman Marvin Pratt underscored how Anderson had used racism to his advantage: "Based on the racist climate, if you say a black male or two black males assaulted you, you would be believed."[39] In August 1992 Jesse Anderson was convicted of killing his wife and sentenced to sixty years in prison.

Moreover, in October 1994, a psychologically troubled white mother, Susan Smith, who was frustrated by a failed romance, drowned her two children in a lake near Union, South Carolina. Initially, she claimed that her car, with the two children inside, had been stolen by a black male carjacker. She helped the police sketch a black suspect. After nine days of useless searching, Smith finally confessed her crime and led the police to the bodies of her children. On August 6, 1995, she was sentenced to life in prison.[40] Since that time a number of similar racial hoaxes have been perpetrated by whites from coast to coast.

Criminologist Katherine Russell considers these racist hoaxes to be serious criminal offenses and "macro-aggressions" against all African Americans. Yet numerous white perpetrators have only been charged with minor offenses, such as filing a false police report. Russell identified sixty-seven hoaxes similar to those described above for the years 1987–1996. Some 70 percent of these were white-on-black hoaxes and were most frequently fabricated by whites in order to allege assault, rape, or murder by a black person. Seven cases involved police officers or court officials. The central importance of racist imagery should be noted here. Russell notes, "The fact that so many White-on-Black hoaxes are successful indicates society's readiness to accept the image of Blacks as criminal."[41] These racial hoaxes are expensive for the police departments that are involved. The two cases described in detail here involved manhunts, extended police investigations, and efforts by numerous officials in police or court agencies. This level of effort has been true for other hoaxes as well. These organizational and other costs show once again the gigantic human waste that is contemporary racism.

The Portland Case

We turn now to a murder case on the West Coast. Portland, Oregon, is a city thought by many to be a liberal place with strong commitments to individual freedom and with little of the racial friction found in other parts of the country. Yet a brutal racial crime took place in Portland in the late 1980s. The perpetrators, white men, made no secret of their racism but paraded it openly. These men, called Skinheads, are not an anomaly but represent the fringe of the larger field of racist practices in the United States.

During the early morning hours of November 13, 1988, Mulugeta Seraw, an Ethiopian American, was beaten and killed by three Skinheads: Kenneth Mieske, Kyle Brewster, and Steven Strasser. These young men were part of a local white gang, East Side White Pride, whose members characteristically had shaved heads and a racist philosophy. They encountered Seraw on the street as he was returning from a party with two friends. The Skinheads yelled at the black men to move their car. As the black men attempted to leave, the Skinheads hit the windows of the car. Then one viciously beat Seraw to death with a baseball bat. Kenneth Mieske was arrested, pled guilty to the murder, and was sentenced to thirty years to life. The others were convicted of manslaughter and received lengthy prison sentences.[42]

Membership in Skinhead gangs in Portland increased significantly between the 1970s and the 1990s, as it did in many other U.S. cities. Most such cities shared similar underlying conditions: substantial unemployment and a growing dissatisfaction among ordinary white workers with their economic condition. Racist gangs with names like Youth of Hitler, Blitzkrieg, Crazy Fucking Skins, and Romantic Violence have attracted young whites. The rituals and uniforms of these groups often resurrect the gestures and behaviors not only of Jim Crow segregationists but also of World War II Nazis.

Prior to Seraw's murder, Skinhead youths in Portland had been involved in a series of overtly racist acts. A number of Skinhead-originated brawls and beatings took place during the 1980s. In 1986 a punk concert at a night club was disrupted by several dozen Skinheads carrying bats and knives; the Skinheads reportedly were angry because they believed that blacks in the club were pimping for white women. Other incidents in the Northwest signaled an increase in overt expressions of racism. Late in 1984 Robert Mathews, the founder of a violent supremacy group called The Order, was being sought by the FBI in connection with a robbery. He fled from FBI agents in Portland and later died in a fiery shootout with the FBI near Seattle. Mathews has since become a hero for white supremacists across the United States.[43]

The National Connection

Initially, the Portland murder appeared to have only a loose connection to white supremacy groups active in other cities and states. As more information came to light, however, a direct connection became apparent. Not long before the killing, WAR, founded by Californian Tom Metzger, had carried out a national campaign to organize Skinheads. Portland was one of WAR's target cities. Members of WAR and its youth division, the Aryan Youth Movement, have spread racist doctrines among white students and workers in a number of cities.[44]

A handful of white men like Metzger have been the catalysts for the white supremacy movement across the United States. One of the most famous of these men is Metzger's mentor, David Duke, who once served as grand wizard of a national Klan federation. In recent years Duke has served in the Louisiana state legislature and has run a primary campaign for U.S. senator in which he received a majority of the white votes. During the mid-1970s, Duke, who later said he has severed ties with the white supremacy movement, recruited Metzger for the Klan in California. Metzger, the owner of a television repair service, became and remains one of the most visible white supremacy leaders in the nation. Soon after joining the California Klan in the mid-1970s, he became active in setting up a Klan chapter at a U.S. Marine Corps base and in organizing a vigilante-type border watch for undocumented workers coming from Mexico.[45]

For a time Metzger published a racist newspaper, which had an estimated circulation of thirty thousand in the early 1990s. WAR's newspaper and pamphlets print derogatory articles about black and Jewish men and women as well as racist cartoons showing people of color as subhuman.[46] WAR's antiblack and anti-Semitic publications have been widely circulated. In the mid-1980s, hate literature of the White Student Union, a southern California organization with reported links to Metzger and the California Klan, was placed in student lockers in several Los Angeles and San Diego public schools. The materials called the Holocaust a fabricated deception and denigrated affirmative action policies for African Americans.[47] Metzger has organized phone message lines in numerous cities and moderated a cable television show, *Race and Reason*: "Hi, this is Tom Metzger, your host for *Race and Reason,* the longest-running show of its type on cable access TV, seen in approximately fifty cities across the United States, blazing a trail of real free speech, free speech for white working people for a change."[48]

Like Duke, Metzger attempted to enter local and national politics. In the late 1970s he garnered eleven thousand votes in an attempt to win a position as county supervisor in San Diego. Two years later, he entered the Democratic party primary in a San Diego congressional district, where he received a plurality in a close three-way race: 32,344 votes out of 87,000.[49] Four-term Republican representative Clair Burgener beat Metzger by a huge margin in the general election. In the campaign, Metzger deemphasized his Klan connections and accented his anti-immigration views. Metzger received 13 percent of the vote, or about 37,000 votes. After his nomination in the party primary, Metzger had tried unsuccessfully to get on the San Diego County Democratic central committee and the state Democratic Party's central committee. In 1982 he announced that he would run again, this time for the Democratic nomination for the U.S. Senate. His platform called for an end to immigration. This time he polled 75,000 votes in a losing effort.[50]

Metzger's racist views attracted a large number of white voters who did not consider his involvement in white supremacy organizations to be a barrier to his holding a major political office. The strength that both Metzger and Duke have shown at the polls suggests that the views of white supremacists may not be as far outside the mainstream of white thought as some white commentators have suggested.

Some white Californians have been outspoken critics of Metzger's activities. For example, California Anti-Defamation League member Morris Casuto has linked activists like Metzger to anti-Semitic incidents carried out by young white people: "Consider what he puts over his telephone hot line. He cannot avoid responsibility for what he puts in his newsletter, in the cartoons that are vicious, obscene. . . . They do nothing but inflame racist hatreds. One cartoon recently showed a black man burning to death and the hooded figure beside him saying, 'This is more fun than football.' This is not an incitement to violence?"[51]

Metzger and the Skinheads

In October 1990 Morris Dees, director of the Southern Poverty Law Center, began civil proceedings against Tom Metzger in Multnomah County, Oregon. One of Dees's goals was to bankrupt Metzger and put WAR "out of business." Working with local civil rights attorney Elden Rosenthal, Dees argued that the legal principle of "vicarious liability" should be applied to the Seraw killing. Dees contended that Metzger was liable for Seraw's murder because he had sent radical organizers to inform and incite the Skinhead gangs in Portland. The jury agreed with Dees and assessed $12.5 million in damages against Metzger and his son, to be paid to Seraw's family. The case again reveals a serious flaw in the U.S. judicial system. Justice is not well served when the primary way a racist campaign of violence can be punished is through a civil case with, at most, monetary penalties.[52]

At the trial Metzger, serving as his own lawyer, argued that he was not responsible for the murder and that he did not advocate violence except in self-defense. He said that WAR is "an association of people who agree on race . . . people who are concerned about their whiteness. I am a white separatist."[53] Evidence presented at the trial clearly tied Metzger to the advocacy of racial violence. Metzger's *Race and Reason* cable program, which first aired in the Portland area in the summer of 1988, has had guests who advocate racial violence. Moreover, after Seraw's murder, Metzger's national phone message stated: "Now that the initial B.S. is waning in the Skinheads' Ethiopian confrontation, we may find that these beautiful people were high on crack and many of these beautiful Negroes had long arrest records. Sounds like the Skinheads did a civic duty."[54] The drugs and arrest records allegation here sounds like a blaming-the-victim rationalization of violent antiblack actions.

Testimony from Metzger's former associates tied him to the Skinhead killing. Michael Barrett, once a Skinhead organizer, provided an affidavit stating that he and other Skinheads had been taught by the Metzgers that black and Jewish Americans were the "enemies" and that violent action was required "to save the white Aryan race."[55] Barrett explained that he and David Mazzella, a WAR national vice president, had organized the Skinheads in Portland and indoctrinated them in the Aryan race ideology: "We told them to use violence if they got an opportunity and to be sure and beat the hell out of the enemy." He stated further that he was following orders from Metzger: "We got the East Side White Pride group all fired up to carry out Tom and John Metzger's goals of harming blacks and Jews." For his part Metzger asserted that Barrett had been coached in what he was to say by the other side.[56]

Mazzella also said that Metzger had a public face that was different from his private face: Publicly Metzger professed nonviolence, but privately he advocated violence against African and Jewish Americans.[57] Mazzella reported that he was one of several organizers sent to cities in several states to build membership in WAR and the Skinhead gangs. Mazzella spoke of the effect of Metzger's racist philosophy on

daily activities: "It was a whole different world once I entered Metzger's world. . . . I'd see blacks and they all looked like monkeys." This
worldview also considered blacks to be inferior, like "bugs you can
step on."[58]

Barrett and Mazzella said that they had kept the Metzgers
informed of their organizing activities. In their view the Portland
Skinheads had been directly influenced by their work and the racist
doctrines they preached. A few months before the Seraw murder, a
dozen members of one Skinhead gang had articulated their white
supremacist philosophy on a Sunday television show in Portland.
They defended themselves with statements such as: "We're trying to
unite the white people."[59]

The court ruling against Metzger did not end his efforts in the
white supremacy cause. In 1990 he was told by authorities that he
could keep his home during his appeal if he ceased WAR activities
and organizing, but he refused to accept the compromise. According
to a *Los Angeles Times* report, Metzger was to "shut down his hate
machine," including his newspaper and hot lines, during his appeal of
the multimillion-dollar award by the judge to the Seraw family. But
Metzger regarded the agreement as a violation of his right to free
speech.[60] Then, late in 1991, he was sentenced to a six-month jail
term for an earlier Los Angeles–area cross-burning, his first conviction in a criminal court and his first jail sentence. Released on probation early because of his wife's illness, Metzger was soon involved in a
controversy regarding a possible parole violation for his role in showing an anti-Semitic film on a local television program. Interviewed in
June 1992, Metzger indicated his continuing commitment to fighting
for WAR causes: "I feel like a military man. I'm going into war—I'm in
a war—and, while I'll lose some of the skirmishes, I'll win most of the
battles, and ultimately, you can bet I'll win the war."[61]

The white supremacists' philosophy recognizes that there are officiants who take violent action to alert the white community and also
passive whites who more or less acquiesce in the actions of the officiants. Both groups are linked by a common mythology that defines
African Americans as less human than whites. The supremacists' racist

ideology is reminiscent of the worst in the racist traditions of the Western world, including the German Nazi ideology. It is based on a "we" and "they" imagery that divides humans into different and opposing racial groups involved in a zero-sum contest for resources and access to power. Many white supremacists are officiants in racist rituals; they often wear ritualized dress and hairstyles. Burning crosses and stalking black victims are racial rites. Supremacists see themselves as militant, even Christian, warriors marching against those who threaten "white power." Their racist rituals are often not just private ceremonies. Skinhead actions are a public revelation of the extreme implications of common antiblack views. Their racist rituals exemplify the objectification of black people in a very consequential form.

The National White Supremacy Movement

At the extreme end of the continuum of white racism, violence-oriented groups such as WAR have grown in recent decades, from perhaps 1,500 members in the mid-1970s to 20,000 or 30,000 activists in the 1990s. Tom Metzger is only one of many influential leaders in the white supremacy movement. Yet the mass media and national political leaders have given little sustained attention to this racist development.

Today's complex variety of sometimes cooperating, sometimes competing white supremacy groups typically target African and Jewish Americans as the major villains in U.S. social and economic problems. Sometimes Latino and Asian immigrants and homosexuals are also targets of white supremacists. Over the last decade the most important of the supremacy groups have included (1) several Ku Klux Klan federations; (2) Skinheads, the youth gangs with racialized names; (3) the largely rural Posse Comitatus, whose ideology is vigorously anti–federal government; (4) the Christian Identity movement, a religious denomination whose members believe that God's chosen people are white Anglo-Saxon Protestants; and (5) the Church of the Creator, a Florida-based group that advocates racial war to advance the interests of the "White Race." Most white supremacy groups have taken on some of the beliefs and other trappings of the Ku Klux Klan or German Nazism. In recent years these groups have increasingly worked together and hold annual gatherings in Tennessee, Idaho, and other states. Elinor Langer has estimated that there are perhaps 20,000 active members in the groups, with perhaps another 180,000 less active supporters who buy or accept their literature. Others have estimated the number of active racist groups to be about 300 and the membership to be even higher than Langer's figure, perhaps as high as 50,000.[62]

One disturbing aspect of the modern white supremacy movement is its increasingly international character. The Skinhead movement originated in Great Britain, where Skinheads were a group that evolved out of the mods—a rock-and-roll subculture that, ironically, viewed black culture positively—to groups of young white working-class toughs who advocated "white power" and beat up Asians in London.[63] The ideas and customs of the British Skinheads migrated across the Atlantic, often carried by punk rock music groups.

Some U.S. white supremacy organizations have maintained ongoing international connections. Commenting on his discussions with German neo-Nazis, Tom Metzger has stated: "There is only one movement. Our goals are similar." As early as 1980, Metzger met with Manfred Roeder, a German lawyer active in anti-Jewish causes. Roeder, a suspect in some bombings, was being sought by the German police. Roeder traveled around the United States meeting with other white supremacy leaders before returning to Germany, where he was arrested.[64] In addition, some U.S. supremacy groups have supported neo-Nazi groups that attack immigrants in German cities. In the early 1990s U.S. Klan leaders met with a few of the estimated 40,000 German right-wing extremists oriented to racial violence and terrorism and helped establish Klan chapters in several German cities, including Berlin.[65] Numerous searches of neo-Nazi homes by German police found Ku Klux Klan publications and other supremacist literature from the United States.[66]

Some observers believe that the white supremacy movement in the United States is quite small in scale. Mira Boland of the Anti-Defamation League has noted that many of the movement's leaders are in prison or deceased, and the others are afraid of criminal or civil prosecution. Boland's perspective was summarized by a journalist who interviewed her: "Although anti-black or anti-Semitic sentiments may be held by a fairly large minority of white Americans. . . . [t]he number who favor denying rights to blacks and Jews, or who support physical attacks, remains relatively small."[67]

Yet some signs indicate that the white supremacy movement is growing and uniting. On August 16, 1992, in a show of national unity honoring the new imperial wizard of the Northwest Knights of the Klan, members of more than a dozen white supremacy groups from a number of states met together in the largest summit of such groups to be held in a decade. The group's ritualized celebration included a cross-burning. Television talk show host Geraldo Rivera traveled to Janesville, Wisconsin, to film the gathering for an August 1992 program. One of the white supremacists reportedly shoved Rivera and insulted him: "You're part Jew, part Spic, you're a piece of shit. Your time is up here." Rivera shoved back, and police had to break up the fight.[68]

Between 1992 and 2000, thousands of hate crimes, including violent attacks against Americans of color, have been carried out by white supremacists in U.S. towns and cities. For example, in the summer of 1993 eight whites were arrested for planning violent attacks they believed would bring racial war to the United States. Among other actions, the group planned to kill prominent blacks and Jews and to bomb a black church in Los Angeles. Media accounts reported that one man who was arrested, Christopher Fisher, was the head of a Los Angeles gang called the Fourth Reich Skinheads. Eventually, Fisher received an eight-year sentence for attacking a synagogue with a Molotov cocktail and for bombing two homes.[69]

For most of 1993 some residents of Billings, Montana, were the victims of white supremacist actions, including many acts of vandalism and violence. Early that year racist literature began appearing on car windshields and in mailboxes in Billings. The leaflets attacked a range of groups, including homosexuals, Latinos, blacks, and Jews. In January 1993 white supremacists put racist literature on the windshields of people attending a Martin Luther King, Jr., holiday celebration. There were numerous acts of racialized vandalism. A posterboard swastika was attached to the door of a Jewish synagogue, a bottle was thrown at the home of the local symphony's Jewish conductor, and a concrete block was thrown at the house of another Jewish family. The local newspaper ran editorials against the violence, and many non-Jewish families and Christian churches put menorahs on display in an act of solidarity with the victimized Jewish families. But this widespread community response did not stop white supremacists' violent actions.[70]

Since the early 1990s one of the more active and growing white supremacy groups has been the World Church of the Creator, which celebrates a religion that envisions a racial war that will advance the white cause. The group has been linked to several violent attacks. In the summer of 1993 one minister was convicted of killing a black veteran in Florida. Currently headquartered in Cincinnati, the organization claims thousands of members in the United States and overseas and concentrates much of its attention on young people.[71] Skinheads recruited into the organization have been implicated in violent racial actions. According to Sarah Henry of the Center for Investigative Reporting, in July 1993 one of the Skinheads thought to have set fire to an NAACP office building in Tacoma, Washington, confessed that he was affiliated with this church.[72]

From Illinois to Texas: A Chain of Hate and Death

Reportedly, the World Church of the Creator attracts recruits who are educated, articulate, and young. Supporters come from schools, workplaces, and the prison system. One new recruit, Benjamin Nathaniel Smith, twenty-one years old, was so active in distributing leaflets and recruiting members that in 1998 he was named "Creator of the Year." Many people who knew Smith have remembered him as a calm person, one who presented arguments regarding the superiority of the "white race" in a seemingly calm way. The son of a doctor, he attended an elite public school, and during high school he was remembered for writing a paper denying the Holocaust. In his high school yearbook, he included the phrase "Sic Semper Tyrannis" (Thus Ever to Tyrants), a phrase shouted by John Wilkes Booth after shooting Abraham Lincoln and the phrase printed on Timothy McVeigh's T-shirt on the day he bombed the federal building in Oklahoma City. On the Fourth of July weekend in 1999, Smith, then an Indiana University criminal justice student planning to pursue a law degree, put his semi-automatic gun and pistol in his car and drove around the states of Indiana and Illinois shooting people who looked to him to be black, Jewish, and Asian. He killed two people and injured four others before committing suicide during a subsequent police chase.[73]

Moreover, in one small city to the south, Jasper, Texas, another young white man, John William King, dreamed of forming a chapter of a white supremacist group, the Confederate Knights of America. He reportedly thought of calling his group the Texas Rebel Soldiers. Jasper, the town in which he grew up, is a logging town of 8,400 in the pine woods of east Texas near the border with Louisiana. The population is 60 percent white, but blacks have long held influential political positions there.[74]

On June 7, 1998, John William King, along with two other young white men, Shawn Allen Berry and Lawrence Russell Brewer, beat up James Byrd, Jr., a black resident of Jasper, chained him to the back of a pickup truck, and dragged him several miles to his death along a rough dirt road. When Byrd's body was discovered, his head and right arm were missing.[75]

James Byrd, Jr., grew up in the area and was working as a dry cleaner. He was known as a friendly person, with a deep affection for his three children.[76] Because of health problems, he did not drive and that night had apparently accepted a ride when it was offered. In letters introduced in the trial, one of the white supremacists described the killing as "rolling a tire," which prosecutors said was a derogatory term for assaulting a black person. "Well I did it," Brewer wrote in the same letter. "It was a rush, and I'm still licking my lips for more." Further, he said that "a life sentence would do them no justice" and the lethal injection would be "a little old sleeping medicine."[77] The mostly white juries in the highly publicized trials of the three white men gave them death penalties without long deliberation. The sentences were unusual. These were the first white men sentenced to death for killing a black person *since 1850* in the state of Texas. The national attention given to the crime and the trials was overwhelming for the town and the Byrd family, who throughout the trial advocated reconciliation and community solidarity against racism. Guy James Gray, the Jasper County District Attorney, argued to the jury: "This isn't our case. This case belongs to everyone in the State of Texas and maybe the whole nation. You are the law. You are the state. You are the nation."[78]

Indeed, he is right, but perhaps in more ways than he thought. White racism is not an isolated phenomenon or something in which only white extremists in rural areas engage. It can be found in larger cities as well as in town and rural areas. This racism is integral to the way our society is organized. Note in this Jasper example that racism is most centrally about racist practices that destroy the lives of its targets. It is imbedded in practices, which are often physically violent, and not just in the minds that rationalize the practices.

White racism is often mixed with various forms of denial. For example, in September 1998, New York City's mayor Rudolph Giuliani spoke about "a disgusting display of racism of a few misguided, possibly sick individuals" when it became public that a Labor Day parade in the borough of Queens included a float mocking James Byrd's being dragged to death. The float included white men in blackface wearing dreadlock wigs standing under a sign that read "Black to the Future, 2098." One man—one of six firefighters and police officers on the float—said they did not originally intend to parody the killing in Texas, but somebody just "did it." The area in Queens is mostly white; in the 1990 census there were 2,200 whites, 2 blacks, 11 Asians, and 41 Hispanics there—making it much more segregated than Jasper, Texas. This was not an unusual event for this neighborhood. Previous Labor Day parades had included other "just for fun" floats, such as "Gooks of Hazzard" and "Hasidic Park."[79]

Even though the city government froze all money and equipment for such floats in the future, this type of integration of racist imagery and action requires more than official denunciation to effectively end it. In his comments Mayor Giuliani accents the action of a few individuals and not the system of racism that undergirds what they did. He does not ask why whites, across the nation, often mock black Americans and their lives. He does not ask why white workers spent so much time building a racist float. It is clear from recurring incidents like this that whites have privilege that allows them to appropriate and transform the extreme pain and death of African Americans into an occasion for white fun and levity. Moreover, once again, it is evident in these cases that white-on-black racism dissipates the valuable human resources and energies of all those involved, resources and energies that would be much better spent on building a truly democratic society.

Conclusion

This chapter is centrally about the racist actions and practices of white-racist activists and supremacists. However, the Skinheads and other white extremists described here are not simply representatives of extreme fringe groups, although they are indeed that. In addition, they are related in some significant ways to mainstream white opinion and actions on racial matters. Clearly, many mainstream whites share some portions of the white supremacy movement's racist stereotypes and ideology. As the Stuart case and similar racist hoaxes illustrate, many whites harbor the racist image of the menacing or criminal black male. The mass media, as well as white supremacy publications, have frequently portrayed black men as threats to whites, and particularly as threats to white women. This image can and does have serious consequences for black men, as it did in Boston. The imagery was also a central feature of the "Willie" Horton advertisement used by the senior George Bush in his 1988 presidential campaign, which we examine in a later chapter.

The Reagan and Bush administrations in the 1980s and early 1990s were characterized by considerable laxness in civil rights enforcement. While these administrations prosecuted some white supremacists, some administration officials reportedly shared at least a few of the supremacists' views on racial matters such as affirmative action and civil rights enforcement. In *Blood in the Face,* James Ridgeway has argued that in the 1990s the white supremacy movement was not an aberration but rather reflected racist views that have now penetrated mainstream politics: "Increasingly, race seems to lie just below the surface of nearly every political debate, and the opinions of the extreme right have been voiced by mainstream figures on both the political and cultural scenes, as ever more visible signs of interracial hostility have emerged. Since the early 1980s, especially, the parameters of acceptable discourse and behavior have broadened, making room for more and more openly racialist viewpoints."[80]

While the extreme actions of organized white supremacists are not considered normal or desirable by most white Americans, their actions and racist mythology are rooted in the culture of white society. A broad array of whites accept some part of the mythological legitimation for supremacists' extreme racist rituals, holding an "I disagree with their tactics, but agree that blacks are . . ." perspective. Organized white supremacists are the officiants in extreme racist rites, but many other whites subscribe to their literature or silently sympathize with aspects of their mythology. Numerous mainstream whites, including top political leaders, have parroted racist stereotypes, sometimes while espousing the need for fair play in racial matters. Very telling is the absence of large-scale organizations of whites in Boston, Portland, or other U.S. cities to counter aggressively white supremacists or common racist images and doctrines. To our knowledge there are no major groups with names like "Whites Against Racism," and the term *antiracist* does not yet appear as a defined entry in most English dictionaries. Yet, communities are making efforts to redefine themselves in this context. For example, in Pennsylvania, the Human Relations Committee helped fifty communities to form groups to confront racism. In Boyertown, a historically all-white community where the Klan has a presence, residents formed a coalition and asked citizens to pledge 5–50 cents for each minute the Klan spent in town distributing racist literature. The money raised was used to sponsor the town's first rally to honor Dr. Martin Luther King, Jr.[81]

Taken together, the Stuart murder in Boston, the Skinhead murder in Portland, and the racist lynching in Jasper, Texas, show some of the ways in which the racism embedded in the everyday rhythms of American life and culture is reproduced. These murders were made possible by widely held racist images that shaped white propensities and actions. In the Stuart case, the responses of the police, politicians, and media were accurately predicted by a white murderer planning an insurance scam. Boston's officials ordered an extraordinary hunt for black men in the racially integrated neighborhood where the shooting occurred. The white-run local and national media targeted black-on-white crime for its alleged heinousness while some white politicians cheered. Republican gubernatorial candidates in Massachusetts demanded the reinstatement of the death penalty, and the Democratic candidate went so far as to say that he would like to pull the electric chair switch.

After it became clear that Charles Stuart had murdered his wife, the media did report that the police lineup in which William Bennett was identified was tainted and that the police relied on coerced evidence. However, despite the accumulating evidence of the role stereotyping played in the Boston events, as Christopher Edley, a Harvard law professor and adviser to presidents Jimmy Carter and Bill Clinton put it in 1990, the politicians, police officials, and media commentators avoided confrontation with "their own racism by saying that they were fooled by Stuart and that he manipulated us all. The whole episode—from murder to strip searches to false grand-jury testimony—becomes Stuart's fault."[82] And Governor Michael Dukakis's final state address made a brief reference to "old wounds reopened" by the deception of *one man*. He made no reference to the role of other whites in this racist tale.

The racial hoax cases clearly show that white racism is not just a matter of feelings in the racist assassins' hearts, for they involve a creative manipulation of the social imagination of the large white audience and an expectation of impunity. Few whites would deny that in the cases here the overt white extremists and supremacists are acting and thinking in racist ways. But how many would recognize as racist the widespread white fear and obsessive indignation over the allegations of black criminality, before the allegations were discovered to be false? How many whites would recognize as racist their passive acceptance, their inaction, over a manhunt harassing many black men, an effort driven by a bogus racial profile? Indeed, the overt white supremacists are often cited by white officials and public as the prime examples of the serious racists that remain in this society (see Chapters 7 and 8), examples that most whites seem to feel are far removed from their own thoughts, feelings, and actions.

Some antiracist action has been stimulated by these violent events. Prodded by white supremacists and their violent attacks, some communities have begun to educate themselves in antiracist ways. One example of this community action can be seen in East Peoria, Illinois, a mostly white town on the bank of the Illinois River. Matthew F. Hale, the leader of the racist World Church of the Creator, has lived there with his parents. When he set up headquarters there, some local white residents regarded it as a joke. Only when a member, Benjamin Smith, went on his racist killing rampage did the community decide to take Hale seriously. Dennis Triggs, the city's attorney, said, "We had the sense that benign neglect must come to an end."[83] The benign neglect he had in mind was overlooking blatant racism. The community got in touch with the Center for a New Community, an organization that fights white supremacist groups, and the mayor led the mostly white town in finding ways of combatting hate. Neighborhoods began to post signs announcing "Hate Has No Home Here," while the mayor suggested that "we are in this for the long haul."[84] (Hale did not leave.) Even these modest initial efforts to deal with overt white racism underscore the point that it is not enough just to take individual action; antiracist strategies must focus on re-educating the larger white community.

In this chapter we have combined an analysis of racial hoaxes and overt acts of great physical violence by whites against African Americans in order to show that white racism in operation is much more than a matter of a few racist images in the minds of white perpetrators of such crimes. It involves a large array of *actions*, including those of extreme violence. Moreover, the racial hoaxes work because the white criminals accurately predicted the feelings, thoughts, and reactions of white police officers, court officials, other government officials, journalists, and much of the white population generally. Many of the stereotyped and hateful images in the minds of the hoax perpetrators and those engaging in extremist acts of racial violence circulate all too freely throughout this society. Racist imagery and racist actions, it is clear, are intimately webbed together in the social whole that is white racism.

5

The Racial Profile of
Police Brutality

On April 30, 1992, the announcement of the acquittals of several Los Angeles police officers in connection with the videotaped beating of Rodney Glen King sparked tremendous anger and a major urban rebellion that lasted for several days. By the time the unrest ceased, thousands of black and Latino residents had been arrested for participating in the rebellion. More than fifty people had been killed, and more than 2,400 people were injured. The verdicts also precipitated urban revolts and organized protests in other U.S. cities. Since the 1940s the majority of major riots by African Americans have been precipitated by an incident involving white police officers and black citizens. In looking at such uprisings white observers have often overlooked or played down the role of police actions in generating the rioting. Yet the role of police actions is harder to overlook in the case of the 1992 Los Angeles rioting because of a videotape that documented the beating of an unarmed black man.

The fact that Rodney King was black and the police officers white, the character of the beating, the communications between police officers before and after the arrest, the selection of the places to hold the trials, the composition of the juries, the verdicts in three separate trials—almost every detail in the complex chain of circumstances was probed and examined in racial terms. Yet in contrast, the officers who were prosecuted strongly denied and continue to deny that any racial motives lay behind their beating of King.

An examination of this paradox may provide some further insights into the shape and nature of the system of racial relations and conflict in the United States. Our analysis explores how this police-citizen incident occurred and what its social, legal, and political repercussions were over a period of several years. In our view the police beating of King and its turbulent aftermath should be understood within larger societal and cultural contexts. Different observers will doubtless identify different aspects of these contexts as important. Yet at the heart of the matter is the issue posed by a perceptive observer of U.S. racial relations, Nobel prize winner Toni Morrison: "As is almost always the case, the site of the exorcism of critical national issues was . . . inscribed on the bodies of black people."[1]

The Police Beating of Rodney King and Its Consequences

Rodney Glen King was born in Sacramento, the son of devout Jehovah's Witnesses. His neighbors reported that he was characteristically polite, an image reinforced by his plea after the jury verdict in Simi Valley: "Please can we all get along here. . . . We all can get along."[2] Six feet tall and weighing 225 pounds, King could be intimidating to some perhaps, but he was not the giant monster that white officers portrayed him as at the Simi Valley trial. His friends knew him as a passive man—"Baby Huey," as one described him.[3]

King was convicted prior to the beating incident for a 1989 robbery. Tae Suk Baik, the store owner, told reporters that King had bought gum and then threatened him with a tire iron while ordering him to open the cash register. Boldly, Baik grabbed King's jacket and pulled it off, whipping King with a rod he picked up. King fled but was soon arrested. Baik told reporters: "I held him, and he didn't hit me. I hit him twice."[4] King served a year in prison for the crime. His parole officer described the robbery as an impulsive act of economic desperation: "It was something that wasn't planned, really."[5] After his release from prison, King was employed at Dodger Stadium, where he was said to be a good worker.[6]

We should emphasize that King's biography is irrelevant to the question of his civil rights being honored by the police. Police officers are supposed to respect all individuals' civil rights regardless of who they are or what they might have done.

The Events of March 1991

When Bryant Allen and Freddie Helms, longtime friends, got into Rodney King's car to go for a drive early in March 1991, they did not anticipate that a year later they would be testifying about that drive in one of the most important trials of the twentieth century. It was chilly, and they were driving with the windows up.[7] That night they were driving around, drinking, and having a good time. King was driving too fast down a freeway when his small Hyundai passed the patrol car of the husband-and-wife team of Officers Tim and Melanie Singer. When King did not stop, one of the officers yelled "Pull over" through a bullhorn.[8]

King drove off the freeway into residential neighborhoods at about 55 miles an hour. He even stopped for a red light but failed to pull over. The officers radioed the license plate number to headquarters, noting that the car had approached them from behind at about 115 miles an hour and that it was occupied by three black males. This speed figure was apparently exaggerated; the highway patrol's tests showed the Hyundai could not exceed 97 miles per hour.[9] Using the bullhorn again, Officer Tim Singer advised King to "Pull over to the right. We won't hurt you."[10] This comment seems significant: It can be read as a promise by a white officer to black citizens that they will not be treated badly by the police. It may even anticipate the fear that many black Americans have of the police. Just after midnight King finally stopped in a middle-class neighborhood. Eventually, no fewer than twenty-seven uniformed police officers, twenty-one from the Los Angeles Police Department (LAPD), the California Highway Patrol, and the Los Angeles School District, in a number of patrol cars and a helicopter, converged on the scene.[11] Only one of the LAPD officers was black. Some officials contended that this was only a "chance development."[12] However, one might well question this contention given that 14 percent of the LAPD officers are black.

Tests given several hours after the incident showed that King had a blood alcohol level just below the .08 percent standard of California law. Police officials speculated that King's blood alcohol level might have been twice that permitted by law at the time he was stopped. The tests also showed that he had consumed no illegal drugs. Why did he not stop earlier? King later told his lawyer Steve Lerman that he was afraid the officers would ticket him, which would affect his parole.[13]

George Holliday, a white store manager who lived in the neighborhood, came out on his balcony when he heard voices yelling, "Stop! Stop!" and "Oh my God!"[14] King and his passengers had gotten out of the car, and King was on the ground. In his testimony at the Simi Valley trial, Bryant Allen stated that King was ordered to roll down the car window and place his arms outside. King did this, but when he tried to obey the order to get out of the car, which was difficult because of his seatbelt, the police yanked him out. Allen got out on the other side and lay down. He remembers hearing King screaming. Helms, the third rider, was also ordered to get out and lie down.

Missing the first two minutes of the action, Holliday started filming with his camcorder. The police car headlights provided light for a seven-minute recording. Eleven officers are shown watching while several hit King. Some twenty people came out of their homes, a few of whom yelled at the police not to kill King.[15] Musicians passing in a bus got the closest look. In an interview one musician said that King put up no resistance; another said he thought that the officers were trying to kill King.[16]

Officer Melanie Singer testified at the Simi Valley trial that King was jovial as he obeyed orders to place his hands on the roof of the car. He waved to the police helicopter with his right hand, the other on the car. When Singer told King to keep his hands away from his body, he "grabbed his right buttock with his right hand and shook it at [me]." When she got near King, Singer said, she saw a white LAPD sergeant, Stacey Koon, but because of the noise she could not hear his commands. She saw Koon shoot King with a taser gun. King was ordered to get on the ground. Singer also saw LAPD officer Laurence Powell hit King with a baton, splitting his face. She testified that Officer Powell continued to strike King on the face while giving him no further commands. Singer told the jury there was no reason for the blow to the head or the subsequent blows. Her husband, Officer Tim Singer, testified that he heard a popping sound and saw King still partially on the ground, his face vibrating in convulsion: "I can recall seeing six blows, five to the head." After the beating, King was handcuffed and left bleeding until an ambulance arrived.[17]

The physician who attended King testified at the Simi Valley trial that King required numerous X-rays and had multiple scalp lacerations and blunt-weapon trauma. The doctor reported that King did not act as if he were under the influence of drugs, as the LAPD officers later claimed. Hospital tests showed that King had not used drugs. ABC's *Primetime Live* reported that one police officer told King, "We had a pretty good, hard game ourselves tonight, didn't we? We hit quite a few home runs. Do you know who we were playing tonight, Rodney?" "Yeah," said King, "me." The officer replied, "Well you lost the ball game, didn't you? We won it."[18] In the federal trial of the police officers a year later it was disclosed that Officers Laurence Powell and Timothy Wind took King from the first hospital and delivered him two hours later to another hospital. The prosecution argued that the officers took so long because they wanted to show King off at the police station. The defense countered that the officers took King to the station only to book him.[19]

Two computer messages sent to the police station by Officer Powell from a patrol car suggested the officer's racist attitudes toward black people. The first, sent shortly before King's arrest, described a black family's domestic dispute as being "right out of *Gorillas in the Mist.*" The second message, sent after the King beating, stated, "Oops, I haven't beaten anyone that bad in a long time."[20] The white officer's overt attitude toward his beating of a black man contrasts with the view expressed by most (92 percent) Los Angeles residents in a *Los Angeles Times* poll that the police actions involved the use of excessive force.[21] Moreover, another *Los Angeles Times* opinion poll conducted a few weeks after the King incident found that six in ten whites and seven in ten blacks and Latinos felt that the officers were racially motivated in their violent actions against King.[22]

The Holliday videotape provides a visual record of the incident. Before they knew of the tape's existence, Officers Powell and Wind wrote reports that King had tried to stand up while being handcuffed, causing an officer to fall, and had reached for a possible weapon. These actions were not on the videotape, which shows fifty-six blows delivered in only eighty-one seconds while King was on the ground. The LAPD officers filed reports saying they struck King in self-defense. Sergeant Koon wrote of King's injuries: "Several facial cuts due to contact with asphalt. Of a minor nature. A split inner lip. Suspect oblivious to pain."[23] Powell and Wind started their report by claiming that King was driving 110–115 miles per hour and ignored repeated orders to get out of his car. The report continued: "Defendant finally laid down on the ground, and I [Powell] approached him to handcuff him. Defendant then started to raise up and I placed my knee on his back to prevent this movement. . . . Defendant started to turn and charge towards me." Koon said he fired the taser gun only once and that King recovered immediately and resumed his hostile charge in Koon's direction. "Officer Wind and I drew our batons to defend against the defendant's attack and stuck him several times in the arm and leg area to incapacitate him." Then the report states that King kept on "kicking and swinging his arms at us. We finally knocked defendant down and he was subdued by several officers using the swarm technique."[24]

Holliday's videotape showed different actions—a portrayal of violence by police officers that has since been seen all over the world.

Commenting on the text of the report filed by Officers Powell and Wind, Deputy District Attorney Terry White stated, "When you read this report and then see the video, you realize they are talking about two different incidents. It's a cover-up, and it's disturbing."[25]

The day after the event, Rodney King's brother contacted the police department to file a brutality complaint on his brother's behalf. A few days later, King appeared on television in a wheelchair and with a leg in a cast; at that time he answered "no" to a reporter who asked him if he thought the beating was racially motivated. He said that he was very scared when the police began to beat him and lay down to take whatever came.[26] Later, he would change his statement regarding police motivation. Some observers familiar with the LAPD's record in regard to minorities were surprised at King's early denial of the officers' racial motivation. However, members of the King family have revealed that immediately after the incident Rodney King's mother persuaded them not to publicize a racial slur made by white officers during the beating. A deeply religious woman, she reportedly felt that revealing the epithet would provoke further division between black and white residents of the city.[27]

King was soon released from the hospital; he was not charged with speeding or driving while intoxicated. The doctors examining him found extensive bodily damage: nine skull fractures, a shattered eye socket and cheekbone, a broken leg, a concussion, injuries to both knees, and facial damage.[28] One of the doctors said that the blows to King's head were so severe that several tooth fillings were knocked out and that he might never recover from some of his wounds.[29] King later underwent an extensive surgery.

On March 8 a California grand jury handed down felony indictments charging Sergeant Stacey Koon and Officers Laurence M. Powell, Timothy E. Wind, and Theodore J. Briseño with assault by force likely to produce bodily injury and with unnecessarily assaulting and beating a suspect. Powell and Koon were charged with falsifying their written report of the incident, and Koon was charged with aiding Powell so that he might escape arrest.[30]

The Background

The beating of Rodney King was more than an isolated incident. It took place in a Los Angeles police department with an extensive record of police malpractice. It was also part of a historical process, a long series of local and national events. The political context of the 1980s and early 1990s was a period of lax civil rights enforcement. Thousands of cases of police malpractice were reported to the Department of Justice each year, but few were prosecuted. Each year in the decade 1982–1992 the FBI investigated about 3,000 cases of civil rights violations by police officers, but the Department of Justice prosecuted only about thirty of these each year.[31] During the 1960s and 1970s, the U.S. Civil Rights Commission, created to review the implementation of civil rights laws and to oversee federal compliance with such laws, actively supported the Civil Rights Movement. Its reports on police brutality and other matters of discrimination were cited by policymakers and in Supreme Court rulings. However, during the 1980s President Ronald Reagan intentionally weakened the commission and tried to get rid of its liberal members. The commission's four-month delay in reacting to the King beating and its failure to make any recommendations for police reform signaled a lack of federal support for those struggling to prevent police malpractice.[32]

The LAPD has long been plagued by allegations of police malpractice. It ranks in the top ten departments nationally in the quantity of malpractice complaints received. During the five years prior to 1991, an average of fifty complaints a month had been filed against LAPD officers. In the first two months of 1991, 127 complaints were filed. The data also indicate that the LAPD has a pattern of malpractice that differentially affects citizens of color. While blacks make up only one-eighth of the city's population of 3.5 million, they filed 41 percent of the complaints against LAPD officers in the period between 1987 and mid-1990. One prior police incident has been described as an "orgy of violence."[33] In this 1988 incident some seventy-seven officers invaded the homes of two black families and smashed windows and television sets in apparent retaliation for a telephone threat to a police station.

The officers beat the residents as they were arrested and scrawled "LAPD Rules" on a wall. In another incident police rounded up a group of thirty mostly Latino and black youths who entered a park in a mostly white neighborhood. The youths were ordered at gunpoint to lie on the ground and were then forced to walk on their knees while officers directed racial slurs at them.[34]

Officer Powell, whom the videotape shows delivering blows to Rodney King, had a history of violence, according to Salvador Castaneda, a fabric cutter who filed suit against Powell and the LAPD for injuries inflicted by Powell in October 1989. Powell's report allegedly did not explain the Latino worker's injuries or coincide with witnesses' accounts. In addition, Officer Briseño had been suspended in 1987 following an administrative hearing regarding his hitting and kicking a handcuffed suspect.[35]

Police harassment has sometimes been directed against affluent blacks in southern California. A former Los Angeles Laker and businessperson, Jamaal Wilkes, who is black, was stopped by LAPD officers and handcuffed because his automobile registration was about to expire. Joe Morgan, a former baseball star, was physically abused and wrongfully detained on suspicion of dealing drugs. Morgan filed a civil suit and was awarded $540,000 in punitive damages.[36]

Most police malpractice goes unpunished. Very few of the hundreds of complaints filed each year (4,400 between 1987 and 1990) against LAPD officers have resulted in felony charges.[37] One *Los Angeles Times* analysis of the malpractice claims against the LAPD from 1987 through mid-1990 found significant racial disparities in the percentage of complaints that were upheld. Most complaints against officers were not upheld, regardless of the race of the complainant, but complaints by whites were more likely to be upheld than were complaints made by blacks or Latinos. Black citizens, who constitute 13 percent of the city's population, filed 41 percent of the complaints, 5 percent of which were upheld. Latinos, who make up 40 percent of the population, filed 28 percent of the complaints, 7 percent of which were upheld. Anglos, who are 37 percent of the population, filed 30 percent of the complaints, 9 percent of which were upheld.[38]

Some victims of LAPD misconduct have sought redress through the courts. Some portion of the money awarded to such victims ($11.3 million in 1990 alone) represents a cost of racism that is borne by taxpayers.[39] Communities across the country face similar problems of police abuse of citizens and expenses for taxpayers.[40] Yet monetary settlements indemnify black victims and communities for only a small portion of the harm done by police violence.

Investigating the LAPD

Initially, LAPD chief Daryl F. Gates did not condemn his officers but called the beating an "aberration," and the brutality complaint made by Rodney King's brother was quickly dismissed. Yet after the videotape was aired repeatedly on national television, a police cover-up of the events became impossible. Between March 1991 and February 1992 several investigations were launched. One was directed by a commission headed by Warren Christopher, who was later to serve as secretary of state under President Bill Clinton. The Christopher Commission report on the LAPD found that although the "vast majority" of LAPD officers did not use excessive force, there was "a significant number of officers who repetitively misuse[d] force" and "receive[d] inadequate supervisory and management attention." The commission found that about 3.5 percent of the LAPD officers were the central culprits in the misuse of force. Few of these officers were disciplined, and many had received glowing evaluations or promotions. Reviewing 103 brutality case settlements in which more than $15,000 was paid to plaintiffs, the commission found that a majority of the cases "appeared to involve clear and often egregious misconduct resulting in serious injury or death to victims." Yet the discipline against officers was usually light or nonexistent.[41]

The commission's review of the communications system that links patrol cars with each other and with headquarters revealed a number of typed computer messages that seemed to condone excessive force and presented evidence of racism. Here are a few samples from the period between November 1989 and February 1991:

I would love to drive down Slauson with a flame thrower. . . . [W]e would have a barbecue.

If you encounter these negroes, shoot first, ask questions later.

U can c the color of the interior of the [vehicle] . . . dig. Ya, stop cars with blk interior.

This hole is picking up, I almost got me a Mexican last night but he dropped the dam gun too quick.[42]

Assessing these messages, other police data, and testimony from community hearings, the Christopher Commission came to the conclusion that expressions of racism were common in the LAPD and that the excessive use of force by some officers was "aggravated by racism and bias."[43] The racially based mind-set, apparently shared by a significant number of white officers, may explain some police malpractice. The Christopher Commission's conclusions on malpractice and mismanagement in the LAPD were echoed in a report of a second commission, chaired by former FBI director William Webster, that was charged with looking into the riot that followed the Simi Valley jury verdict on the King beating.

The police hierarchy in Los Angeles, a city whose population is substantially made up of people of color, did not include many senior officers from communities of color. In 1991 two California Department of Fair Employment and Housing cases pending against the LAPD alleged that the police department had systematically denied promotions and advancement to black and Latino officers. The 8,300-member department included seven Latinos, seven blacks, and not one Asian American above the rank of lieutenant. There was a single representative from the city's communities of color among the department's seven deputy and assistant chiefs. Although 27 percent of white officers had been promoted to the rank of detective between

1986 and 1987, only 12 percent of black officers received similar promotions. One-quarter of the white officers who applied for the rank of lieutenant were promoted, compared with only 4 percent of black officers who applied.[44] The two discrimination complaints were settled in 1991 when the city council entered into a consent decree designed to improve diversity at all police ranks.

The Simi Valley Trial

Much legal maneuvering followed the indictments of four LAPD officers. Defense attorneys were particularly concerned that widespread publicity on the case in Los Angeles County would jeopardize their clients' chances for a fair trial. After several months of debate, a California Superior Court judge rejected the prosecution's proposal to move the trial to Alameda County, choosing instead Simi Valley in nearby Ventura County, which has few black residents. Moreover, a large proportion of the LAPD's white officers live in Ventura County and are neighbors of the Simi Valley jurors, not one of whom turned out to be black.[45] The prosecution had argued that Alameda County's racial diversity would give black citizens a better chance of participating on the jury. The judge, however, felt that moving the trial to Alameda County would be "too costly and inconvenient."[46]

John R. Hatcher III, president of Ventura County's NAACP chapter, wrote a letter to local newspapers describing the decision to move to Simi Valley as "a slap in the face" of African Americans. He said that most black residents view that county as "the home breeding ground" for white supremacists. He added that "they would be better off going to Mississippi. . . . King is on trial, not those officers. King will lose and the officers will win." A *Los Angeles Times* story juxtaposed Hatcher's statements with local white officials' expressions of outrage and disappointment at such views.[47]

The trial of the white officers began at the Simi Valley courthouse on March 4, 1992. After summarizing the indictments, Prosecutor Terry White introduced the Holliday videotape, stating, "The evidence is going to show that the beating you are going to see in this videotape is unjustified." Then he continued, "You are going to see the videotape a number of times during this trial, but we believe the evidence will show that you'll see that you have a man who was down, a man who was not aggressive, a man who was not resisting, yet those blows from Powell's and Wind's batons continued and continued and continued—for no just reason."[48] White conceded that the evidence would show that King had been speeding.

Bryant Allen, the prosecution's first witness, testified that he and his companions were drinking over the course of the evening. He said that after he got out of the car he could "only hear Mr. King howling, screaming."[49] The prosecution's expert witness on the use of police force, LAPD commander Michael Bostic, testified that from the time Officer Briseño reached out to push away Powell's baton (see below), about 20 seconds into the tape, the officers' use of force was excessive and inappropriate.

Defense attorney Darryl Mounger, representing Stacey Koon, told the jury in his opening statement, "There's only one person who is in charge of the situation: Mr. King."[50] The defense intended to put Rodney King, not the police officers, on trial. Defense strategy rested on an attempt to define the empirical evidence presented to the jurors as the routine reactive behavior of professionally trained officers. Mounger recounted the facts, starting with the officers' initial sighting of a speeding car and their request for a backup unit. He described King as "under the influence of something." The lawyer told the jurors that when Koon saw this big man not complying with officers' orders, "He knew the danger. He knew how his officers are trained. It is the suspect who controls what happens." A police attorney then showed the jurors a chart listing six steps in the escalation of force: "1. Verbalization, 2. Firm grip, 3. Chemical agent, 4. 50,000 volts, Baton." He explained that when the less severe tools are ineffective, an officer goes to the level of deadly force: "5. Neck hold," which can cause death, and "6. Deadly weapons." The chart presented a concrete justification for the use of force, implying that these were written procedures by which police officers lived. Although no source was provided to authenticate the list, it remained in the courtroom within sight of the jury for part of the trial.[51]

Powell's attorney concentrated on refuting the testimony of California Highway Patrol officer Melanie Singer, whom he referred to as "Mrs. Melanie Singer," and on challenging the reliability of Holliday's videotape. He told the jury that Singer's testimony that Powell had hit King five to seven times was wrong, that the medical evidence "will be that there were no head shots. . . . [A] strike to the head or a strike to the face can be fatal with this baton." Such blows, which are against LAPD regulations, are visible on the videotape. If the medical evidence failed to show the results of such blows, the jurors could not trust the videotape. This was a surprising line of defense, since the press had already reported that physicians treated King for serious facial and head wounds. This lawyer summarized his defense by telling the jurors that the tape contained "a lot of things that you do not see at first. A lot of things that you only see after examination."[52] In his testimony Officer Powell denied that his comment over the radio about "gorillas in the mist" had a racial connotation and claimed that he used the word "beating" to describe what he had done only because it was a professional term used among police officers.[53]

Contradicting the argument of Powell's lawyer, Theodore Briseño's attorney informed the jurors that his client "saw Powell hit Mr. King in the face" and pushed Powell away when he saw the torrent of blows. He said Briseño perceived that his fellow officers were "out of control," and he yelled to King to "stay down." Briseño's own testimony earned him the nickname of "the choirboy" among the jurors. Briseño was charged with assault with a deadly weapon and use of force under cover of authority for allegedly kicking King in the head as he lay face down on the pavement, yet he sounded more like a witness for the prosecution than a defendant on the witness stand. He described the "beating" as "wrong" and stated that he yelled at Powell, "Stop, that's enough." Briseño was yet another witness who testified that Powell "hit [King] on the right side of his face," adding that Powell continued to strike King "from the shoulders up."[54] While apparently damaging his fellow officers' case, Briseño's testimony also emphasized the same point with which the defense opened the trial: that Rodney King was in control of the events.

One expert witness for the defense, Sergeant Charles Duke, Jr., who was in charge of recruit training for the LAPD, testified in a frame-by-frame analysis of the videotape that all the blows hitting King were "reasonable." In his view, each baton swing or kick was a direct response to "aggressive," "combative," or "resistive" moves on the part of King. "This sounds cruel, but it may come to the point that you have to break a bone or so incapacitate a suspect to where he can no longer rise and pose a threat," Sergeant Duke told the jury.[55]

Sergeant Koon's testimony was perhaps the most effective. Looking jurors in the eye, he emphasized his street experience. His testimony paralleled the expert testimony of Sergeant Duke. Both countered the testimony of Commander Bostic, who testified for the prosecution. Self-assured and articulate, Koon argued that the task of subduing black men like King required strong police force.

The Simi Valley Jury Deliberations

Late in April 1992 the California Superior Court judge instructed the jury, which then convened in a room with a television set and videotape player. D. M. Osborne, a legal researcher who later conducted interviews with seven jurors and two alternates, commented that the jurors' reverence for the police shaped the way they saw the trial: The jurors accepted the negative view of King offered by the defense, that of a "hulking, ferocious criminal suspect" who posed a physical threat to the officers.[56] The jurors' mind-set evidently incorporated the objectification of black men as dangerous monsters.

The matter of race was rarely explicitly mentioned during jury deliberations. The jurors began with the case of Officer Briseño. Four jurors told Osborne that they were very surprised when Briseño's lawyer let him testify that Powell had hit King hard on the head.[57] The jury ultimately believed Briseño's account of his own actions, and he was the first to be acquitted. However, according to Osborne some jurors were reportedly hostile to Briseño because of his criticism of the other officers.

One juror told Osborne about the jury's approach to the videotape: "We all agreed that it was a bad beating. But we had to kind of leave the emotional impact of the evidence behind, and just weigh things on the physical evidence." Another agreed, saying, "Maybe that's the reason why we got the verdicts we did. I wasn't into it emotionally."[58] These comments are important in understanding not only the jury verdict but also much white thinking about black targets of police violence. When the jurors decided to agree cognitively that it was a "bad beating" but to ignore its emotional impact and suppress their feelings, they ceased to see the victim as a human being. Racism made King an objectified villain.

The jurors moved on to the case of Officer Wind, the only defendant not to take the stand. The prosecution had seldom mentioned Wind during the trial. Wind's lawyer argued that he was merely following orders and showed that each time Wind struck King he moved back to assess the impact. To exonerate Wind, the jurors had to dismiss Commander Bostic's expert testimony on force and accept Sergeant Duke's testimony. Wind was the second to be acquitted.[59]

The jurors then considered the case against Officer Powell. After some initial confusion, the jurors narrowed the question to whether the force Powell applied was legal. A first poll of the jurors counted nine votes for acquittal and two for conviction. One woman resisted the group's analytical method for assessing the tape: "I kept [looking at the tape and] saying, 'This can't be right.' What I saw was wrong." However, heated exchanges convinced her to join the other jurors in acquitting Powell. Osborne quotes her as saying, "There was no clear area [on the tape] where blows were given that could have been construed as a head shot. I could not show it."[60] Yet four eyewitnesses, including Officer Briseño, described blows to the head by Powell, and medical evidence confirmed that there had been blows to the head. To reach its conclusion, the jury had to reject both the eyewitness accounts and the medical evidence. They also had to dismiss Officer Powell's own description of his actions as a bad beating. One of the jurors also told Osborne, "[Powell] could have called [King] the worst name in the world. . . . What he did [to King] didn't show that he was a racist or hated black people or anything like that."[61]

The jurors interrupted their deliberations regarding Powell to consider charges against Koon, who was in command of the officers at the scene. The jurors basically agreed that the "mistakes" in the police reports by Koon and Powell—for example, their misrepresentation of the wounds King sustained and of the situation as one of self-defense—were not significant. Koon was acquitted.[62]

The jurors discussed whether the videotape showed the blows to King's head by Officer Powell that the witnesses described. (In the second trial, held in April 1993, an FBI-enhanced videotape showed those hits so clearly that the jury came to the conclusion that they were inflicted as the witnesses described.) The discussion then moved to a detailed analysis of how King's movements should be interpreted on the videotape. Eventually, the jury deadlocked 8 to 4, with the majority favoring acquittal. Briseño, Wind, and Koon had been acquitted on all charges. Powell was acquitted on all charges except that of excessive force, on which charge a hung jury had to be declared.[63]

Community Response: An Urban Rebellion

The acquittals precipitated a major urban rebellion by angry Angelenos. The black rioters were joined by Latinos on the second day. Los Angeles, which had been the site of the first large-scale urban black revolt in the 1960s, was now the scene of the largest urban rebellion by black and Latino Americans in the twentieth century. By the end of the rioting, thousands of black and Latino rioters were arrested, and more than fifty people had been killed. Property damage, much of it to Asian American and other nonblack businesses, exceeded a billion dollars. At one point twenty thousand police officers and National Guard soldiers patrolled large areas of Los Angeles, and their numbers made the area resemble a military dictatorship. The verdicts also precipitated black revolts in other U.S. cities. As in the riots of the

1960s, the underlying conditions generating the violent protests in Los Angeles included not only police violence but also racial discrimination, poverty, unemployment, and poor housing conditions.

Since the 1930s, white media analysts, police officials, and politicians have interpreted urban rebellions by African Americans as wild rampages of local felons, young delinquents, outside agitators, and other "riffraff." Rioters are viewed as motivated by greed or "fun." However, research on black rebellions of the 1960s and 1980s has shown this view to be inaccurate and highly biased. Rioters are substantially motivated by anger over oppressive living conditions, which are rooted in racism and the terms of capitalism. Although the majority of black rioters have typically been under thirty years of age, most have not been young teenagers. The majority are typically native-born or long-term residents of the riot areas.[64] Although we have no detailed statistics for the 1992 Los Angeles rebellion, the available data mostly confirm the earlier pattern.[65] In the past, moreover, white observers have tended to overlook the central role of police malpractice in generating black rioting. However, the role of police violence is harder to overlook in the 1992 Los Angeles rioting because it was generated by a videotape that documented the police beating of an unarmed black man, and fueled by acquittal of the police officers who did the beating.[66]

The National Reaction: Congress and the Press

The Simi Valley jury apparently saw something different from what most viewers in the nation and around the globe saw on the Holliday videotape. Most Americans who viewed the videotape were shocked by the actions of the police officers. Statements found in the *Congressional Record* provide insight into how the beating was seen by U.S. elected officials. Representative Louis Stokes, an Ohio Democrat, described the experience of watching the videotape on national television: "We felt each brutal blow, as the nightsticks raised up by police officers fell repeatedly on Mr. King's head, shoulders and body. In horrifying detail, we all witnessed 7 minutes of a brutal beating by police officers sworn to uphold the law and protect citizens like Mr. King."[67] Representative Craig A. Washington, a Texas Democrat, stated on the floor of the House that "most good-thinking people in this country would have attempted to stop another citizen, or even a police officer, from beating a dog like they beat Rodney King."[68] Ron de Lugo, Democratic delegate to Congress from the Virgin Islands, stated his "deep sense of horror, frustration and despair in the wake of the recent brutality."[69]

Many elected officials called for action. Representative Howard L. Berman, a Democrat who represented the district where the beating occurred, asked for an immediate FBI investigation of what he feared was "systemic police brutality in Los Angeles." He called the FBI director's contention that the FBI lacked authority to conduct systematic investigations of police malpractice "unadulterated hogwash."[70] Representative David Dreier, a Republican from Los Angeles County, stated that he was "embarrassed and outraged." He asserted that racism was clear in the officers' actions and asked that we "as a Congress, and we as a country, do everything we can to ensure that it is stopped."[71] Representative Julian C. Dixon, a California Democrat, said of the incident: A "vicious and brutal beating was administered. . . . Since then, Americans throughout the Nation have viewed the unprovoked and horrifying attack on a helpless, unarmed black motorist. . . . The videotape reveals solid, undeniable evidence that the Los Angeles Police officers engaged in street justice and brutality."[72]

Across the country, newspaper editorials reflected the national shock at the injustice of the Simi Valley jury verdicts. Some writers denounced the verdicts and noted that the rioting was one of its consequences; others interpreted the verdict as yet another type of beating. New York law professor Susan Herman wrote in *Newsday*: "What happened to Rodney King in the courtroom was the same as what happened to him on the highway. Having been judged by a predominantly white police force, he was judged by a predominantly white jury."[73] Herman also noted the jurors' explicit denial of racial bias in the officers' actions, a common element in white thinking on police matters. Significantly, most media reports we have seen that expressed outrage over the Simi Valley verdicts focused on the actions of the police officers or the jurors rather than on the broader problem of institutionalized racism in policing across the United States.

The Second Trial

In a second trial in the spring of 1993, a federal jury convicted Officers Koon and Powell of violating King's civil rights when they ordered or used excessive force to subdue him. Officers Timothy Wind and Theodore Briseño were acquitted on the federal charges. The racially mixed federal jury (one Latino, two African Americans, and nine whites) had the benefit of a new specially enhanced videotape on which it reportedly relied heavily in its judgment that the officers were guilty. In this trial Rodney King testified about his beating for the first time in court, telling the jurors what he remembered. After admitting to drinking, he testified that he stood up and ran when he heard the words, "We going to kill you, nigger!" However, in his testimony Sergeant Koon denied that the officers used the racial epithet, and in cross examination King said he was not sure and that the officers could have used the word "killer" instead of "nigger." King also explained that initially he had not spoken about the epithet following his mother's advice not to make a racial issue out of the beating. Commenting on the impact of the beating, he said: "My whole body was hurting. It felt like I had a mouthful of bones." He stated that the shock delivered by the taser gun made him feel "like my blood was boiling inside me." King told the jury that he never attacked the police officers and was "just trying to stay alive."[74]

Officer Powell's lawyer called California Highway Patrol officer Melanie Singer to the stand. In moving testimony she repeated much of what she had said in the first trial. She said there was no doubt that Officer Powell "struck him in the face." Again she portrayed King as horsing around and acting like an uncooperative drunk. While the lawyers for the officers portrayed King as sweating greatly and saying things in gibberish like he was on PCP, Singer said that just after the beating King was not sweating a lot, was not saying strange things, and did not have the typical smell of PCP. She went on to say that she personally had wanted to assist King after the beating but didn't because she feared "heckling" from the other police officers. She also spoke of King's cries of pain. The testimony of both King and Officer Singer contradicted the LAPD officers' claims that King appeared impervious to pain.[75]

According to a *Houston Chronicle* story, an early draft of Sergeant Koon's book on the King incident referred to King's shaking his buttocks at Officer Melanie Singer as a "Mandingo sexual encounter." According to Koon, "Mandingo" is a term for a black slave. In a hearing before federal judge John Davies without the jury present, federal prosecutor Steven D. Clymer argued that this Koon comment was "racially explicit" and was needed to help show the thinking of the officers at the time of the beating. However, the judge decided against the prosecuting attorneys' request to introduce this manuscript into evidence on the grounds that the phrase was "inflammatory."[76] In the printed version of his book *Presumed Guilty*, Koon removed the term "Mandingo" but left in his construction of King's gesture toward officer Melanie Singer as explicitly sexual.[77]

This book also provides Koon's views on whether there was racism in the King incident and in the Los Angeles police department at the time. Koon agrees with other observers that, "Of course racism exists in the LAPD, as it does throughout American business and society at large."[78] He relates several incidents in which he observed blatantly racist comments or actions on the part of white LAPD officers and their supervisors, instances that he found offensive. However, he does not consider this departmental racism as having any effect on his actions or those of the other officers the night of the King beating. In assessing the beating, Koon rejects as "personally repulsive" the suggestion that he or the officers under his command might have singled out Rodney King for special punishment because he was black.[79]

At the second trial Koon and Powell were convicted of violating King's civil rights. The federal prosecutors sought prison terms of up to ten years for those convicted. However, based on his conclusion that King was "uncooperative and combative" and that he had led the officers on a chase, the judge sentenced Koon and Powell each to 2½ years in prison. They would be eligible for release after 25½ months. The judge declined to assess any fines, which could have been as much as $250,000, because in his view the fines would cause hardship. The police officers appealed their sentences, requesting that they be allowed to remain free while they pursued appeals. However, the federal appellate court denied their request because they had been convicted of a crime of violence. The prosecutors also appealed the lenient sentences.[80]

The jury verdicts were the source of some controversy. The national board of the American Civil Liberties Union, after a heated debate, voted 37 to 29 to oppose the federal trial of the four officers on the grounds that it violated their constitutional protection against double jeopardy. However, the U.S. Supreme Court has ruled that second trials such as this are constitutional because the federal government is a sovereign government distinct from state governments.[81] The protests coming from the black community were not about the trial's constitutionality but about the fact that two of the officers were acquitted. A key black leader, Jesse Jackson, condemned the decision.[82] Isabel Wilkerson, a *New York Times* reporter, interviewed several dozen middle-class African Americans in Los Angeles after the first verdicts and again after the second verdicts. She found more anger after the second verdict than after the first. This response would likely puzzle most whites, who might expect blacks to be gratified that two white officers were convicted. Like many other African Americans, however, these middle-class respondents viewed the second court decision as a strong indication of bias in the U.S. judicial system. Wilkerson's respondents noted that only two of the four officers seen in the videotape of the beating were convicted, and then only after two trials, millions of dollars for legal and court costs, an urban uprising, and many deaths and injuries. Because of persisting racism, these African Americans—who have "made it" in the eyes of most whites—did not feel themselves to be first-class citizens and were not hopeful about the future of U.S. racial relations.[83]

The Third Trial

In 1994 Rodney King appeared in yet another trial, one that dealt with his attempt to secure compensatory and punitive damages for what was done to him. In April a federal jury awarded him $3.8 million in compensatory damages to cover lost earnings from his injuries and medical expenses. City of Los Angeles officials did not dispute their responsibility for these damages but did contest the $9.5 million King sought. Moreover, at the trial the city attorneys tried to deemphasize King's losses by arguing that the beating was somehow justified.[84]

A second phase of this trial, which dealt with punitive damages, initially focused on fourteen LAPD officers, those who delivered or witnessed the beating, and then-chief Daryl F. Gates. For the first time Officer Timothy Wind testified, telling the jury that he saw officer Laurence Powell strike Rodney King: "I saw the end of his baton hit Mr. King in the right cheek." LAPD regulations prohibit baton blows to the head because they can be fatal. Had such testimony been given in the earlier trials, it might have helped document the charge of excessive police force against King.[85] Officer Theodore Briseño, who had given testimony against the other officers at the earlier trials, again testified that the beating was wrong. He also stated that he had been ostracized by fellow LAPD officers because of his candid testimony at the first trial. Sergeant Stacey Koon reiterated his position that the King incident involved a managed use of force and was triggered by King's own combative behavior.[86]

The judge dropped Chief Daryl Gates from the lawsuit, justifying his decision this way: "Bad management is not enough. Allowing racism is not enough. Poor supervision is not enough. There is no evidence of causation."[87] Apparently, the judge saw no significant connection between Gates's management procedures that allowed racism in the LAPD and the King beating. This view contradicts that of the

Christopher Commission, whose report strongly criticized Gates for presiding over a police department where sexism and racism were permitted to be common. The judge also dropped all but two of the other officers from the lawsuit because he viewed their role as observers of the beating as a minor matter. On June 1, 1994, the jury decided against awarding Rodney King any punitive damages. The lawyers for the police officers had argued that their clients had no money left to pay any punitive damages. Although the jurors agreed with the earlier verdicts convicting Officers Powell and Koon of violations of King's civil rights, they apparently agreed with the defense lawyers that Powell, Koon, and the other officers had suffered enough.[88]

The Beating of Reginald Denny

The way in which the media and many white officials repeatedly presented the police beating of Rodney King and the rioters' attack on Reginald Denny as closely parallel events illustrates just how distorted most whites' understanding of racial matters has become. During the 1992 Los Angeles riot a television crew videotaped an attack on Reginald Denny, a white truck driver, by several rioters who left him bleeding on the pavement. One of the assailants was filmed doing a little dance. After the initial attack, four black citizens, each acting separately, came forward to protect Denny from further violence and get him to a hospital. Damian Williams, one of the rioters captured on videotape in the process of hitting Denny once in the head with a brick, was tried on charges of attempted murder and aggravated mayhem against Denny and also on charges of assaulting several other people. The jury acquitted Williams of aggravated mayhem and attempted murder but found him guilty of the lesser crimes of simple mayhem (an unpremeditated violation) and of four misdemeanor assaults. Henry Watson, another black man who participated in the attack, was acquitted of attempted murder and found guilty only of a misdemeanor assault. The defense argued, and the jury apparently agreed, that both Williams and Watson were caught up in the rage and mob hysteria of the ongoing rioting.[89]

Many white commentators transformed the Reginald Denny trial into a test of whether a racially mixed (four blacks, four Latinos, two Asians, and two whites) jury would punish black defendants severely for attacking a white man. Most whites were not pleased with the diverse jury's verdicts. A poll of Los Angeles residents conducted a few days after the court decision found only 28 percent of whites agreeing with the verdicts; in contrast, half of the blacks polled agreed with the verdicts.[90] White media commentators across the nation condemned both the verdicts and the jury. Samuel Francis, a syndicated columnist writing in the *Washington Times,* went so far as to speak of a "racially rigged case" indicating that whites "no longer enjoy the same legal rights . . . as non-whites."[91]

Most media presentations assumed that the similarities between the two beatings were self-evident: Both took place in Los Angeles, both were caught on videotape, and both were linked to a riot. However, the causes and significance of the two cases are quite different. The likely motivation for the attacks on Denny and other nonblacks during the Los Angeles uprising was rioters' pent-up rage not only over the King incident and the Simi Valley jury's verdicts but also over years of suffering the oppressive consequences of white racism. The fact that King's beating was carried out by representatives of law and order was highly corrosive of the sense of legitimacy granted to government authority by black citizens.

The context of the King incident was different from that of the attack on Denny. The police officers were not participating in an event that takes place every decade or two at most. In addition, the King beating took place in a department, as the Christopher Commission and others have noted, with a historical problem of police violence targeting black and Latino citizens. The beating of King was carried out by government agents trained and sworn to protect all citizens equally.[92] In contrast, the assault on Denny was carried out by rioters with no government authority in the midst of an explosion of community rage. Significantly, even in the midst of this collective rage several black residents rescued Denny and helped him get to a hospital. In contrast, however, numerous white officers watched the violence against King without making serious efforts to stop it or to give him first aid once it was over.

Why did the mass media and white officials interpret the two incidents as so closely comparable? One reason seems to be an attempt to minimize the broader social and political significance of the King incident. Many media analyses implicitly argued that police violence is not a significant or widespread national problem. Some white analysts seemed to want to match each beating of a black person by police with the beating of an innocent white individual by blacks.

In an interesting commentary on his personal reactions to the Denny and King cases, David B. Oppenheimer, a white professor of law, wrote that when he saw the attack on Reginald Denny on videotape he felt fearful: "There, I thought, but for the grace of God, go I." Because he could see himself in Denny's shoes he had great feeling for him. However, when he viewed the videotape of the Rodney King beating he was "horrified, but not afraid. For King I had sympathy; for Denny, empathy." Reflecting on this differential reaction, Oppenheimer notes that his black acquaintances could see themselves caught up in such an incident, which was a clear reminder that police violence is possible anywhere for black men and women. Yet this everyday threat is one with which most white Americans cannot empathize, for it is too foreign and remote. Whites do not face a "history in this nation of racial violence against whites."[93]

Racial Profiling and Guilt Marked by Color

On January 27, 2000, Robert Schenck, a twenty-nine-year-old black man from South Carolina, was visiting his family in New York City. Picked up in a police sweep of apartment buildings, he spent that night in jail before finding himself in Manhattan court charged with trespassing. A construction worker with no criminal record, he pleaded guilty to trespassing and paid a fine, in a proceeding that lasted less than a minute. After the incident, he said that he was in the apartment building with friends looking for his cousin's apartment when they were arrested by officers who had already arrested several other men for trespassing. Even though he told them he was visiting a friend, "before I could knock on the door, the police had a gun at my head." Most people arrested in the sweep that night were black or Latino, and they were brought to the night court of judge Martin Murphy, who usually sees nearly one hundred people each night. Murphy has defended the city's aggressive policy: "[T]respassing sweeps in apartment buildings sometimes capture innocent people, but they also lead to major arrests." Steven Fishner, New York's criminal justice coordinator, has argued that the arrests were justified: "[T]hey have had a tremendous beneficial impact on decreasing crime and improving the quality of life in the city."[94]

On December 30, 1998, in Riverside, California, police officers shot to death a young black woman, nineteen-year-old Tyisha Miller. After arriving to help with a flat tire, a friend and a relative of hers found Miller unconscious in her car, with the doors locked and a gun in her lap. Fearing that she was having medical problems, they called 911 for an ambulance. Instead, four police cars arrived. Police knocked on her window and asked her to unlock the doors and get out. According to witnesses, she remained reclined in her seat, shaking as if from a seizure, and holding the gun in her lap. After breaking the car's window, one of the officers, under the impression that she was reaching for her gun, began firing. The officers fired some twenty-seven shots at a woman who appeared to be unconscious and having medical problems. Afterwards a friend of hers said "that they might as well have lynched her."[95] Within the context of law enforcement and court systems dominated by whites, with racist images and stereotypes of black Americans in numerous white heads, this type of police violence is an everyday experience for black communities.

Ironically perhaps, the 1960s Civil Rights Movement was fought and won victories by declaring the moral obligation of fair and equal treatment under the law. Equality and justice frame the possibilities of freedom, and greater freedom becomes attainable only when people are united and believe "injustice anywhere is a threat to justice everywhere."[96] The racist principles that the Civil Rights Movement fought against are inconsistent with international principles of social justice and human freedom. Under the system of white racism, racist norms and values are accepted as the basis of much morality, often making existing laws and informal policing norms—such as those dictating racial profiling—unjust, inhumane, and destructive.[97] Many existing laws and rules protect and celebrate white privileges and the racist images and understandings of whites in regard to African Americans and other Americans of color. Along with millions of people of color, Americans like Robert Schenck, Tyisha Miller, and Rodney King must experience daily the racist images dancing in white heads and the consequent injustice and violence that constitute white racism.

Serious investigations of racism in law enforcement are rare, especially police misconduct and malpractice in the United States, and they seldom lead to punishment or changes in the system. A few research studies indicate that police abuses disproportionately target citizens of color. For example, in a search of major national and regional newspapers for a period two years, Kim Lersch found reports of 130 incidents of serious police brutality against citizens. White police officers were centrally involved in 93 percent of these brutality cases; black or Latino citizens were the victims in 97 percent of the reported police assaults. Significantly, an officer was punished for brutality in only 13 percent of the incidents, and then the typical punishment was a brief suspension from duty.[98] Whether the malpractice occurs in the process of investigating a crime, as in Boston, or in direct police brutality and violence, as in the Lersch study, perpetrators need have little fear of punishment when their victims are not white.

The use of racial profiling has been common in U.S. law enforcement agencies. One black dentist in East Orange, New Jersey, has reported that he was pulled over more than fifty times in three years on the New Jersey Turnpike. He finally sold his BMW so that he would no longer attract white officers' attention.[99] Similarly, Alvin Penn, a black New Jersey state senator, was stopped by police officers while turning his car around on a dead end street. When he asked why he had been stopped, the officer replied that "he didn't have to give a reason for stopping me and said if I made an issue of it, he would say I was speeding."[100]

This racial profiling by police officers often involves routine stops and searches targeting people of color, especially blacks and Latinos. In 1996, a New Jersey state judge ruled that New Jersey troopers had an informal policy of targeting blacks for stops and arrests on the turnpike. According to one study, even though 14 percent of the motorists were black, they made up 46 percent of those stopped and 77 percent of those searched. In the late 1990s the controversy came to the surface after state troopers opened fire on three unarmed black and Latino men in a van stopped on the turnpike. The New Jersey governor and attorney general acknowledged that state troopers used racial profiling. This type of policing involved some state troopers engaging in "spotlighting," the shining of lights into cars to see the race of the driver. It also involved "ghosting," the falsification of records to conceal the disproportionate number of motorists of color stopped by police officers.[101]

The nation's media have been full of accounts of tragic cases of racial profiling. One recent instance involved Amadou Diallo, an unarmed black man who was shot to death on February 4, 1999, by four New York City police officers who were members of an elite plainclothes police unit designed to clean up the streets through aggressive policing. The officers fired forty-one shots, hitting Diallo nineteen times. The officers saw him standing in the vestibule of his apartment building. Initially, Diallo apparently tried to show the police officers his wallet to prove who he was. During the trial of the four officers, in which they were accused of second-degree murder in addition to other lesser charges, one of the officers' lawyers said his client saw Diallo "reaching into his back pocket, saw this black object come out. My client yelled 'Gun.'" All four officers pled not guilty.[102] The trial was moved from a predominantly black area to a predominantly white area in Albany, New York, where a jury trial ended in the officers being acquitted of all charges, apparently because their lawyers succeeded in convincing the jury that the police officers really thought Diallo's wallet was a gun. It seems likely, however, that if Diallo had been white, the officers would have been much slower in their judgment that Diallo was a life-threatening danger to them. The change of venue in this case, as in the case of Rodney King, no doubt contributed to the acquittal.

The Diallo killing resulted in civil rights demonstrations from New York to Washington, DC. Carrying placards and shouting, "No justice, No peace," the demonstrators demanded a federal response to this and other cases of police brutality. For several months demonstrators demanding justice engaged in protest and civil disobedience around the City Hall and the Bronx building where Diallo was shot, and throughout New York City. Amadou Diallo became a symbol of police brutality and a way to nationalize the fight against it. The NAACP's president Kwesi Mfume said, "The Diallo situation is emblematic of a larger set of social ills. What we hope to do here today is to keep this issue before the American public."[103]

Amadou Diallo's killing came at a time when the New York police department was confronting accounts of another white officer's torture of Abner Louima, a thirty-two-year-old Haitian immigrant, while he was handcuffed in the restroom of a police station on August 9, 1997. One police witness, a police sergeant, said officer Justin Volpe thrust a stick into Louima's rectum, causing severe injuries. Later officer Volpe told two other police officers, "I broke a man down."[104] During the trial of Volpe and four other officers accused of aiding in the torture and cover-up, the local newspapers concentrated on Volpe, portraying him as a "big brother" to local children. One of his parents' neighbors said, "[H]e's always been a great kid, very helpful around the neighborhood. Everyone makes mistakes. I hope the judge can give him some leniency." His neighbors felt bad: "It's a shame that this has happened to such a nice family." Not realizing the irony of his statement, Volpe's father, a retired police officer, said his son "was the victim of a modern-day lynching." Who was indeed the victim of a lynching here?[105]

During the federal court trial, Volpe's father still insisted that his son was a "political prisoner" and a "sacrificial lamb" to satisfy a public demand for vengeance.[106] Sincere fictions of the white self seem evident here—the idea that white officers are basically good and should not be held accountable for their apparently racist actions. Asking mercy from the court during his sentencing to thirty years in a penitentiary, Volpe admitted his guilt and apologized, not to Louima, but to his own family.[107]

The Centrality of Racism in the Criminal Justice System

Public opinion surveys on crime in the United States generally find that majorities of both blacks and whites favor the death penalty for persons convicted of murder, want juveniles who commit violent crimes to be prosecuted as adults, favor much gun control, oppose the legalization of illicit drugs, and believe there is too much violence on television and too few police officers on the streets.[108] In contrast, however, a majority of blacks, but only a minority of whites, answer "yes" to a question as to whether they would be afraid to walk alone at night in their neighborhood. Significantly, three-quarters of black respondents, but only 35 percent of whites, believe that black citizens are treated more harshly than whites by the U.S. criminal justice system.[109]

Ironically, there is in U.S. criminology a common argument that the data show little evidence of racial bias in the criminal justice system. Much of the support for this view comes from studies of criminal justice procedures and sentencing. Some major studies show that, controlling for arrest records and similar factors, white and black defendants get similar sentences.[110] However, these criminology studies do not research the quality and fairness of the evidence on which these criminal justice procedures and sentences are based. As we are learning from recent revelations about policing in a few U.S. cities, there are compelling data and testimony that the evidence on which defendants of color are convicted is often fabricated by the police.

In southern California, for example, the case of Javier Ovando and the linked scandal in the Rampart Division of the LAPD have dramatized the quality of the evidence on the basis of which a large number of defendants of color have been incarcerated. Ovando was the first to be released from prison when former LAPD officer Rafael Perez revealed to investigators that he and his partner had shot Ovando numerous times, planted a gun on him, and then testified falsely that Ovando had attacked them. Ovando was paralyzed and served two years before his release. Officer Perez had been arrested for allegedly stealing cocaine from his police evidence locker, and as part of a plea-bargaining process, he said that he and officers in the Rampart division of the LAPD had framed, beaten, and shot many innocent suspects.[111]

As a result of the Perez testimony and other investigations, in September 1999 eleven of the Rampart officers were suspended. In a string of related events, city and county officials took a variety of actions. In fall 1999 the LAPD Chief Bernard Parks set up a board of inquiry to investigate police corruption and urged new officers at a police ceremony to be honest. The Los Angeles County District Attorney publicly said that he would bring back into operation an old police unit that would more aggressively inquire into police violence. The city attorney abandoned weapons charges against one accused man because Officer Perez had been a witness for that case. Two men convicted on drug charges were freed because of tainted convictions. Late in 1999 a decorated war veteran filed suit in federal court charging that officer Perez had fabricated evidence that resulted in a long prison sentence. Another man brought a lawsuit seeking more than $100 million from local authorities; he too alleged that he had been framed by local police officers. Most strikingly, the Los Angeles district attorney and public defender admitted that there might be some 3,000 criminal cases that were contaminated by police malpractice. By January 2000 some twenty officers were facing criminal charges or had been relieved of duty, and judges were continuing to dismiss corrupted criminal cases. In February 2000 police chief Parks estimated that it might eventually cost some $125 million to compensate the victims of police corruption, and he submitted an "integrity package" to the local police commission with various reforms, including lie detector testing for new police officers. Also in February the FBI began its own investigation of LAPD corruption.[112]

This list of events stemming from the corruption scandal in the LAPD is only the beginning, for other data on police corruption and malpractice are still coming out as we write. Recently, the U.S. Department of Justice has gotten involved, and there are growing disputes among city and county officials as to how to handle the deep-lying problem of police corruption. Eventually, the cost of the Rampart scandal will likely climb to hundreds of millions in damages alone. Additionally, there is the cost of the time and energy of police and court officials. Most important, there is the pain from years wasted in prison by those, usually people of color, who are wrongly convicted. Once again, we see white racism as a set of institutionalized arrangements generating large-scale societal waste. Taken together with other data revealing police malpractice, framing, and evidence-planting in other urban and rural police departments, these data directly confront the notion that there is no racism in the criminal justice system. There is, indeed, much racist practice and ideology in the criminal justice system, if only because the whites who generally control that system are not much different from those outside it. Thus, the Rodney King case and similar cases are but the tip of the iceberg in regard to racist practice and other related corruption in the U.S. policing and judicial system.

Conclusion

The Rodney King beating, the shooting of Amadou Diallo, and the torture of Abner Louima are evidence of racism within mainline police and court institutions. Within the context of criminal justice, the "justice" is not the same for whites and those who are not white, especially African Americans. The question of trust, a pivotal issue in establishing the relationship between societal institutions and the individual, rests on a reality of fairness and justice set in the foundations of institutions. Some scholars have argued that with the rise of modernity, the sources of citizen trust have altered, leaving the society to experience rapidly varying forms of uncertainty and certainty, irrationality and rationality. Even though the fading of trust in institutions may be integral to the modern world, without trust societies experience dissipation of sense of self and of community. White racist practices generate and facilitate an erosion of this trust among black citizens and other people of color. This society faces a challenge when its citizens of color conceptualize cooperation and peace after being faced with savagery, brutality, and death from institutions supposedly functioning to protect them and their communities. The cases of Rodney King, Tyisha Miller, Abner Louima, Amadou Diallo, and Robert Schenck are not aberrations but are markers of how human possibilities are limited by the practices of white racism.

The Christopher Commission found that within the LAPD organization, in the summary words of a *Los Angeles Times* article, "racially motivated brutality" was "institutionalized."[113] The fact that racialized actions are routinely allowed within organizational structures like the LAPD is far more significant than are the attitudes or actions of particular police officers.

The views of some black officers in the LAPD add depth to the findings of the Christopher Commission. Assistant Chief Jesse Brewer, the highest ranking black at the LAPD until his resignation in February 1991, told the Christopher Commission that he could not indict the whole department but that "it is the [police] culture we must deal with . . . the culture of 'us' against 'them.'"[114] In a striking op-ed piece, Brenda Grinston, a black woman and former LAPD officer who resigned from the force in 1985, wrote: "The racism was built into the department's system." She reported experiencing "more terror and racism from the police brotherhood and administration than I ever did from suspects in the street." She reported working under a lieutenant who had been a member of a white supremacist organization. As a black female, she reported: "I saw overt, blatant hatred for the black constituency we were supposed to be serving with equality under the law." Giving us an insight into how some officers, even some officers of color, can become what we have called acolytes in racist events, she explained that minority officers like her are "continually faced with the question: 'Which side are you on?'"[115] These officers know that coming forward to speak the truth will end their careers because of the police code of silence, silence toward racism and violence.

White racism is a form of domination that shares some of the features of other forms of domination, such as sexism and class oppression. Dominant groups may use physical force, economic force, or symbolic force against subordinate groups. Pierre Bourdieu has argued that conditions of domination are easier to perpetuate when symbolic mechanisms are established that make people automatically accept those conditions as legitimate. Once such mechanisms are in place, the dominant group needs only allow the "sordid system" to take its course. But until these mechanisms are fully operational, the dominant group must "work directly, daily, personally to produce and reproduce conditions of domination which are even then never entirely trustworthy."[116] Police violence against black men and women is a commonplace in the United States because physical backup for symbolic domination is still required. Yet the dehumanization of any segment of a society reduces the entire society to a less civilized state.

In the United States, clearly, we need to establish a system that delivers real social justice, not just a whitewashed justice. Establishing such a just system will require a firm commitment to social equality. Antiracist strategies demand accountability, the establishment of trust, and the elimination of oppression by established authorities. As the civil rights demonstrators gathered in front of the court house after the Amadou Diallo shooting, they doubtless carried in their minds the belief that the fight for civil rights must continue. From the point of view of many Americans, and especially African Americans, the only way to confront the violence, destruction, and death inflicted on them by established institutions is direct action and protests. As Dr. Martin Luther King, Jr., once said about the protests that were carried out in defiance of police repression in Birmingham, Alabama, "[O]nce on a summer day a dream came true. The city of Birmingham discovered a conscience."[117]

Racism in the Halls of Power: The Texaco, "Willie" Horton, and Sister Souljah Cases

Prominent white Americans, in both the private and the government sectors, have periodically revealed negative feelings and views about African Americans and other Americans of color in their public statements. In the late 1980s television sports personality Jimmy "the Greek" Snyder's public statement that African American success in sports was genetic led to his dismissal by a major network. African Americans were successful as athletes, Snyder had argued, because long ago they had been bred for physical prowess by slaveholders. Later, Los Angeles Dodgers official Al Campanis explained the absence of black Americans in the administration of baseball teams with the argument that they lacked the "necessities" to do well in management positions.[1] These widely noted comments by Snyder and Campanis prompted a *U.S. News & World Report* journalist to ask: "Has it come to this: Are titillating racist jokes a new coin of mirth in Ronald Reagan's

America these days? Was CBS-TV commentator Jimmy "the Greek" Snyder giving public voice to the silent beliefs of many whites?"[2]

In the early 1990s Marge Schott, owner of the Cincinnati Reds, allegedly remarked to an employee, "I'd rather have a trained monkey working for me than a nigger." She was also alleged to have called black baseball players "million-dollar niggers."[3] Schott admitted using racial slurs such as "Japs," "niggers," and "money-grubbing Jews" in private conversations. After extensive public debate over her remarks and whether she *meant* these epithets to be offensive, the Major League Executive Council fined and suspended her.[4] In each of these cases, the influential protagonists publicly defended their remarks by claiming that they did not view them as racist. These denials are not surprising since those who enjoy the privilege to proffer offensive comments and epithets also have the ability to hide them from scrutiny and to deny them publicly if the need arises. These denials are commonplace as a defense to such comments. What is rare is the public debate of the offensiveness of these racial epithets.

Indeed, the most detailed accounts of racist attitudes in corporate suites can be found in discussions of lawsuits, such as the Texaco case noted in this chapter, or in some literary fiction. Charles Powell, a former telephone company executive, started a company that published a novel *(Servants of Power)* focusing on discrimination against black managers and recounting tales of racist attitudes or racial insensitivity in corporate America.[5] In addition, we should note that black managers working in predominantly white businesses have periodically confirmed that racism does exist across corporate America.[6]

Not all influential whites keep their feelings covert. In the media some are open about their negative views of blacks and other people of color. Several white hosts on talk-radio stations are noted for racial joking and other such comments on the air.[7] Some focus on immigrants. For example, radio commentator Paul Harvey used to accuse recent immigrants, who are now mostly people of color, of bringing disproportionately "less industry and ambition" and more crime and drug problems than others to the national population mix, arguing that "limitless immigration" is a serious threat to the "stability of our nation."[8]

Syndicated newspaper columnist James J. Kilpatrick once called affirmative action programs "manifestations of racism, pure, undefiled, and contemptible" in an article that praised the Reagan administration for redirecting the U.S. Commission on Civil Rights away from research on racial discrimination and toward research on issues of concern to conservative white Americans.[9] The white supremacist press reprints and applauds articles like these, using views expressed in the mainstream media to legitimate their extreme positions.

The Texaco Lawsuit and Racism in Corporate America

The case of corporate executives at Texaco became important only because of a surreptitiously recorded high-level corporate meeting that was made public. In January 1999, Texaco, one of the world's largest corporations, agreed to pay $3.1 million to 186 women who had been paid less than men holding similar jobs in the company. This was the largest affirmative action compliance settlement ever obtained by the U.S. Labor Department. This remedial action came on top of the result of the 1996 Texaco agreement to pay $176 million to 1,348 black workers as part of a class-action racial discrimination lawsuit against the company. The average award to each worker was around $63,000, the largest such award in a class action racial discrimination suit in U.S. history.[10] According to the evidence presented at the trial and the tape-recorded conversations among senior Texaco executives it surfaced that the executives had called black employees "black jelly beans" who cannot rise up the corporate ladder because "all the black jelly beans seem to be glued to the bottom of the bag."[11] They referred to the very few black executives at Texaco as "porch monkeys," meaning those who sit out as window dressing to make the company appear to have more high-ranking blacks than it really does. They also indicated that they were going to fight the complaints of black employees pursuing a discrimination lawsuit.[12]

Blacks make up 12 percent of the U.S. population, but at Texaco, out of 873 executives, only 6 (0.7 percent) were black. The number of executives in the highest salary bracket grew 44 percent, to 49 people in the 1990s, but not a single black person was promoted to that level. According to analysts, promotions of employees of color at Texaco were often not made. For example, black accountants at Texaco took 6.1 years to gain their position, while whites obtained the same position in 4.6 years on the average. A black person seeking a supervisory position in accounting had to wait 15 years, compared to only 9.8 years for similar white employees.[13] The first complainant in the discrimination case against Texaco, Bari-Ellen Roberts, said that she was not surprised when she heard racist conversations taking place between executives. The financial analyst has noted that "I had heard from managers that I was refereed to as 'that little colored girl,' and that I was called 'uppity.'" Prior to the release of the tape-recorded accounts of racial slurs, she had also heard that during meetings, high-level executives had referred to black executives as "orangutans" and "porch monkeys."[14]

Her experience was similar to that of Sil Chambers, who joined Roberts to launch the lawsuit in 1994. He related the following event: "[W]e had somebody in California say the company was doing a training exercise with the acronym NIGGR, and when she objected, they told her 'You are being too sensitive.'" Roberts and Chambers drew the attention of the human resources vice president at Texaco. During the middle of their presentation regarding discrimination against blacks in the company, this vice president "banged his hand on the table and said, "[Y]ou are making all these requests, the next thing we know you'll have Black Panthers outside in the circle [driveway] of Texaco. You guys are too militant."[15]

In the midst of the lawsuit—which grew increasingly acrimonious with the release of the taped conversation of top white executives—in November 1996, Texaco chairman and chief executive officer Peter Bijur went public with a corporate apology.[16] Yet what happened at Texaco was not a matter of isolated events, nor were these events confined to the executive level. In 1998, Sheryl Joseph, a secretary in one of Texaco's Louisiana offices, was invited to a party by her colleagues to celebrate her birthday together with her pregnancy. When she looked at her cake, she saw it was decorated with an image of a dark-skinned, apparently pregnant woman, with an inscription reading, "Happy Birthday Sheryl. It must have been those watermelon seeds." She later said, "[W]hen I saw the inscription, I just kind of stared at it and said, 'Oh, thank you.' I didn't feel I could get angry. I had just found out I was pregnant. I needed my job."[17]

The workplace is a battleground for civil rights. One of the plaintiffs in the Texaco case, Bari-Ellen Roberts, argued:

> I had based my life on a myth. I believed that the American Dream was for everyone, regardless of race, even in Corporate America. I believed it when the men of Texaco repeatedly assured me that they really meant what they said in their glossy recruiting brochures: They welcomed diversity; it made good business sense; it was merit, not color that counted.[18]

It seems that Roberts heard a common pretense about diversity in U.S. society. Texaco and its executives are not alone. After the Texaco suit, five black employees at Shell Oil filed a lawsuit. One of the black employees of Shell said that his manager pointed out that Shell does not have a good record of promoting blacks and added that he had "shackles around his ankles" because he was black. Recently, too, the Coca-Cola company has faced a large-scale lawsuit by black employees asserting that there is significant discrimination in the firm.[19]

In contrast, a few corporations are making some efforts to change the racist culture by confronting their own policies and employees. For example, IBM now has recruited many employees of color. Now 22 percent of its employees and 13 percent of its managers are people of color. For its work on diversity, IBM has been recognized by the American Association of Minority Business, the National Minority Business Council, the National Society of Black Engineers, *Black Enterprise* magazine, and *Hispanic Business* magazine.[20] In addition to IBM's diversity policies, it has also been named one of the best companies in terms of creating a hospitable workplace for gay employees and those with disabilities.

Some groups have made connections between the racial policies of large corporations and other of their social and environmental policies.

For example, in 1999 the Committee for the Defense of the Amazon began to draw parallels between Texaco's racial discrimination case and its practices in dumping toxic wastes in the Amazon rain forest, which had caused health and environmental problems for people in Ecuador and Peru. According to the data presented by the Committee, Texaco has dumped more than 16 million gallons of oil and toxic wastewater into the Ecuadoran Amazon over the past 21 years, causing cancer and other diseases to perhaps 30,000 people.[21] According to these reports Texaco's actions in the Amazon have revealed a lack of concern for the impact of its decisions on people of color in other parts of the globe. Moreover, government and international organization officials have publicly given support for such policies. In December 1991 Lawrence Summers, chief economist of the World Bank, argued that the toxic waste of industrial nations should be dumped in poor countries. He argued that many poor countries have little pollution and thus that these dumps would not effect human health. He also averred that "health impairing pollution should be done in the country with the lowest cost, which will be the country with the lowest wages." He added that "the economic logic behind dumping a load of toxic waste in the lowest wage country is impeccable, and we should face up to that." Furthermore, the editors of the prestigious journal *The Economist* agreed that "on the economics, [these] points are hard to answer."[22]

From the Texaco case, and certain of its domestic and international policies, we learn that white racism is not just the practice of poorly educated, disgruntled white supremacists, but it is intimately tied to the logic of some corporate profit-making. The same lack of essential human empathy that led Texaco executives to exclude its black employees from the earned fruits of their efforts on behalf of the company also seems evident in the economic logic of its toxic waste-dumping.

The Federal Government

While employment discrimination through the denial of raises and promotions observed in the policies and practices of private corporations like Texaco has had devastating effects on black Americans (as well as other Americans of color and women), these private policies and practices are far from the only form of discrimination that African Americans must endure. For example, a brief examination of a lawsuit brought against the U.S. Department of Agriculture (USDA) allows us to illustrate the differential treatment the U.S. government gives to people of color. We draw here on research by Phyllis Craig-Taylor, who has spoken of the situation we outline as "open door days on the last plantation."

The federal lawsuit arose out of racial discrimination faced by frustrated black farmers, who in this particular case faced abuse from the USDA from the early 1980s to the late 1990s. Government denial of legal redress to the aggrieved black farmers who were protesting discrimination in Farm Service Agency (FSA) programs lead to a class-action lawsuit against the U.S. Department of Agriculture.[23] Across the nation black farmers gave evidence about widespread discrimination in many aspects of the process of getting FSA loans and benefits. This discrimination took the form of FSA officials misinforming black farmers that there were no loan applications or benefits available in particular local FSA offices. Or, if a farmer somehow got an application, some FSA agents held back the information necessary for its completion. In many cases, completed applications were lost, delayed in the extreme, or denied for no legitimate reason. Once complaints from black farmers started coming in, the USDA went into a stonewalling mode for more than ten years and refused to deal with them.

Eventually, the targets of this discrimination had their day in court and won a major settlement of the class-action suit, which was approved by the U.S. District Court for the District of Columbia. The black farmers involved could choose among three options: Reject the settlement, get $50,000 if they could show injury, or petition for more in binding arbitration. However, for many farmers the standard compensation offered was insufficient as a response to many years of discrimination, for they had lost their homes, farm equipment, and land, some of which had been in the family for generations. In the initial complaint, the requested damages had been for $1 million for each farmer, which appears to be more appropriate compensation for the damages and pain incurred by most of those involved. Clearly, officials of the U.S. government have often behaved in much the same manner as the corporate executives noted in previous pages. At bottom are attempts to exclude black workers and farmers from the just rewards and benefits they have earned.[24]

Other Public Officials

Periodically, statements by important government officials have revealed negative views of black Americans and other people of color. These deserve special attention because they come from appointed and elected leaders, who are often seen as role models in the nation and are usually given broad media coverage. In 1976 Earl Butz, a former Purdue University dean, was forced to resign his position as Secretary of Agriculture after making racially offensive comments. Joking about what Republicans should offer black Americans, he stated that all a black man wants is "loose shoes," warm toilet facilities, and sex.[25] Butz later denied that he was a racist, claiming that his derogatory remarks did not indicate his true opinion of African Americans.

In the early 1980s the *NAAWP News*, a newspaper published by the National Association for the Advancement of White People, quoted Clare Boothe Luce, onetime U.S. ambassador to Italy, as saying that immigrants from Haiti and Latin America are a greater threat to the nation than the atomic bomb. According to the article, Luce said that in the nineteenth century the "good immigrants" were "all white." The article added, "If everyone in positions like those of Clare Boothe Luce spoke out publicly with such candor, the first step toward the Majority Renaissance would be taken."[26]

In the mid-1980s Arizona governor Evan Mecham vetoed a bill making the birthday of Martin Luther King, Jr., a state holiday. Mecham also publicly defended his use of the slur "pickaninnies" to refer to black children.[27] In 1987 the western region commissioner of the U.S. Immigration and Naturalization Service (INS) reportedly said that illegal aliens should be "skinned and fried" and deported.[28] The same year, a Glendale, California, judge caused a controversy when he used racial epithets to express irritation over a case of a white man assaulting a black man. According to the court transcript the judge asked, "Another one where this nigger business came up?"[29] After reaction from local black leaders and some justice system officials was quite negative, the judge apologized for his remarks but argued that they were innocent. In most of these cases the central actors, all powerful white Americans, did not see their comments or actions as racially offensive.

Since the early 1980s several political candidates with overtly racial philosophies have polled significant numbers of white votes. We noted in an earlier chapter that former Klan leader David Duke ran for high political office several times and was elected as a representative to the Louisiana legislature. He also received a majority of white votes in a primary contest for the U.S. Senate. Tom Metzger (see Chapter 4) also received a significant number of white votes in two California elections.

Pat Buchanan, a White House staff member under Richard Nixon and Ronald Reagan and periodic presidential candidate, has voiced stereotypical views.[30] While working as an adviser to President Richard Nixon in 1971, Buchanan became interested in psychologist Richard Herrnstein's argument that blacks have lower intelligence than whites because some black groups scored lower on IQ tests than did some white groups. In a memo to Nixon, Buchanan argued that "every study" showed that blacks had significantly lower IQs than whites and that Herrnstein's views about race and IQ provided "an intellectual basis" for reviewing and perhaps trimming government social programs. Buchanan has denied that he accepted these views; he says he only wanted to advise Nixon properly.[31]

Numerous incidents and reports revealed a racialized atmosphere in some parts of the White House during the Reagan and Bush administrations. James Watt was forced to resign from a cabinet position because of his racially insensitive comments.[32] A *Chicago Tribune* report on Michael Deaver's role in setting up Reagan's much-debated trip to a Nazi cemetery in Germany in May 1985 also noted that "Deaver's penchant for telling racist jokes about blacks has sometimes jolted associates and members of the White House press corps."[33] In Chapter 2 we noted that Reagan White House aides reportedly told racist jokes; referred to Martin Luther King, Jr., as "Martin Lucifer Coon"; and spoke of Arabs as "sand niggers." Reagan cabinet member Terrel Bell reported encountering widespread bias among midlevel aides and was shocked at their "racist cliches."[34] Bell stated in his memoirs that at White House meetings he often argued for equal opportunity issues. Yet he "never received any encouragement from others in the White House or from those in the Department of Justice to support enforcement of civil rights laws."[35]

Since his first election campaign for the U.S. Senate in 1972, Jesse Helms, a Republican senator from North Carolina, has received the support of white supremacy groups, and he has never repudiated such groups. During the 1960s Helms argued that the Ku Klux Klan was as politically legitimate as the black Civil Rights Movement: "No court has declared that the Klan is in violation of any statute law on the books."[36] Despite the Klan's record of violence, Helms publicly advocated the group's right to organize. During Helms's 1984 re-election campaign, the Klan organized an aggressive voter registration effort to counter black opposition.[37] While Helms did not openly solicit the Klan's efforts, he did not discourage them. In his re-election campaigns Helms has manipulated the fears of white voters. During the 1990 campaign he used a television advertisement that implied that his Democratic opponent, Harvey Gantt, a black man who had led in the polls at the time, favored racial quotas. The ad showed white hands holding a job rejection letter while the commentator said: "You needed that job and you were the best qualified. But they had to give it to a minority because of a racial quota. Is that really fair?" Helms won two-thirds of the white votes in the election. It is important to note that Helms is not on the fringe of the Republican Party. One of Helms's political consultants in the 1990 campaign was concurrently a top consultant for then-president George Bush.[38]

Presidents and presidential candidates have also made remarks reflecting racial and ethnic stereotypes. In taped White House conversations, Richard Nixon commented that he kept his daughters away from art functions because, "The Arts you know—they're Jews, they're left-wing—in other words, stay away."[39] The diaries of H. R. Haldeman, Nixon's chief of staff, offer a window into attitudinal racism at the highest levels of the federal government. As Nixon's chief aide and friend, Haldeman probably spent more time than any other official with Nixon. His detailed diary entries have revealed Nixon's negative views of Jewish and black Americans. Diary excerpts were first broadcast on a May 16, 1994, *Nightline* show anchored by Ted Koppel. This is the entry for April 28, 1969, as quoted on *Nightline*:

> President emphasized that you have to face that the whole [welfare] problem is really the blacks. The key is to devise a system that recognizes this, while not appearing to. Problem with overall welfare plan is that it forces poor whites into the same position as blacks. . . . Pointed out that there has never in history been an adequate black nation, and they are the only race of which this is true. Says Africa is hopeless.[40]

Nixon's Oval Office discussions were ill-informed about past and present black nations and also about U.S. welfare recipients, more than half of whom at the time of his comments were white. An April 2, 1970, entry revealed Nixon's unwillingness to work with black leaders who spoke out on discrimination: "[Nixon] broods frequently over problem of how we communicate with young and blacks. It's really not possible except with Uncle Toms, and we should work on them and forget militants."[41] These and other diary entries document the hidden racism that African Americans must contend with in the political sphere and demonstrate the way in which racist images can corrode a white leader's ability to think clearly about important matters of state.

In his 1980 presidential campaign, Ronald Reagan privately told an ethnic joke that suggested that Polish and Italian Americans were criminals or buffoons. Reagan later stated that he disliked ethnic jokes, except those about the Irish.[42] Speaking to her husband in a telephone call being carried by a loudspeaker during the campaign, Nancy Reagan said she would like for him to be with her in Illinois with "all these beautiful white people."[43] She quickly retracted the remark, but at a minimum the slip suggested how white that Republican campaign was.

During the presidential campaign of 2000, one Republican candidate for president, Senator John McCain, used the racial slur "Gooks" to refer to his former Vietnamese captors.[44] One can certainly understand an ex–prisoner of war's grudge against those who imprisoned him. What is significant, however, is that he expressed his feelings using a racist term of abuse and not in terms making reference to the ideology or actions of the Vietnamese soldiers who imprisoned him. It seems too that McCain used the term expecting not to suffer any protests from Asian Americans.

The following cases focus on two powerful political actors—presidential candidates who used racially defined symbols in calculated ways to win public office. Their actions illustrate the important role of icons in America's racial rites. The first case examines the "Willie" Horton advertising campaign of George Bush in 1988. The second looks at Bill Clinton's attack on rap musician Sister Souljah in 1992. It is significant that both candidates had a record of public statements deploring racism as a scourge to be eradicated; yet both used racial images and icons to manipulate white voters' fears about black Americans.

"Willie" Horton and the Politics of Racism

William Robert Horton, who was given the nickname "Willie" by white commentators during the 1988 campaign, became a widely used symbol of the menacing black criminal. "Willie" Horton is a real black man, but his name now symbolizes far more than his personal biography. In 1988 he became a racial icon in a series of paid television advertisements run by several Republican groups.

The first ad, paid for by the Republican National Security Political Action Committee (NSPAC), aired in September 1988 during the heat of the presidential campaign and ran for a month. The ad opened with side-by-side photographs of George Bush, smiling in a picture filled with light, and Democratic candidate Michael Dukakis, looking downward in a dark picture.[45] A voice-over read the title: "Bush and Dukakis on Crime." Then a photograph of Bush flashed on the screen as the voice-over said: "Bush supports the death penalty for first-degree murderers." A picture of Dukakis, who was then the governor of Massachusetts, followed, with the commentary: "Dukakis not only opposes the death penalty, he allowed first-degree murderers to have weekend passes from prison." Captions under the Dukakis picture included: "Allowed Murderers to Have Weekend Passes." The next frame showed a mug shot of a bearded William Horton. "One was Willie Horton, who murdered a boy in a robbery, stabbing him nineteen times," the voice said, as the name "Willie Horton" appeared under the mug shot. A blurred photograph of a black man being arrested appeared as the voice continued with a reference to Horton's weekend passes. The words "kidnapping" and "stabbing" appeared on the screen, followed by "kidnapping," "stabbing," and "raping," as the voice-over added: "Horton fled, kidnapping a young couple, stabbing the man and repeatedly raping his girlfriend." The final photo showed Dukakis with the caption "Weekend Prison Passes. Dukakis on Crime."[46]

Later, several analysts would point out the factual errors in the ad. Horton was convicted of the gruesome murder of a young gas station manager, but there was no evidence that it was he who stabbed the victim because three men participated. He said he was driving the getaway car, but Massachusetts law charges all participants in a murder with felony murder. Ten months after Horton had failed to return from a forty-eight-hour prison furlough, he was apprehended in a stolen car that belonged to Clifford Barnes, the man Horton was later convicted of stabbing.[47]

A second ad, paid for directly by the Bush campaign, aired on October 5 and featured an image of convicts walking toward the viewers through a turnstile. The caption read "268 escaped." The voice-over said that Governor Dukakis had vetoed the death penalty in Massachusetts and had given prison furloughs to "first-degree murderers not eligible for parole. While out, many committed other crimes like kidnapping and rape." In her book *Dirty Politics,* journalism professor Kathleen Hall Jamieson noted that this ad contained several false statements. "Many" first-degree murderers did not escape from the furlough program. Of the 268 convicts who jumped furlough during Dukakis's first two gubernatorial terms, only four had been convicted of first-degree murder. Just one, not many, had been convicted of kidnapping and raping while on furlough.[48] And the number of escaped convicts was not as great as the long lines of convicts going through the turnstile implied.

Several local and state Republican organizations used the Horton story in brochures or television ads. George Bush referred to Horton and the furloughs in his campaign speeches. Maryland's GOP committee sent thousands of fund-raising letters signed by its chair featuring side-by-side pictures of Dukakis and Horton with the question: "Is This Your Pro-Family Team for 1988?" The letter added: "By now, you have heard of the Dukakis/Bentsen team. But have you heard of the Dukakis/Willie Horton team? . . . You, your spouse, your children, your parents and your friends can have the opportunity to receive a visit from someone like Willie Horton if Mike Dukakis becomes president." Later, Bush campaign chair James Baker stated that the Maryland letter was "totally out of bounds, totally unauthorized; it was not authorized by this campaign."[49] Unfortunately for his campaign, Dukakis was slow to react to these ads. In a belated October 22 statement he said, "To use human tragedy for political purposes has to be one of the most hypocritical and one of the most cynical things that I have ever seen in my 25 years of public life."[50]

Some of the Horton ads were created by organizations separate from the Bush campaign. However, decisions to air the ads generally came from campaign headquarters, as the following excerpt from a September 1992 congressional speech by Republican representative Robert K. Dornan of California makes clear: "This Congressman told the late Lee Atwater [Bush's campaign manager] to his face, 'Don't use "Willie" Horton. It is a great crime issue, but because the man is a black, the liberal media will twist it and say you are trying to use . . . it for race.'"[51] Dornan's speech confirms that the issue of race was present in discussions of the ads by top Bush campaign functionaries.

The question of whether the Bush campaign was guilty of playing on racial fears was the primary subject discussed at a meeting of campaign managers convened at Harvard's John F. Kennedy School of Government following the campaign. At the conference Lee Atwater explained that the Bush campaign chose the prison furlough issue after conducting studies of focus groups with white Democrats. The Republicans felt that this strategy would win them Democratic votes. Susan Estrich, Dukakis's campaign manager, addressed Atwater directly concerning the racist nature of the Horton ads: "I happen to have been a rape victim. . . . My sense . . . is that it was very much an issue about race and racial fear. . . . It was, at least on my viewing of it, very strong—look, you can't find a stronger metaphor, intended or not, for racial hatred in this country than a black man raping a white woman. And that's what the Willie Horton story was."[52]

Atwater replied that he himself had made the decision not to use Horton in campaign advertisements. In an attempt to distance the Bush campaign headquarters from the Horton ads, Atwater said he decided that if the Horton ad was used by an independent committee the campaign would condemn such actions. He added that "we resent the fact that it was used racially in the campaign because we certainly didn't, and we were very conscious about it."[53]

When asked to reconcile these comments with his June 1988 statement that he would make Willie Horton's name a household word, Atwater said that was the one time he had used Horton's name and that he had apologized for it.[54] Atwater apparently had forgotten that in a speech at a Republican gathering in Atlanta reported in a July 31, 1988, *Washington Post* article he had also spoken of "a fellow named Willie Horton, who for all I know may end up being Dukakis's running mate."[55] Pressed on the issue of the Horton ad as a racist strategy, Atwater said: "There is no question in my mind that Republicans, Democrats, blacks, and whites all reject racist politics. If there were any racist politics in this campaign, it would have back-fired on us, on the party."[56]

This argument rests on the false premise that the white electorate rejects racist politics. The Bush campaign commercials worked precisely because many white voters do respond to racist political appeals. Clearly, the image of "Willie" Horton was deliberately associated with the GOP's opponent to evoke white voters' deep-rooted fears and widely held stereotypes of black men as criminals.

Later, in a *Life* magazine statement just before his death in 1991, Atwater admitted that the decision to make an issue of Willie Horton was made at the top levels of the Bush campaign: "Well before the Bush campaign decided to make an issue of the Willie Horton case, I overheard a couple discussing it while I was attending a motorcyclists' convention in Luray, Virginia." Atwater apologized for saying that Dukakis would "make Willie Horton his running mate." He said that "makes me sound racist, which I am not."[57]

After the 1988 campaign, Michael Dukakis and William Horton were regularly intertwined in media commentary and in the memory of the electorate.[58] Jamieson discovered from focus group research that some voters "remembered" that Dukakis had pardoned Horton and that Horton had gone on to commit another murder, yet neither event had actually occurred. Jamieson uses the Horton ad campaign to illustrate the ways that voters and reporters collect political information; the Republican ad-makers influenced the news media to adopt "such words as 'torture' and 'terrorize' to describe Horton's actions while on furlough, [to define] the furlough program's purpose as dispensing 'weekend passes,' and [to define] the policy as a 'revolving door.'"[59] These assessments, all of which are exaggerated or inaccurate, served to bias discussion of the actual events.

Whoever controls the language in which issues are discussed controls the issues. Horton's given name is William, as court records indicate; he calls himself William. Yet the Republican advertisements refer to him only as "Willie" Horton. Virtually all reporters, and even Democratic candidate Dukakis, used "Willie." Jamieson suggests the familiar "Willie" summons up more sinister images of criminality than "William." Diminutive names like "Willie" are reminiscent of the naming practices of white slavemasters or of adults nicknaming dependent children.[60] Horton himself has strongly objected to being called by the nickname "Willie": "It's part of the myth of the case. The name . . . was created to play on racial stereotypes: big, ugly, dumb, violent, black—'Willie.'"[61] Media language about the furlough program was also shaped by the ads, which described the Dukakis policy as weekend passes for first-degree murderers. Several commentators have pointed out the inaccuracy of these and other ad (and media) phrases: The furloughs ranged from 1 to 170 hours and could begin on any day, not just on weekends.[62]

Jamieson shows how the ads used an intentionally distorted story to construct the view of a savage black murderer-rapist in the white viewer's mind.[63] This view was reinforced through campaign fliers, press conferences, and candidate speeches. Bush, for example, referred to Dukakis as "the furlough king" and spoke of how the "victims of crime are given no furlough from their pain and suffering."[64] In fact, Horton was actually the exception to the rule; he was the *only* person imprisoned in Massachusetts for first-degree murder to be accused and convicted of a violent crime committed while he was on furlough. The ads also ignored the fact that the furlough program was initiated by Dukakis's Republican predecessor and that sitting Republican governors, including Bush's friend Bill Clements in Texas, had presided over similar prison furlough programs in other states.

Why was Horton, an atypical criminal in a number of ways (for example, he was convicted of raping a white woman, and most rapists of white women are *white*), selected rather than other criminals in the state of Massachusetts, including serial killers and admitted first-degree murderers? Would the face of a white man who raped a black or white woman have had the same effect on the white voters that Republicans were seeking to influence? Clearly the ads achieved the intended aim of scaring white voters and helping to defeat Dukakis. In particular, white southerners interviewed in the media admitted the ads influenced their votes. Nationwide, 61 percent of white men voted for Bush. Andrew Kohut, president of the Gallup polling firm, reported that his opinion polls indicated that racial intolerance was a factor in whites' choosing to vote for Bush.[65]

Who Is William Horton?

In the national media coverage that followed the Horton ads, the victims of his reported crimes became real people telling about their ordeals. Horton himself remained unknown as a person; he was only a threatening mug shot for the voters. The media and candidates repeated the distorted story again and again until "Willie" Horton became more than one black criminal. In the minds of many whites he became an icon symbolizing the quintessential violent black man.

William Horton was born on August 12, 1951, in Chesterfield, South Carolina. His father was a trash collector, a heavy drinker, who shot and injured Horton's mother when William was five. When Horton's father went to jail, his mother left the children with an aunt and moved away. William did average to poor work in school until the eighth grade, when he dropped out. First arrested at age thirteen for breaking and entering, he served six months as a juvenile offender. His first adult crime was assault with intent to kill and carrying a concealed knife. After serving three years in prison, he moved to Lawrence, Massachusetts. Between 1971 and 1974 he was charged with eleven offenses, including public drunkenness, assault and battery, and distribution of a controlled substance.[66]

Horton developed a serious drug problem, and in 1974 he was charged with the stabbing murder of a Lawrence gas station attendant in the course of a robbery. During the 1988 presidential campaign these events would be embellished with the false allegation that the attendant was mutilated. The police never determined who actually did the stabbing. According to a law enforcement source, one of Horton's codefendants allegedly confessed to the murder, but the confession was not admissible in court because the police officers had not read the suspect his rights.[67] All three robbers were sentenced to life in prison without parole, and Horton began serving his sentence at a maximum security prison.

After serving several years of his sentence, Horton was placed in a minimum security prison, where he acquired his first marketable skill, the ability to cook. He was granted nine successful furloughs, then failed to return from his tenth. On June 7, 1986, after learning that his daughter was experiencing serious problems, he became involved in a family argument. When he realized that he would not be able to reach the prison by the end of his furlough time, Horton decided to flee. Using money he had won in a lottery, he traveled to Florida, where he worked in construction, then later moved to Maryland. On April 3, 1987, he was apprehended while driving a stolen car and charged with assault and rape. He was convicted of these charges and sentenced in October 1987.[68] Horton has consistently maintained his innocence of the violent crimes of which he has been convicted.[69]

In order to move beyond superficial discussions of race and crime in the United States and to understand the function of racism in creating black criminals, we must listen to the voices of black men and women and know them as human beings. A 1989 *Playboy* interview by Jeffrey M. Elliot revealed that Horton is an intelligent and articulate man who, given better opportunities, could have led a productive and useful life. When asked about the origin of his menacing photo in the Republican ads, Horton answered: "Hell, I agree with you—that picture would have scared the shit out of me, too. . . . They moved me to a segregation unit in the hospital, which is designed for the so-called rough criminals—those who they can't control. I remained in that cell for six to ten months, during which I wasn't allowed to shave or get a haircut. That's when they took the picture."[70]

Asked by the interviewer whether he thought President George Bush was racist, Horton replied that he could not know: "I . . . take strong exception to what he did—which was to fuel fears by implying that if Governor Dukakis were elected, he would unleash monsters like myself on an unsuspecting public."[71]

Horton as Political Icon: The 1990s

Horton's image did not disappear with the 1988 campaign. The political use of the Horton icon was debated well into the 1990s. In 1991 then-president George Bush finally discussed the Horton ads, which he argued were not racist. Dukakis, however, replied that the ads were a "thinly veiled attempt" to bring racial issues to the campaign: "The Republican strategy for many years has been to break up the Democratic coalition by emphasizing patriotism, crime and race. The Willie Horton ad satisfied two of those criteria. If the ad did not have a racist base, then why did Lee Atwater apologize for it?"[72]

Between June 1988 and March 1993, no fewer than 148 speeches or extensions of remarks in the *Congressional Record* contained references to the Horton ads. According to some Democratic members of Congress, "Willie" Horton has became a symbol of politics at its lowest level. In a 1992 speech to the House, Major R. Owens, a Democrat from New York, argued:

> There is an undercurrent of racism through all the dirty tricks, and it pays off very well. Willie Horton helped elect a President. Millie Horton, his aunt, an image of a welfare queen, a person who is swindling the American people because she is on welfare, will do it the next time, it is believed by the perpetrators of dirty tricks. Nothing is more immoral than this steady stream of dirty tricks. Nothing is lower than the subversion of the democratic process by using all the organs of government, the organs of the media, to perpetrate upon the people a big lie which is divisive and racist.[73]

In 1992 Senator Bill Bradley, a Democrat from New Jersey, told the U.S. Senate: "The Willie Horton ad was an attempt to demonize all black America. If you do not believe me, ask any African-American who tries to hail a cab late at night in an American city."[74] Bradley explained that the demonization of black men like Horton is but one of the divisive walls created by whites: "How can we achieve a good life for ourselves and our children if the cost of that good life is ignoring the misery of our neighbors? The answer has been to erect walls. The wall of pride: We are better and deserve what we have. The wall of 'ignore the problem and it will go away.' The wall of 'blaming the symptoms.' . . . And finally the Willie Horton wall of demonization that says they are not like us."[75] Senator Bradley is one of few white political leaders willing to speak out openly on the problem of white racism. In 1999 Bill Bradley ran for the presidential candidacy of his party but failed in his effort.

The Black Man in the White Mind: An Old Image

Chapter 4 described how Charles Stuart used the image of a fictitious black male criminal to deflect attention from his crime. The Horton ads illustrate how a real black criminal became a negative racial icon of national dimensions. Both cases share a common historical and cultural context. In Chapter 4 we cited research suggesting that many whites view young black males as dangerous.[76] However, according to national victimization surveys, only about 17 percent of the attackers of white victims in violent crimes are black; approximately three-quarters are white.[77] As a result of the exaggerated white images, most black men suffer from negative reactions by whites who, for example, move away from them in elevators or on sidewalks or call the police when seeing them walking in a white neighborhood.

We have noted previously that the negative stereotyping of African men as uncivilized and fear-inspiring "savages" who are threats to white women dates back several centuries.[78] Winthrop Jordan has suggested that the origin of this mythical image lies in the belief of early white colonizers that black men were particularly promiscuous and virile and lusted after white women, an image rooted in "deep strata of irrationality." According to Jordan, white men parroting this myth have projected their own passions for black women; the racist image of black men lusting after white women has eased white male guilt.[79] Dr. William Lee Howard, a nineteenth-century physician and defender of black enslavement, once explained the common white view of black men: "The attacks on defenseless white women are evidences of racial instincts that are about as amenable to ethical culture as is the inherent odor of the race." He added, "When education will reduce the size of the Negro's penis as well as bring about the sensitiveness of the terminal fibers which exist in the Caucasian, then will it also be able to prevent the African's birthright to sexual madness and excess."[80] The fear of many white men for the safety of "their" women is an exercise in sexual possessiveness. The same white male mind that transformed African men and women into slaves transformed white women into possessions that must be protected and repressed. As we suggested in earlier discussions, this view often lay behind lynchings. The obsessive fear of the mythical black rapist monster is one of the major costs that white Americans, male and female, have paid for the brutal subjugation of African Americans.

Today the fear of the black rapist monster continues unabated. Recall Joel Kovel's speculations about the deep psychological atavism expressed by such white fear.[81] Sociologically, the fear of the black rapist is used to legitimate whites' continued bad faith toward blacks in the United States. The lurid image of the black male also defines black crime as the expression of twisted minds and savage desires rather than the product of widespread racial discrimination and the consequent horrible living conditions. Republican campaign officials had confidence in the utility of this image to discredit the "liberal" view that street crime is bred by racial discrimination and related poverty. Using the myth of the black rapist is yet another way to evade the responsibility that whites as a group have for the effects of white racism.

Bill Clinton and Sister Souljah

What presidents say in political speeches and what they do in political practice are often quite different. This has become a truism in U.S. politics, but it is especially true for matters of racial relations. The same George Bush who allowed the Horton icon to be created also said in his 1990 State of the Union address that racism and bigotry must be condemned "not next week, not tomorrow, but right now." Although Bush, like most white Americans, is willing to accept this view at an abstract level, at no point in his four years as president did he take an aggressive role in enforcing or extending the antiracist actions of the federal government.

Bush was followed into office by Bill Clinton, a moderate Democrat who had served for several terms as governor of Arkansas and who had expressed more liberal attitudes on racial matters than Bush had. During the primary and national campaigns in 1992 candidate Clinton occasionally spoke of his good civil rights record and publicly condemned racial discrimination in general terms. Yet Clinton also attacked the black activist and rapper Sister Souljah for comments she reportedly made to *Washington Post* reporter David Mills. The attack was made in a speech before the Rainbow Coalition, a progressive multiracial organization led by the black civil rights leader Jesse Jackson.

On May 13, 1992, just after the Los Angeles rebellion generated by the Simi Valley verdict on the Rodney King beating, Mills quoted comments by Sister Souljah that he characterized as "a chilling extreme":

> I mean, if black people kill black people every day, why not have a week and kill white people? You understand what I'm saying? In other words, white people, this government and that mayor were well aware of the fact that black people were dying every day in Los Angeles under gang violence. So if you're a gang member and you would normally be killing somebody, why not kill a white person?[82]

Mills's article, like the writings of most other white commentators, made little effort to understand the depths of the point of view Souljah was expressing—the world as seen by alienated black gang members. Instead, most white commentators accused her of personally supporting the killing of white Americans.

The setting Clinton chose for his comments was a meeting of the Rainbow Coalition. Clinton confronted Jesse Jackson, who was then the nation's most prominent black Democrat, on his connections with Sister Souljah, who was being honored at the meeting for her efforts to encourage young blacks to vote. Clinton quoted Souljah's remarks from the *Post* interview, focusing on the words: "If black people kill black people every day, why not have a week and kill white people?" Clinton said: "I know she is a young person, but she has a big influence on a lot of people. . . . If you took the words white and black and you reversed them, you might think David Duke was giving that speech."[83] Clinton used a clever white debating technique: Distort what your target, a black victim of white racism, has said, then compare that black target's views with the views of a white supporter of the oppression of black Americans.

Jackson later criticized Clinton's ill-considered remarks as an attempt to please white voters and to sabotage the coalition meeting. Jackson was upset that Clinton, who was his guest that day, had implied that Jackson himself condoned black-on-white violence. Noting that he had supported Clinton politically "at his lowest moment," Jackson suggested that Clinton should be as sensitive to blacks "in their low moments as he wants people to be to him in his low moments." Clinton subsequently claimed that he was not trying to embarrass Jackson.[84] Nonetheless, a few days later Clinton repeated his argument that Souljah's views were extreme.[85]

Several weeks later, while visiting the lower East Side of Manhattan, candidate Clinton was asked by a black teenager to explain his verbal attack on Souljah. Considerably softening his criticism, perhaps because of the strong black response to his earlier remarks, Clinton replied: "That's an example of how alienated we are today. She obviously believes that the system values white people's lives over blacks. . . . What we ought to do is find a way to talk to each other across racial lines and not to make it worse. I thought those comments made it worse."[86] Clinton again appeared to be out of touch with young black people like Souljah, who clearly view this type of talk across racial lines as an insufficient response from a white political leader in a nation where white racism is deeply entrenched.

Clinton's strategy worked well with many whites. White commentators usually agreed that Clinton's critique of Souljah, and of Jackson for allowing her to play some role in coalition activities, benefited his presidential campaign because Clinton had shown that he could stand up to the so-called interest groups (code words used increasingly to mean black, Latino, feminist, and gay groups) in the Democratic Party.[87] The political significance of Clinton's attack was not lost on

African Americans. Jackson made it clear that he viewed Clinton's attack on Souljah as an attempt to move away from the liberal multi-ethnic wing of the Democratic Party: "This was a move by the right wing of the party to pull away from the DNC [Democratic National Committee] because the DNC was too multiracial for them and too democratic. . . . The further attempt to isolate the Rainbow is just another dimension of their strategy."[88]

Unlike Horton, Sister Souljah was able to fight back and to criticize vigorously the intentional misreading of her statements. On CNN's July 2, 1992, *Crier & Company* show, Souljah explained her interpretation of Clinton's motivation for attacking her: "America needs Sister Souljah to be the black monster, to scare all of the white people to the polls because they were disinterested in a very boring, very sloppy political campaign that's been put forth by not only Clinton, but George Bush himself."[89] Elsewhere Souljah noted it had taken Clinton no less than five weeks to comment on her remarks and that a Clinton aide had undoubtedly brought her comments to his attention, believing that it was a "strategic political move to show how macho he is."[90] In her view Clinton was also trying to discredit Jackson as a political contender for vice president.

What Did Souljah Really Say?

Before she became a rapper, Sister Souljah, born Lisa Williamson, pursued a college degree at Rutgers for several years, then became a community activist. After Clinton's attack, Souljah spoke in her own defense. On a radio talk show in June 1992 she said, "White people should not be surprised" about the attacks on whites in a black riot because in a black gang member's view, the killing of blacks has become casual and commonplace in this racist society.[91]

On the *Larry King Live* show Souljah pointed out that her controversial comments were in response to a *Washington Post* reporter's question about whether the black rioters thought the violence "was wise." The reporter was seeking her interpretation, and Souljah responded in the voice of those blacks. She added, "White people have known that every day in Los Angeles black people are dying from gang violence, but they did not care. But when it became a question of white people dying and a billion dollars in property being lost, that's when it became a concern." Then she explained that, from a gang member's point of view, "If the social and economic system has neglected your development and you have become a casual killer who will kill even your own brother, in your mindset, why not kill a white person?" In her view the violence directed against non-blacks during the Los Angeles riot was not surprising because gang killings are so common; injustice anywhere threatened justice everywhere.[92] Souljah's analysis of Clinton's actions, and of racial oppression, is generally sharper and deeper than that of her white critics. She articulates a clear and nuanced view of the wastefulness of white racism for whites as well as blacks. The constant reminder by whites that they are different can produce a sociological acumen that allows many black individuals to see through common white rationalizations of racist thought and action.

Souljah's original interview with reporter David Mills in the *Washington Post* confirms that she was indeed referring to how black gang members in Los Angeles thought. Replying to a question about how the rioters were thinking, Souljah stated: "It's rebellion; it's revenge." Pressed on whether such revenge was morally acceptable, Souljah stated, "I don't think that anything we can do to white people could ever even equal up to what they've done to us. I really don't." She added that the underlying cause of black violence was the system of white supremacy. In the white reporter's view, however, Souljah was an extremist arguing that "white people are born guilty" and are beyond hope of redemption.[93] Such an extreme conclusion, however, cannot reasonably be drawn from Souljah's actual words.

A few weeks before his interview with Souljah, the same *Washington Post* reporter, David Mills, had offered a substantially negative view of black rappers: "Rap lends itself well to didacts, zealots, sloganeers and blowhards. Some of them are even worth listening to." Mills argued that Souljah's lyrics pushed the limits of "anti-white rhetoric" as she openly shows her disgust for "white people as a class."[94] Mills criticized Souljah for cataloging the weaknesses of whites in her music.[95] Referring to a line in Souljah's lyrics to the effect that two wrongs may not make a right, but "it damn sure makes it even," he argued that centuries of "systematic white oppression" cannot be "an excuse for merchandising artless anger and bad vibes."[96] It seems to us that this insensitive attitude toward black anger after four centuries of white oppression lacks historical perspective: Only a century and a half of English oppression led white leaders like Thomas Jefferson to assert in the Declaration of Independence that the abrogation of the rights of "life, liberty, and the pursuit of happiness" justified *violent revolts* against such oppression.

Souljah used the media interviews and talk show appearances that proliferated during this controversy to discuss racial politics. On NBC's *Today* show in mid-June, she pointed out that it was "absurd" to believe she was an advocate of murdering white people; then she noted the hypocrisy of many white politicians: "Bill Clinton is like a lot of white politicians. They eat soul food, they party with black women, they play the saxophone, but when it comes to domestic and foreign policy, they make the same decisions that are destructive to African people in this country and throughout the world."[97]

After the Clinton attack, Sister Souljah became active in trying to get white Americans to look beyond the violence of the black gangs to the underlying conditions created directly and indirectly by white racism. In 1992 a mass media public service message in Evanston, Illinois, argued that gangs of black youth bring more deaths to black communities than all the white supremacists like the Skinheads and the Klan. The announcement presumably intended to reduce the tendency of black young people to join gangs. Yet many blacks were offended by the contrast, as black gangs cannot be compared to organizations reinforcing centuries of white oppression. Souljah explained, "I think that what's wrong with it is that, repeatedly in the United States of America, we fail to address the real problems that cause young African men in this country to join gangs."[98] Many white commentators, both liberal and conservative, have adopted this strategy of blaming only the black community for the proliferation of youth gangs.

A white caller to a *Larry King Live* show where Souljah was the guest asked how she differed from "a David Duke." Souljah replied that Duke belonged to a group with a history of terrorism, then added that she "does not own a gun, has never shot anyone, has never killed anyone, does not have a criminal record, and has never been a member of a terrorist organization that advocates the murder of white people."[99]

Reaction: White Political Leaders and the Mainstream Mass Media

Just as "Willie" Horton became an icon of the dangerous black male criminal, Souljah became an icon of the dangerous black revolutionary. White politicians and media commentators agreed with Clinton's attack on Souljah the revolutionary. Former president Jimmy Carter remarked, "Jackson is wrong, and so is Sister Souljah. . . . I don't blame Bill Clinton at all. I admire him for being brave enough to say it in that particular forum."[100] In congressional discussions, Souljah became a symbol of black extremists advocating anti-white violence. Senator Robert Byrd, a Democrat from West Virginia, claimed that he had confirmed that Souljah really had uttered the remark: "If black people kill black people . . . why not have a week and kill white people?" Insisting that this statement constituted Souljah's call to kill whites, Byrd also made no attempt to understand the comment as an interpretation of a gang member's perspective. Instead, Byrd asked the Senate, "Why advocate killing anyone, white or black?"[101]

In comments to the House, Robert K. Dornan, the Republican representative from California who earlier stated that he had counseled Atwater not to use the Horton ad, criticized Time-Warner for continuing to produce records by black rap artists like Sister Souljah. Dornan also alleged that Souljah "recommends that one group of Americans take time out from killing themselves and kill another group of Americans."[102] Although Dornan had resisted the Republican distribution of the distorted and racist image of Horton, he would apparently ban the antiracist words of articulate black rappers like Souljah from public distribution.

In contrast to the increasingly common interpretation of the "Willie" Horton ads as "dirty politics," Clinton's treatment of Sister Souljah and her comments became synonymous with smart political strategy in both Congress and the media. After the election, a *Newsweek* writer referred to the "Sister Souljah gambit," meaning a politician's demonstration of toughness toward "special interest groups" in his or her political party.[103]

Of the many comments by white media analysts on Clinton's critique of Souljah that were reported by the American Political Network's hotline, as far as we can determine, *not one* major white commentator revealed a deep understanding of Sister Souljah's point of view.[104] The *Washington Post*'s Colman McCarthy wrote harshly: "Souljah's soul mates defended this rant with the customary defense that the quote was taken out of context. An examination of that context—the interview was taped so the I-was-misquoted alibi is out—shows Sister Souljah to be little more than another minor celebrity pushing violence and hate as solutions to conflict."[105] He chided Souljah for thinking that violence can ever lead to anything good and for blaming racial problems on "the demon white power structure."[106] In this opinion piece McCarthy made no effort to understand the black perspective on racism, attempting instead to shift the focus away from the white power structure.

A white writer for the *Detroit News*, Nickie McWhirter, expressed outrage for what she saw as Souljah's call for black killers to put "variety in their sport. Perhaps we should establish killing seasons," she wrote. McWhirter minimized the continuing significance of discrimination even while acknowledging it: "The oppression and discrimination *may be*, certainly historically have been, real. And abominable. Souljah's suggested response in the here-and-now is just damn foolishness."[107] McWhirter refused to understand the reality of racial discrimination as a major U.S. problem. Some white commentators attacked Souljah personally and accused her of using rap radicalism for economic gain. A *Time* magazine writer attacked her "dubious achievements," sarcastically calling her a "capitalist tool."[108] Showing no understanding of why a young black rapper might be angry about persisting racism, he viewed her "eye-for-an-eye message" as a direct departure from the liberal objectives of the United Church of Christ's Commission for Racial Justice, with whom she had once been employed.[109] Moreover, like Horton, Souljah received attention in the international press. One Canadian paper, the *Vancouver Sun*, interpreted Clinton's "Sister Souljah attack" as a critique of a rapper who had said that blacks should "take a week off and just kill whites."[110]

The Black Reaction

A remarkably diverse number of black commentators voiced objections to Clinton's attack on Sister Souljah and his choice of Jackson's Rainbow Coalition meeting to make the attack. The Reverend Timothy Mitchell, a prominent New York minister, said that Clinton was rude and offensive in selecting a meeting of this organization to air his comments: "You don't invite a person to your house for them to insult your daughter."[111] Similarly, New York mayor David Dinkins argued, "I think it could have been handled differently." He added, "Nobody condones a call for murder, and she certainly did not mean that."[112] Derrick Jackson, a prominent black journalist, offered a nuanced view of Sister Souljah and her fellow rappers in an op-ed article in the *Boston Globe*: "The horrific fantasies of race wars by rap musicians give us a choice. We can deride them. . . . [Or] we can take their words as a sincere warning to prevent a real race war." He argued further that Souljah's tough language is that of a black rapper exhibiting great pain: "The wound is not healed by castigation. It is healed by curing sick urban conditions." In his view, heeding her words might have averted recent urban riots. Jackson concluded that although rap is criticized as violent, much in the popular media is also violent: "Schwarzenegger murdered women in a Terminator movie, yet remains a Kennedy and President Bush's emissary."[113] Sister Souljah is not the problem; she is only a

messenger with bad news about the state of white racism in the
United States.

The Case of Lani Guinier

A few months after taking office President Bill Clinton nominated
Lani Guinier, a distinguished law professor and civil rights attorney,
for an assistant attorney general post in his administration. Because
she was black and supported vigorous enforcement of the voting
rights law, Guinier was quickly labeled a "Quota Queen" by a *Wall
Street Journal* headline writer, a coded reference to the hostile label
of "welfare queen" often applied to black women. Many white politicians and journalists took up the theme articulated in the *Journal* by
conservative activist Clinton Bolick, who inaccurately charged
Guinier with supporting "racial quotas."[114] Guinier became yet
another black-radical icon. President Clinton and his advisers refused
to allow her to defend herself against the racist attacks because it is
customary for appointees to maintain silence on their views until con-
firmation hearings. Yet without a public defense of her position on
voting and other civil rights, Guinier soon found her nomination with-
drawn. Later, in July 1993, Guinier told a group of journalists: "I
became the Quota Queen because I talked openly about existing
racial divisions. . . . It did not matter that I, a democratic idealist, had
suggested race neutral election rules such as cumulative voting as an
alternative to remedy racial discrimination. It didn't matter that I
never advocated quotas."[115]

   Guinier's views on voting rights, contrary to much of the public discussion, were not outside the mainstream of political discussion and
action. In the late 1980s and early 1990s she had clearly stated her
reasonable ideas for empowering black voters in several law journal
articles.[116] While the traditional enforcement of the 1965 Voting
Rights Act has increased the number of black-majority voting dis-
tricts, it has not reshaped local and state legislative bodies to give
black elected officials a proportionate influence on daily operations.

In her writings Guinier has suggested additional remedies that might increase black influence on these government bodies, among which is cumulative voting, a procedure in which each voter is given a number of votes equal to the number of positions to be filled in a legislative body. If ten members of a commission are being elected, each voter gets ten votes and may use them to vote for one candidate for each of the ten different positions or cast all ten votes for one candidate for one position. This strategy is thought to increase the probability that a person of color might be elected in an area where the majority of voters are white. Cumulative voting is a departure from most existing voting rules, but it is not unprecedented. Some small areas of the country, such as Alamogordo, New Mexico, and Peoria, Illinois, have already experimented with this voting procedure, and it is used in selecting members of corporate boards of directors. Guinier has suggested in her law journal articles that other mechanisms, such as "minority vetoes" and the requirement of legislative "supermajorities" to pass most laws, should be considered if cumulative voting and traditional strategies do not improve black political influence. Interestingly, in the 1980s the conservative Reagan administration agreed to a super majority mechanism to redress voting rights complaints in Mobile, Alabama. This remedial procedure stipulated a five-vote majority on Mobile's seven-member city commission to pass legislation. The intention was to ensure that at least one of Mobile's three black commission members would have to vote in favor of any new law.[117]

It is significant that while Clinton allowed Guinier to be pilloried as a "Quota Queen" by whites with undisguised racial motives, her actual views were not radical or outside the political mainstream. Moreover, as of late 1999, Clinton's civil rights record was better than that of his predecessors Ronald Reagan and George Bush: He appointed considerably more blacks and women to important government positions, including judgeships, than they did, and his administration put greater emphasis on the enforcement of civil rights laws. Yet Clinton's actions regarding two talented black women, Sister Souljah and Lani Guinier, reveal a president who often pays more heed to the racial concerns of the majority of white Americans than to the desires for empowerment of the majority of African Americans.

Conclusion

Taken together, the Texaco and the William Horton and Sister Souljah cases, different though they are, reveal the distortion that racial symbols and icons bring into critical national issues. Even white liberal commentators who chastise white supremacists have used these images to communicate racial ideas to the larger society. Both Horton and Souljah became such icons, with the realities of their personalities and situations twisted to transform them into violent black Frankensteins to be used at will by white politicians and commentators. Both became symbols of senseless attackers of whites, but for different reasons.

Since the 1988 Bush-Dukakis presidential contest, numerous political and media discussions have raised the issue of whether certain people or groups were becoming "Willie Hortons," that is, politically damaging figures or issues. In the 1992 campaign, for example, gay groups in the Democratic party were sometimes called the "Willie Hortons" of that campaign. "Willie" became a shorthand and ritualized way of saying, "Black men are criminals," or of more generally typifying any person or issue as a political pariah. Images in the ads suggested that men like Horton are not in any significant way like the rest of us (that is, like whites). Few whites questioned this iconization of Horton; most are born into a social world where a range of negative images of African Americans is automatically accepted. The Bush campaign did not create the icon of the dangerous young black man, but it did intentionally and successfully exploit that image.

Sister Souljah is a different icon, although one that is also feared by whites. Since 1992 Sister Souljah has become a larger-than-life symbol of a black person out of control, a so-called proponent of black revolutionary violence. In the Clinton incident, a white candidate sought political gain by disassociating himself from the black icon. In contrast, in the Horton ads Bush succeeded in damaging Dukakis by linking him with the dreaded black icon. In both cases, black icons were used to evoke white fears about black crime and violence directed against white Americans.

White racism is based on concepts that are part of the normal "order of things." Racist images are not just the product of intentional propaganda and manipulation of symbols by political leaders or the media. They are first and foremost fundamental perceptions of the world generated in everyday socialization, perceptions often so subtly inculcated that most whites accept them as self-evident. The common images, symbols, and icons of U.S. racial rituals have been created in white American homes, schools, workplaces, and political and media institutions. Moreover, these icons were not created by a few isolated white actors but were the product of the collective efforts of many white Americans, including those officiating at the highest levels of the power structure, from the halls of the White House to the board-rooms of corporate America.

We also see how some Americans fight back against racism. There are several ways to confront racist words and actions, as we see in other chapters. One way is by talking back and becoming an inter-rupter, bringing the reality of prejudice and discrimination into set-tings where seemingly benign racial comments are being made. In the Texaco case Bari-Ellen Roberts and Sil Chambers, by talking back and stopping the process, were able to show the costs of racism in the lives of black workers. Still, the overwhelming white control of U.S. institutions makes this fighting back very difficult.

7

Sincere Fictions of the White Self

In previous chapters we have focused on what whites actually do in cases of racial victimization. On the assumption that some of the meaning of these antiblack actions can be found in "the souls of white folk," we now turn to an examination of what whites say and believe about racial matters. This chapter explores the complicated views of whites about African Americans and U.S. racial relations and offers some explanations for white perspectives.

Our concern is not just with how whites see black "others" but also with how whites see themselves. Antiblack prejudice denotes sentiments directed toward others; it makes no reference to the sentiments about the white self elicited by encounters with the "others." However, racialized attitudes and actions require not only a representation of the stereotyped other but also a representation of oneself. This self-definition involves the creation of "sincere fictions," personal ideological constructions that reproduce societal mythologies at the individual level. In such personal characterizations, white individuals usually see themselves as "not racist," as "good people," even while they think and act in antiblack ways. Sincere fictions are both about the other—those fictions usually called prejudice—and about one's group and oneself.

We have previously noted white racism's ancient heritage. Europeans held negative views of African peoples before the founding of European colonies, although these views did not develop into thoroughgoing racist ideologies until the 1700s. As early as the 1600s, however, white theologians and political leaders in the North American colonies were constructing racist theories of biological, mental, and moral inferiority to legitimate their exploitation of Africans as slaves. Early on, the dark color of the African American slaves was defined as ugly by white Americans, and by the 1700s racist defenders of slavery were portraying Africans as an inferior species, as apelike and subhuman. Whites used this image of African peoples to rationalize their exploitation of individual African slaves. Even in the early colonial period strong societal and personal fictions were required to allow a brutal slave system in the midst of a society white settlers considered to be committed to strong egalitarian ideals. As we noted in Chapter 1, these fictions were accepted and used by waves of European immigrants seeking to establish their own identities as "whites" in America.

After slavery, the white mythology about African Americans continued to evolve during a century of legal segregation, which officially ended with the civil rights acts of the 1960s. Yet many white Americans continue to depict African Americans in negative terms. Today a well-developed white mythology about African Americans still contains many sincere, if often outrageous, individual and collective ideas.

White Attitudes in Opinion Polls

Social science analyses of opinion surveys generally show significant improvements in white attitudes toward African Americans since World War II. White survey respondents' decreasing acceptance of old-fashioned stereotypes and increasing acceptance of civil rights laws and the idea of equality of opportunity are often cited.[1] We do not argue with research findings showing that in recent decades whites as a group have become less negative in assessments of civil rights or of African Americans. But we do argue, on the basis of survey data and our own in-depth interviews, that many whites still hold negative images of and stereotypes about African Americans.

Consider, for example, the views white respondents expressed in a National Opinion Research Center (NORC) survey. Asked to evaluate on a scale of 1–7 how prone to violence blacks are, half chose the violent end (ranks 1–3) of the spectrum. When asked the same question about whites, a small proportion (16 percent) placed whites as a group in the same ranks. When asked to rank blacks and whites on whether each group preferred living on welfare aid (versus being self-supporting), just over half the white respondents ranked blacks toward the welfare preference end of the spectrum, while only 4 percent ranked whites as a group in that same direction. Asked to evaluate blacks and whites on whether they tended to be hardworking or lazy, 17 percent ranked blacks at the hardworking end of the spectrum compared with 55 percent who ranked whites similarly. Asked to rank blacks and whites on "intelligence," 29 percent of whites placed blacks toward the unintelligent end of the continuum, while only 6 percent ranked whites similarly.[2] Judging from this major national survey, a majority of whites still stereotype black people as violence-prone, inclined to live on welfare, and disinclined to hard work, and a substantial minority still stereotype black Americans as unintelligent.

The Anti-Defamation League conducted a national survey of white attitudes toward black Americans. White respondents were given a list of eight stereotypes of black Americans, including "more prone to violence," "prefer to accept welfare," "less ambitious," and "less native intelligence." Fully 76 *percent* of this national random sample agreed with one or more of the antiblack stereotypes; 55 percent agreed with two or more stereotypes, and about 30 percent agreed with four or more. This survey provides clear evidence that the majority of white Americans are still willing to profess publicly their allegiance to relatively crude conceptions of African American culture, values, and propensities.[3] Some slavery-era arguments are very much alive, albeit sometimes translated into a modern idiom.

Other surveys have examined an array of white attitudes. In surveys from 1973 to 1990 the proportion of whites supporting a law prohibiting antiblack discrimination by homeowners selling their homes increased from 34 percent to 51 percent. By 1990 a majority supported an open housing law; however, 44 percent of white respondents nationwide did not, preferring a law giving a white homeowner the right to refuse to sell to a black buyer.[4] In NORC's 1990 survey a majority of white respondents also expressed a negative view of intermarriage: two-thirds were opposed to a close relative marrying a black person. In addition, about one-fifth of the whites interviewed nationwide favored a law banning marriages between blacks and whites.[5]

A majority of whites hold the opinion that, while some racial discrimination still exists, it is no longer of great significance. A Louis Harris survey discovered that seven in ten did not believe that black employees in white-collar jobs faced discrimination.[6] More than six in ten white respondents in a NORC survey believed that discrimination was not the main reason that blacks, on the average, have worse jobs, lower incomes, and poorer housing than white people. Almost six in ten said the differences were mainly because most blacks "just don't have the motivation or will power to pull themselves up out of poverty."[7] Blaming African Americans for their own poverty has been a characteristic white opinion for decades.[8]

NORC's 1991 survey also asked respondents whether "government is obligated to help blacks." Fifteen percent of whites chose the help end of the continuum offered, 30 percent took a middle position, and half felt that "government shouldn't give special treatment" to black Americans.[9] John McConahay and his associates have described whites' unwillingness to support government programs as "modern racism," defined as a white perspective that views black Americans as illegitimately challenging cherished white values and as making unreasonable demands for racial change. McConahay reports that in opinion surveys most whites publicly state their support for freedom of opportunity; he argues that extreme antiblack stereotypes and white opposition to legal desegregation have been replaced by "modern" prejudices and stereotypes.[10] However, one must not exaggerate the positive changes that have taken place in white racial attitudes since the days of legal segregation; there is much continuity from the past to the present. White actions are still often legitimized by an overt or barely disguised racial mythology. Perhaps the greatest change is in the content of the sincere fictions undergirding racist action. By defining black people as too demanding, paranoid, or pushy, whites rationalize their opposition to aggressive programs that might end racial discrimination.

Opinion surveys provide a view of the whole nation comparable to looking at a city from a satellite in the sky. We see the city as it dissolves into the countryside, the broad pattern of streets and blocks. But to understand the daily rhythm of life in that city, we must come down to earth and walk the streets. A close-up view cannot be obtained from a satellite. Data from opinion polls, typically brief answers to short questions, yield at best an overview or distant portrait of the social issues under scrutiny. In-depth data are required to better understand those issues.

Living in a White Bubble

Having looked at survey results to give us the overview picture, we can now walk the streets of our cities and examine interview excerpts from some of the ninety exploratory interviews we and our students have conducted with white Americans in several states (mostly in New York, California, Texas, and Florida). These interviews were designed to probe in some depth how whites think about racial matters and to explore an area largely neglected in the social science literature. The sample is a convenience sample of white adults who were accessible to us or our students.[11] Most interviewees held white-collar jobs or were attending college to prepare for such jobs. In examining the responses of these white men and women we move closer to understanding how whites construct racial issues in their minds and what racial issues mean for them.

The cases analyzed in previous chapters suggest that relatively few whites think reflectively about their whiteness except when it is forced on them by encounters with or challenges from black Americans. Indeed, white supremacists seem to be the only group that has articulated an explicit and highly developed ideology of whiteness. Surprisingly little research has been done on how whites view themselves as a racial group. Significantly, most white respondents in research conducted by Robert Terry said that they had rarely or never thought about being white.[12]

In the interviews analyzed in this chapter, several respondents indicated they rarely thought about what it means to be white. One forthright college student gave this reply to a question about what being white is like:

> You really don't think about that much, at least I don't. It has its advantages; and then again it has its disadvantages. There is always a feeling of comfort, usually, but sometimes disadvantages because you feel you may miss out because they are looking for a minority or something like that, so it has its good points and bad points. But . . . I don't think about it much.

Changing interracial dynamics appear to have pressured this student to give some thought to his whiteness and to his comfort with that status. Apparently, for most whites, being white means rarely having to think about it. This attitude contrasts sharply with the reports of many African Americans that their blackness is forced into their consciousness virtually every day by contacts with white Americans.[13]

To a substantial degree the lack of daily reflection on whiteness appears to come from social isolation. While the actual proportion is unknown, many whites have lived their lives totally or mostly isolated from black persons of any age or any social status. Most whites have not had significant contacts with black Americans apart from the occasional maid or other service worker, or perhaps brief contacts with a few black employees at work or in shopping rounds. There is little interracial contact in most of the nation's residential neighbor-hoods; most historically white neighborhoods still remain overwhelm-ingly white.

This white isolation is not a new problem. The desegregation that followed the 1950s and 1960s Civil Rights Movement broke down some racial walls, but it did not alter the way most whites live out their lives. A few earlier research studies have briefly explored this issue. In Bob Blauner's study of white Californians in the 1970s, one dock-worker spoke of white isolation: "I never knew much about black peo-ple until I went on the waterfront. . . . Black people used to scare me. 'Cause I didn't know anything about 'em. You know, I never heard of greens. It's just like anything else, if you don't understand it, you're suspicious and you're off it."[14] Isolation thus seems to feed misunder-standings and suspicions.

The response of another college student in the interviews suggests that whites view blacks from a distance and construct their limited knowledge about black people from within an encapsulated white "bubble":

> Most white people feel, I think, detached from blacks in the sense that they are kinda in their own world and blacks are kinda in their own world. You look at them through a looking glass and say, "Hmm, isn't that interesting what that black family's doing or what that black cou-ple's doing, or what those black teenagers like to listen to, or like to dance, how they like to dance." And things like that. But they don't really identify that well or aren't that close with them totally.

A white professional offered some biographical insight into whites' isolation from blacks:

> I never even saw a black person when I was younger. I grew up in [a south-ern area]. There weren't any black people in our neighborhood. I had never been to school with a black person until I got to college; and then there was a woman in my dorm who was half black, half Asian, and every-body thought that was totally bizarre. And I, I don't know, it didn't faze me too much. I had a friend from the South, and she almost had a heart attack that we were in the dorm with somebody who was half [black].

Because of the everyday demography of black-white relations, many of the places that most whites traverse still have few, or no, black people present. This woman's early isolation from contacts with African Americans was not broken until she entered college, and then the general reaction of white peers to cross-racial acquaintances was consternation and hostility. Her comments on racial animosity bring to mind statements by students at Olivet College that were discussed in Chapter 2.

The Meaning of Whiteness

Whether or not they give their whiteness much thought, at some level, conscious or half-conscious, many white Americans do have some knowledge of what whiteness means. In a study of how white men think about African Americans, Margaret Moore has suggested that there are white "systems of knowledge . . . used for the discovery and organization of the dominant group reality. . . . Whites' knowledge of racism is also presumed to have been generated over time and transmitted among whites from one generation to the next."[15]

Seeing Blacks through the Mass Media

Much of what whites today know about African Americans comes from the media. One of the white respondents, a government official, cited the media as an important window in the white bubble:

> I think it's changing; and it has changed tremendously within the last five years. Previous to that I think it was not very good. I think it is changing more because we are being more sensitive to . . . we are getting to view more of their culture through TV and sports. And the media have made these people who once were not considered to have feelings, were inferior, now we are seeing that they have just as much pain as anyone else. They have families, and they care like anybody else. I think it's come a long way. I will be honest with you. I get a little upset when I hear black people disagree that it has . . . come a long way. I don't buy

that. I can't tell you the last time that I heard a joke where the black person was the punchline and "nigger" was used.

This man not only attributes his awakening from isolation to the media but also credits media images of black people with increasing white sensitivity toward racial issues and improving racial relations in general. He communicates a strong sense of change. Blacks' media presence, notably in sports or entertainment roles, may make them more legitimate members of society in the eyes of many whites. Changes in images in the artificial world of television are also sometimes accepted as evidence of real-world changes. This can have both positive and negative effects. The media play a major role in shaping the white public's attitudes and beliefs, and distorted media images of contemporary racial relations can contribute to the construction of whites' sincere fictions, in this case to an exaggerated view of the improvement in racial conditions. In his statement that "now we are seeing" that blacks have as much pain as other people, the speaker notes the earlier acceptance of the less-than-human image of black Americans among whites. Could it be that many whites were unaware that black people felt and suffered pain until the television networks chose to show black families as fully human, perhaps in programs like *Roots* or *The Cosby Show*?

Concealing Racism

Gunnar Myrdal wrote about the tension that exists in U.S. society between the widely proclaimed ethic of equality and the reality of everyday racism and inequality. He called this tension "the American dilemma" and predicted that over time the tension between ideals and practice would be resolved in the direction of the ideal.[16] The white respondents seem to adhere, at least at an abstract level, to the principle of equality for all. Among the most important of the myths to which whites cling is that the United States is a land of equal opportunity for all racial and ethnic groups. A white businessperson com-

mented on this freedom: "In this country, you are free either to experience the American dream, or you are free to fail. You have that freedom. So it's up to you as to what outcome transpires. So if two
individuals are applying for a job, race should absolutely not enter
into the decision whether that person's hired or not."

This freedom-and-equality ethic can make the expression of overt
racism uncomfortable for many prejudiced whites. There is some
awareness that racism goes against the basic principles of the nation.
Indeed, a few psychological studies have found that some whites in
interracial contexts avoid acting in what they feel to be blatantly racist
ways.[17] In certain public settings many whites will try not to appear
overtly racist. One educator was clear on this point: "There is a lot of
racism that no one wants to talk about because they are afraid to say
anything, because it is not accepted to be racist. You know it is not
accepted to say anything against blacks. So I think a lot of white people have some feelings that they won't even say, so I think [this causes]
more racial tension." Drawing on his own observations, a student
echoed the educator's sentiment:

> Most white families like to say that they're not prejudiced. They like to
> say that they don't discriminate, that they want true equality, that they
> want all these things, but if you ever put them to the test there is a lot
> that would back off. A lot of whites still, the majority I'd say, will say the
> right, politically correct things at the right times, but behind closed
> doors, or with their friends, their small circle of friends, will be
> extremely bigoted in their comments.

Erving Goffman has written about the distinction between the
frontstage and backstage actions of everyday life.[18] Backstage, the
majority of whites, who know what to say publicly, are bigoted. Bot-
tled-up prejudices can explode into the open in critical situations like
those in Dubuque or at Olivet College. One white student noted the
character of racism in his experience:

> I know a lot of people who are very racist. And that makes it hard on me
> too because they'll be saying stuff. And I'll be like, "You need to quit

saying that." They'll be "nigger this and nigger that," and I'll be going, "Come on, Man." [How does it feel for you?] I'm like "ahhh" [sighs]. But like I'll call my [white] roommate, I'll say, "Shut up, nigger" and stuff like that to my roommate in the same way that blacks call each other that. I use that word in that context, but I never . . . well, I don't know if you can say that word and not be racist. Well that's like the only time I ever say that word. But sometimes if one of my roommates say, "Oh, look at that nigger." I'm like, "Oh, come on." I think white people are making a general effort, I know I am, and it's disappointing to me when black people don't make the same effort.

Many whites recognize and condemn virulent racism, even while continuing to practice racism themselves, if only to get along with other whites. Like the government official quoted earlier, this student presumes to argue that whites are more insightful about or active in racial change than blacks. This sincere fiction again privileges whites and seems essential to many whites' conceptions of themselves as nonracist.

Sometimes whites justify antiblack hostility and discrimination by citing what they consider to be the good intentions or good character of white discriminators. One student spoke of a relative:

I just don't want to be there when [a relative] says "nigger this and nigger that." This [black] guy that my [relative has] had forever, I think since they were slaves. . . . But, see, they are like [her] family. She had a little house set up for them, and they drive her around and stuff—it's like driving Miss Daisy around. . . . It's not derogatory, I mean that's just how she grew up. . . . I mean it is derogatory realistically, but she doesn't mean anything.

This student, like the previous respondent, is aware of, and uncomfortable with, overtly racist attitudes and practices, both in the past and in the present. Both respondents express concern that racist attitudes should be eradicated. Yet the omnipresence and routinization of antiblack behavior—often in a family or friendship context—soften the harshness of the racist realities for these white observers. This softening makes it easier to exonerate offending whites, especially if they are relatives or friends who do not really "mean anything" by their antiblack views and actions.

The White Sense of Privilege

When whites do speak specifically about the meaning of being white, they usually talk of their privileges and seldom mention any negative aspects. Conviction about some type of white superiority is a key part of the racial thinking of many whites. The government official quoted earlier had this opinion about what it is like being white in a multiethnic society: "It's, I'm sure, better than not being white. I really think that's depending on your white person's place. If he's well-to-do, upper middle class to upper class, there is probably no problem. It's the low-income/middle class—I'm sure it's not as great as it used to be." His was one of the few mentions of class given in answers to this interview question. It is unclear whether he means simply that lower-income and low-middle-income whites are having a harder time economically or whether he means to say that whites at those status levels have suffered more than others from the advancement of people of color in U.S. society.

One business executive's answer was clear: "Well in certain regards sometimes you feel like you're the minority, but you know I still think that we are probably a lot better off as a whole than the majority of the blacks are." A man of substantial power, he senses that white power has begun to slip. Addressing the same issue, a college student answered somewhat differently:

> I think although despite strides toward, you know, equality and things like that . . . whites in a way still have an easier row to hoe in the society. I'm not exactly sure why that is, but maybe . . . if you're white you have, your odds of being in a better family, or having a better upbringing, or having education emphasized more, is more there than being black.

Another student provided an insightful comment on the white sense of hierarchy:

Whites feel that they should stay above blacks. I mean I was born in the sixties, so I feel like, maybe, at least whites my age and older feel like when they came into this situation, and by America's standards on how everything works—status and hierarchy and classification—that you should at least . . . jump off the plateau your parents are on. You should have it a little better than your parents. And I feel that a lot of whites feel that way. When they came into the picture, they were better off than most blacks, so that should continue.

An understanding of whites' higher status and privileged circumstances was pervasive in the interviews. The taken-for-granted position of white superiority in the social world was accompanied by feelings that ranged from hatred to indifference to guilt.

Some white Americans, such as the white activists in Dubuque or the Skinheads in many cities, express the sense of superiority in a hardened, hateful language of supremacy. Other whites, such as most of the speakers here, express an enlightened recognition of racial differences that are more or less regretted. When asked to explain their position in a multiethnic United States, many whites do so in vertical terms. This propensity is embedded in U.S. culture and in the English language. Racial denotation implicitly involves a vertical dimension, a hierarchical meaning. The racial group designation is different from other stratification terms in that it not only places white and black people in a vertical classification of social status but also classifies them and sets them apart. For whites, the category "black" labels a group as physically (for example, dark-skinned or athletic), culturally (for example, promiscuous or lazy), and morally (for example, dangerous criminals or welfare queens) different, all in a single "race" appellation.

White Men as Victims

In the Dubuque, Olivet, and Portland case studies, young white men felt very angry, in part because they felt like victims of a changing racial system. Today white male supremacists like Skinheads and Klan members present themselves as victims. Yet they are not the only white men to feel this way. Opinion polls and media reports have emphasized that white men in all segments of society feel targeted and harassed and have a sense of losing political, social, and economic status. For example, a white father quoted by a *Boston Globe* reporter stated: "Everyone wants to know what the African-American and the Haitian and the Native American think, but no one really cares what the white man thinks. I am a known quantity. I am invisible."[19] The reporter suggests that some white men feel that they are "being held singularly responsible for the travails of Western civilization."[20] During the white/male backlash days since the 1980s, numerous books have been published attacking the advances made by blacks and women. One of these, *Invisible Victims: White Males and the Crisis of Affirmative Action,* was written by Frederick Lynch, who has argued that white men have suffered terribly and unfairly under persisting affirmative action policies. He sees the diversity movement and the multiculturalism thrust as serious and enduring attacks on white men.[21]

Some of the white male respondents saw themselves as victims. One college student spoke strongly on this matter:

> As a white male, I feel like I'm the only subsection of the population that hasn't jumped on the victim bandwagon. And I feel from a racial perspective, as the white man, I have been targeted as the oppressor, and frankly I'm getting a little tired of it, because I haven't done a whole lot of oppressing in my life. . . . I feel like I'm branded with this bad guy label. There was a time when I enjoyed what might be called "white man's privilege." And that came at a time when I was working very very hard in business. . . . Supposedly, as we study gender and race, as white men, we run the world; I never knew that.—I haven't oppressed anybody, but I've experienced feeling oppressed.

Until recently, it appears, most white men were not challenged and felt quite comfortable with their privilege. But today the challenges from white women and men and women of color have forced many into a rethinking of the white male self, to the point that some white men argue they are not (or are no longer) the beneficiaries of privilege.

A well-educated professional admitted his displeasure with recent attempts to achieve social equality: "I have experienced the backlash. As a white male, I have felt some resentment. But I have never lost a job to someone because of affirmative action. At this point, I think things have been equalized, and I am not sure quotas are the best operation to continue with." A white man who is apparently secure in his job, this speaker still states that he has "experienced the backlash" and "felt some resentment." The attitude of vulnerability sometimes expressed by white male interviewees is significant, in part because it is rather new for most.

White men have been decentered, to some extent, in public discussions, especially in the comments of those influenced by civil rights and women's liberation movements. The challenges of these civil rights movements have left many white men feeling vulnerable. For most, however, this feeling is not buttressed in their personal and collective realities, particularly at the material level. One thoughtful professional addressed the status of white male power in his definition of what being white and male in America means:

> It means you're part of the ingroup on the [matter of] power. My wife made a comment this morning, "You better tell them that you're prejudiced against this, this, this, and this, and against this, old white man." Basically, I feel like the world has changed, and most of the old white men are, first of all have the political power, and have the industrial power, and they're going to hold on to it until it's taken away from them, and so they are basically looking at it as [theirs]. . . . They hold the power away from the old white women too, it's the old boys' network, it's starting to be taken away, but it's going to be a long process. . . . I'm talking about the presidents in corporations, and the old boy network within corporations. That sometimes is what people think is being white in America. People who hold the power are going to hold on to it until it's taken away from them.

A major reason for white male concern about change is the challenge to white men's power by those who have been oppressed. Many find it hard to accept the fact that they have been (or are) oppressors. They sense they are losing legitimacy and power, and they wish to stop this process. National discussions of "reverse discrimination" and the "excessive demands" of people of color led by white male conservatives since the 1980s have had a profound effect on many white men. They sometimes feel like part of an embattled minority. Some are concerned that white men will not be hired or not get promotions because of competition from women and people of color who were once excluded from their workplaces.

Yet in reality white men as a group still have great advantages over women and men of color in the social, economic, and political realms, whether at the bottom or the top of the class system. At the top white men control most major institutions, from Fortune 500 companies and elite universities to state legislatures and highway departments to large hospitals and major law firms. Tom Dye's analysis of who holds the top positions of power in U.S. economic, political, and educational institutions found only 20 black people and 318 non-black women in the 7,314 positions he examined. These numbers are less than 5 percent of the total.[22] Since Dye's 1980s analysis there appears to have been little change in this proportion. Today, white men make up 39 percent of the population over thirty years of age, yet they hold all but a handful of the most powerful positions in this society's major institutions, even with recent "diversity" changes taken into account.

Stereotyping African Americans

In Studs Terkel's book *Race,* a civil rights lawyer spoke of the consciousness of race every white person carries. He noted that during black urban riots, whites in faraway places armed themselves in the foolish notion that they might be attacked. Then he described a trip his wife made down a street through a black neighborhood:

> The people at the corners are all gesticulating at her. She was very frightened, quickly turned up the window and drove determinedly. She discovered, after several blocks, she was going the wrong way on a one-way street and they were trying to help her. Her assumption was that

they were blacks and they were trying to get her. Mind you, she's a very enlightened woman.[23]

Such assumptions are not uncommon. For example, many whites lock their car doors or take other defensive precautions when a black man even comes near, revealing the embedded and personal character of the negative images of black men that we analyzed in earlier chapters. These racial predispositions may often be half-conscious or unconscious. Their source may be familial, peer group, or media socialization. The inclinations and orientations of whites toward African Americans are so much a part of everyday life, so "normal," that many whites do not realize they are present.

White Antipathies

The crude form that racist images of African Americans sometimes take is illustrated by the Skinheads' view of blacks as "monkeys." In Chapter 1 we noted that white views on racial matters have both cognitive and emotive aspects. Often these dimensions blend together, as in this comment from a white female college student: "Blacks are dirty. And just some of their habits and things. . . . They're so different than whites. It's kind of a tough question. I don't know. It's just something that you see and something that you're taught but you don't do. . . . You [as a young white girl] don't bring home black boys."

Many white Americans seem to view black bodies as dirty, something to be kept at a distance. Black shoppers report that some white clerks refuse to touch their hands in giving them change. One white woman we interviewed recoiled in disgust at the idea of giving a black person mouth-to-mouth resuscitation. As we noted in previous chapters, Joel Kovel has argued that such reactions may occur because whites are projecting onto the dark otherness of black Americans their own deepest fears. Somehow, for many whites the blackness of African Americans comes to symbolize the disgusting.[24]

The topic of interracial sex, including dating and marriage, is perhaps the most revealing about the depth of white attitudes. We noted earlier that about two-thirds of white respondents to one opinion poll were opposed to a relative marrying a black person. The following opinion about an adult child dating or marrying a black person, expressed by a white male respondent, shows how deep white feelings can be:

> I'd be sick to my stomach. I would feel like, that I failed along the way. I'd probably take a lot of the blame for that. It, I would feel like probably I failed out on the job along the way or they would not have those tendencies to do that. I'd feel like I probably failed as a father, if that was to happen. And it's something that I could never accept. I would probably be in big-time trouble over that. It would truly be a problem in my family because I could never handle that, and I don't know what would happen because I couldn't handle that, ever.

This statement indicates the emotional roots of this man's racial attitudes. Protecting his family from interracial relationships seems to be part of his self-conception as a father. White disapproval of interracial dating and marriage can involve concerns about blacks having sexual desires for or relations with whites, as was apparently the case among some white men at Olivet College who reportedly objected to black men dating white women and, doubtless, among some white voters influenced by the "Willie" Horton ads to vote Republican. The almost instinctive negative reactions to even the idea of whites having sexual contacts with black people underscore the link between conceptions of the white self and the negative images of black people.

The Work Ethic and Racism

Even the famous American work ethic is sometimes overlaid with racialized images; whites tend to have an almost obsessive concern about the work ethic of black Americans. A few of our students have paraphrased informal conversations with whites who spoke privately to them of "jigaboos," "niggers," and "coons" not being willing to work hard. Such harsh language, usually uttered backstage, would probably not be used by most whites. The following statement from a white professional is more typical. After expressing sympathy for the plight of black people, he replied to the question, "What do you think blacks need to do to become truly equal?"

> For them to be as successful as we are, they are going to need to adopt our values. Be a part of our system or whatever. . . . Not values exactly, but, it is like, it is just that thing, like wanting the money but not wanting to actually show up, being reliable. The basic things we try to teach clients, or a high school kid about work, you know, like you need to be there, you need to work hard, so I guess it is the work ethic.

A college student who stressed his own belief in egalitarian values cited the work ethic in a critique of black pride: "Maybe they can take that pride, and do something better with it—like try to work every-thing out. I don't know. Instead of trying to be like 'It's a black thing,' because all that is to me is fostering racism. Instead of talking a bunch of flak they should take that pride and do something with it . . . like work hard!"

Repeatedly, whites advise blacks to work hard, as though hard work were not already part of the black repertoire. The gospel of the work ethic is central to the white conception of self. Its essential beliefs typ-ically include: (1) Each person should work hard and strive to succeed in material terms; (2) Those who work hard will in fact succeed; (3) Those who do not succeed (for example, poor people) have only themselves to blame: their laziness, immorality, and other character defects.[25] Whites' articulation of the work ethic ideology often tends to present whites as virtuous and the black poor as enduring justifi-able punishment for being nonvirtuous.

White criticisms of the black poor frequently focus on welfare recipients, who are seen as villains violating the work ethic. Earlier in this chapter we noted survey data indicating the white stereotype of blacks as preferring welfare to being self-supporting. Critics of the

Lani Guinier nomination, which we discussed in Chapter 6, evoked the stereotypical black "welfare queen" image in opposing her nomination as assistant attorney general. Research studies over the past three decades have shown that stereotypes of lazy black welfare recipients are prevalent among white Americans.[26] This imagery is also common in the literature of major white supremacy groups.[27] One white respondent stressed the threat certain of the poor pose in the minds of white people:

> Most white people feel that any minority is a threat. I think they see people on welfare as the scum of the earth, and I think that they think most black people except for Bill Cosby are on welfare. It's not something that we talk about. I'm sorry. What happened to the good old days where we did talk about things like that? I guess that that's what the majority of people feel.

Asked about programs to compensate African Americans for discrimination, a white educator changed the subject to blacks in social welfare programs:

> There is this welfare system that enables young mothers . . . who can't support their children to have children anyway. I see that system intact. And in a lot of ways [it] encourages poor people to have children, and they don't have to work. And I see public housing, and Headstart . . . and free daycare, and free services, and free medical. . . . I guess this is my prejudice; it's toward education: I don't think you need to have money so much, just have some values towards certain types of things, like education or intellect, or something like that. Instead of, you know, just loafing, and watching TV, and getting welfare. And you know, getting fat, and being angry, and taking your anger out on robbing people, and killing people.

Mimicking what he views as black dialect, another white respondent added to the list of white notions about black weaknesses:

> They'll sit there on talk shows and say, "I'se got to stay home and take care of my babies, I can't go to work." Well, hell, my wife has to go to work. I work, you know, we work, we go out and earn a living. We pay taxes and make it possible for this dumb ass to sit home on her butt and

not do anything. And yet she's going to justify to me that she's got eight children there, that we're taking care of, and she cannot go out and work because she needs to take care of those children. Now, and yet, we only have three children. . . . It's not responsible to have any more than that. We both have to work. . . . Well how the hell did they get the eight kids? And why do you need anybody paying for them?

The last two respondents hold harsh and gendered images of black women, with large broods of children, sitting and doing nothing. Their views are out of touch with empirical reality. Most poor blacks are not on welfare. Most low-income black families, including welfare families, are relatively small, with one to three children. A study in Wisconsin by Mark R. Rank found that women on welfare had *lower* birthrates than nonrecipients in their age brackets.[28] Moreover, the average time on welfare is about two years, not the lifetime of the myth. Whether or not they have received welfare, most poor black parents try hard to support their families with work as they can find it, and they doubtless try at least as hard as typical white parents. Part of whites' racial mythology seems to involve transforming the white self into one with a superior work-ethic morality.

Blacks Viewed as Deviant

The case studies in earlier chapters revealed a common white belief in black people's propensity for serious crime and deviance. White residents of Dubuque worried about black newcomers being gang members. The Boston police viewed black men in Mission Hill as potential murderers, and Charles Stuart fooled much of white America with his fiction of a black mugger. Stereotypes of blacks as violent played a significant role in the ways George Bush and Bill Clinton conducted presidential campaigns.

Popular white commentators reveal this biased thinking as well. In *The Way Things Ought to Be,* Rush Limbaugh, whose talk shows reach millions of white Americans, writes about his view of himself and racial issues but denies he is racist. In a chapter on the "Rodney

King affair" he seeks to demonstrate that white racism played no role in the events: "The fact that racial epithets were tossed back and forth between officers in squad cars unrelated to this incident is disgusting, but totally irrelevant."[29] Limbaugh blames black riots like the one in Los Angeles in 1992 on a poverty of values in black communities and defines them as primarily a criminal rather than a social problem. For many decades white Americans have expressed similar opinions about black protests against oppressive racial conditions.

One of our respondents, a college-educated woman, admitted that she and some of her neighbors automatically assumed that blacks were responsible for crime in their neighborhood, even though they had no evidence to support this assumption:

> In the past three years, we are suddenly having robberies that have never happened before. We are one of two houses on the street that have not been hit. . . . The man across the street has theorized that a bunch of lowlifes have moved in into a local government housing area. I don't know where it's coming from, but I think that it's flashed through every mind that it's probably blacks, including mine. And I'm so ashamed of that. I immediately shake myself and say, "No, it isn't." [Where do you suppose that feeling comes from?] Society. You hear it all the time. I think that it gets grilled into us.

Notice how racism can insinuate itself into every nook of the individual mind and society. Even this insightful woman, who recognizes the source of the white stereotypes and fears, finds herself initially inclined to accept racial myths.

Many whites seem to have a strong feeling that African Americans are somehow not like white people. This is evident in the notions that blacks do not work as hard as whites, that blacks are more likely to be on drugs than whites, that blacks have numerous children to get welfare aid, and that blacks are far more likely to be criminals than whites. One white professional summarized this point of view: "I think it's just a matter of values, of blacks having lower standards and lower values than whites, if you're going to put it black versus white." One striking thing about negative white commentaries is that *very rarely* is the law-abiding majority of black America mentioned, much less given credit for surviving under serious economic and racial difficulties. Reality is sacrificed for sincere fictions; most whites' lack of empathy makes them unable to relate to the black struggle to survive in a hostile white world.

White Views on Discrimination and Affirmative Action

One remarkable effect of the relatively conservative political ethos of recent decades is the circulation of the myth that racial discrimination is no longer a serious problem in the United States. A white professional expressed no doubt that blacks have achieved equality:

> They are equal; they do not need to become equal. In my mind, they are. Progress has been made in the laws and in jobs. And there are thousands and thousands of blacks who are making twice as much money as I am making and have better jobs than I have. But what is happening, and I think many of the blacks—take Bill Cosby for example; [he] is making very strong inroads in providing equal opportunities for blacks in entertainment and sharing his wealth with colleges.

The survey data cited previously suggest that a majority of whites assume that civil rights laws today provide African Americans with all the protection against discrimination they need. Apparently, media representations of black people, and stories about a few successful black individuals, have convinced whites like this man that African Americans have achieved equality.

Criticism of Affirmative Action

Because of this view that black progress has been significant, many, if not most, whites believe it is time to revise, scale back, or end affirmative action policies, which have increasingly been defined as racial "quotas." A government official reflected some ambivalence in his comments:

In a way, I oppose affirmative action as far as quotas and discriminating against any particular class of people to [bring] additional benefits to any other class of people. But I can understand why . . . it is necessary to have some type of affirmative action. Without some type of affirmative action, the people who are being discriminated against would continue to be discriminated against even more so.

This man, who deals with Americans of color in his job, has some sensitivity to discrimination. Yet he opposes rigorous affirmative action.

A white administrator also expressed some ambivalence about present-day affirmative action programs:

If you come down to two candidates that are equal in many respects— obviously no two people are equal—I have no problem with it [affirmative action] in an effort to move towards a goal of a truly multicultural society, helping, I guess, the minority. However, what I am strongly opposed to is a situation where you have, maybe, for instance, I know personally of a situation where a person, a white male you know, WASP person, scored very high on a standardized test and there was a minority who scored very low, barely passing. . . . And because she was a minority she received a job. I mean, to me that is not good because I think it does a disservice because . . . it builds up resentment. I think the person that is in this new position maybe is not quite as capable of handling it, and that is a problem. So I think when things are close, I have no problem at all. . . . But when there is a big discrepancy between the two candidates, I think giving the minority the position just because they are a minority is a mistake.

This respondent focuses on the relatively rare case in which a demonstrably less-qualified black candidate is hired simply because of an affirmative action program. Many whites seem to believe that wide racial discrepancies in candidate qualifications are common in the hiring process and that white candidates are usually better qualified.[30] Yet there is no research evidence to support this idea. Most candidates who are hired, black and white, are qualified. It is likely that the percentage of black candidates who are better qualified than their white counterparts is greater than the percentage who are less qualified.[31] Interestingly, there is not a hint in most white male comments on affirmative action that many white men, especially older ones, currently hold high-paying jobs to a substantial degree because they are white and male. When older white men were hired, there was little or no competition from black or female candidates, who were then excluded in the hiring process.

Here too we also see the idea that "merit" can be adequately and objectively measured by the commonplace standardized paper-and-pencil tests that are crafted mostly by white workers in testing organizations. Much research on the tests given in higher education shows that tests like the SAT, ACT, GRE, and the like are biased in cultural, racial, and class terms. Scores on such limited skills tests have often been taken to represent "objective merit" by generations of white parents and students. However, this type of "merit sounds like white people's affirmative action."[32] Generally speaking, native English-speaking whites from upper-middle-class backgrounds or schools (and with no learning disabilities) tend to do the best on such tests because they are the most familiar, and can likely cope best, with the language of the tests, their content, their framing, and their time-limited nature. The Educational Testing Service and the American College Testing Program, the creators and marketers of two popular college screening tests, have begun to recognize the racial and class biases in their tests. They have developed a "strivers" test score that takes into account a student's racial group and parental socioeconomic background to adjust upward the scores of those students who suffer from these social biases. Clearly, both in college admissions and in job settings white privilege can often be measured in test score points.

Interestingly, whites with access to substantial information on affirmative action may come to a more realistic view than the notion that unqualified blacks are often hired over better qualified whites. Another white administrator who oversees her organization's hiring policies was clear about the need to recruit black candidates more seriously and effectively:

> I favor affirmative action, and I don't believe that quotas exist. I think that's a myth brought on by the media. That it's a very simple term to

apply. And I think that the whole concept of what I do for a living involving affirmative action has been misunderstood under that label of quotas. Quotas are an absolute requirement that you hire "x," "y," or "z," and there is no system in the world that requires that. . . . . I look at our hiring figures, and I find in so many areas that we don't meet our goal for black professionals or Hispanics. And I always have to go out and find out why were the people less qualified, and if so then I agree with the decision we should go with the best-qualified person. But where are the well-qualified black employees, and that is where affirmative action comes in, what are we going to do next time to make sure that there are some fairly well-qualified black folks in there, that black people have the opportunity to be the best and that you're not out on the street corner recruiting for one group and recruiting in the professional society for the white professional? So I think the chances of that horrible myth, I don't think that exists very much at all.

Blacks Are to Blame

One white solution to black problems is for African Americans to accept the blame and the responsibility for their conditions, as this college student suggested:

> I don't agree with their [black] rationale because they seek to blame white people for all of the problems that they encounter, refusing to take responsibility for those problems themselves. It's like the academic performance thing, you know. The blacks score low on the SATs. Well, it's got to be because "the whites in control of everything have given us the short end of the stick with our schools."

A police officer made a similar argument: "It's everybody else's fault but black America. We are born in this world in times that are tough. But times have changed; there's equality. We're actually past equality. We're actually into favoritism now based on sex and race, and it's not easy to understand their anger." Here we can see that the white backlash against recent advances for African Americans often presents blacks as paranoid about racism or as being given unfair advantages.

Whites have also blamed black problems on black attitudes, even charging black leaders and entertainers, such as Sister Souljah, with "black racism." One white respondent commented explicitly on this issue:

> Black people are bigger racists any day of the week than white people are. I mean white people, for all intents and purposes don't give a shit. . . . . Black people teach their children the white power structure is the root of all of their problems. It's not that they all come from single-parent homes, or what have you, it's all the white man's problem! Now how [do] they ever expect for racism to die? See, what they want is for racism to die on one side. They don't want us to be racists anymore. [But] they want to be as racist as they want to be.

This speaker, like many white Americans, shows no understanding of why blacks are angry about racial discrimination. By an odd quirk of the white mind, the consequences of white discrimination—black anger and frustration—become a form of racism.

Additional Costs of Racism for Whites

In previous chapters we have shown that real-world incidents of racism have serious costs for white Americans. Moreover, most white Americans, including many white liberals, are often unwilling to take antiracist actions if there is a significant loss attached. Derrick Bell has pointed out that moderate and liberal whites may idolize black athletes, even have a few black friends, but oppose selling houses in their neighborhoods to blacks they do not know. They may also oppose hiring more than a few token blacks in their workplace. In Bell's view, many liberal whites will advocate integration only where there is little cost.[33]

One particularly insightful respondent, a white professional who manifested an enlightened awareness of the barriers that black men and women must face, discussed childhood experiences illustrating the waste of energy that racism can entail for white Americans:

We lived in a neighborhood that was, I guess, about a mile and a half from a black neighborhood. So I can remember early on, during my youth, we had a black park. I can remember the difficulty I had when I told my father that I was fishing there. It came to a point where we did-n't go fishing there because it was a black neighborhood. I thought that it was really sad. I used to enjoy to go there, and the idea was that it was somehow dangerous now to go there. We had a swimming lake there, and I was ten or eleven, and blacks were allowed then to go to that park. It was just overnight that, "Well, son, you're not allowed to go there because there are black people swimming there now." Basically we had to go twenty miles out to a different lake to go swimming. They just said, "You don't want to go there because it's dangerous. Black people are there. You never can tell what they might do to you."

The boy's image of dangerous blacks was not based on his own experi-ence but rather on family stereotypes rooted in a history of segregated living patterns. The price paid for white isolation and fear was more than just having to go to a more distant lake. The respondent paid an emo-tional price; his sense of sadness even now was palpable in the interview.

Racial images and attitudes are learned from many sources: par-ents, neighbors, peers, even strangers. Discussing black paper dolls she bought as a child with money found on the sidewalk, one white woman now in her twenties described the role whites other than par-ents play in prejudice:

I'm playing with my black paper dolls, having a good time. Then some-body comes to visit my parents, and they saw these dolls. And they say, "Oh, you let her play with nigger paper dolls? You let her do that?" Later, when this person leaves, my parents come over, and it's, "She bought nigger paper dolls! What's with her!?" And they took my paper dolls away. To this day there's this little something in me that, I want those paper dolls back. Because that just wasn't where my head was at, I wasn't about black or white, I just wanted those paper dolls.

This is another example of white racial thinking that occurs in response to the views of other whites. Interestingly, two decades after the event, this respondent still feels some sense of irritation and unfairness. Racial attitudes limited her choices just as they constrained the choices of other whites quoted in this and previous chapters. Racial attitudes can restrict even the thinking that whites undertake. Sometimes these limits can create consternation, if not resentment, especially in children who have not internalized the taboos such racial attitudes produce.

Parents' racist teachings can cause children much unnecessary pain. A retired white-collar worker described what her mother had told her about black people:

> "The niggers would come in the night and steal us away and use us for their pleasure," that's what my mother told us. What an awful thing to do, don't you think, frightening little children like that. There weren't even any colored people in our little town. I think she must have done that to make us behave. It worked; she scared us to death. The first time I ever saw a colored person I just about had hysterics. I was raised on a farm and did not go to town until I was about four. And there he was, right in front of the door to the shop we were going shopping at. I remember him as an absolutely huge black man, menacing and very frightening. I burst into tears and would not go into that store.

This woman added that she does not have such extremely negative responses today, but she still has a funny feeling when she comes near a black man. One wonders how many white children have been and are now being raised with this image of black people as frightening monsters.

White fear of black men or women can exact a heavy price. One white woman in a northern city said she lives in constant fear of black men. She was horrified at the thought of a black president:

> I'd move. I'd leave the country. Black people scare me. And I think that they would, first of all, I think that we'd be taxed from here to hell. . . . . People who have any money would be taxed terribly. . . . . I'd definitely leave. I don't trust them. I don't think they like white people very much, so that's not for the good of the society, either. I think that. . . . they'd work for their part, you know, the 20 percent of America.

This woman overestimated the black proportion (actually about 11 percent) of the U.S. population by nearly 100 percent, yet another sign of the exaggerated character of her racial fears. Leaving her country because a black person became president would be a high price to pay for her prejudices about black Americans.

Conclusion

The focus we take in this book represents a departure from previous attempts to understand the attitudes and actions of white Americans. As we have noted previously, we are not at all interested in labeling particular white Americans as "bad" or "good," for this name-calling will not lead to meaningful remedial action. The examination of white thinking as racialized, racist, or antiracist is of interest only as it aids the understanding of the system of white racism in the United States. In our interviewing and in our personal experience we have found that few whites view themselves as racist. When asked what was the first thing she learned about racial differences, one white woman replied:

> The very first experience I had was back in [elementary school]. I switched from a. . . . school which had no blacks to a public school, and I was thrown in the middle of a bunch of apes, no I'm just kidding. . . . . It always seemed like they were trying to be bullies; they were always bigger than the whites. And I don't know, my parents have always instilled in me that blacks aren't equal, because we are from [the South]. That's how they were brought up, and that's how they brought me up. [Did they scare you or anything?] Yeah, they look like apes. . . . . [How do you feel about them now?] The same. I dislike them, except when they treat me with respect and they're nice to me, I'm nice to them. I think there are differences. I don't say I hate every black person, but the majority.

Several times in a lengthy interview she referred to black people as "apes," a term that suggests a range of negative stereotypes in her thinking about racial matters. She also criticized affirmative action and favored racially segregated neighborhoods. Yet for all her negative views of African Americans, she did not see herself as racist: "I don't consider myself racist. I, when I think of the word racist, I think of the KKK, people in white robes burning black people on crosses and stuff, or I think of the Skinheads or some exaggerated form of racism."

Even whites who hold stereotyped images of African Americans usually do not acknowledge to themselves or to others that they are racist. Strong sincere fictions often hide everyday racial realities. One mechanism of sincere denial is distancing oneself from those whites who are considered to be racist, such as Klan members or Skinheads, who are viewed as uneducated or psychologically disturbed. Such distancing allows whites to deflect attention from their own role in promoting and implementing antiblack views.

The interviews examined in this chapter contain many insights into white thinking that help explain the antiblack actions seen in the case studies. The majority of whites have a developed mythology that can direct socially destructive practices and rituals. This mythology typically includes a sense of white superiority and privilege. Most whites wish to enjoy their privileges not by brute force but legitimately. One way that whites do this is to find something intrinsic in themselves to justify their array of racial privileges. A majority of whites adopt sincere fictions to the effect that, compared with whites, blacks are less competent, more likely to prefer welfare, less likely to work hard, or less likely to live upstanding lives. These sincere fictions usually undergird the racist rituals examined in earlier chapters and thereby perpetuate the great racial divide.

Antiblack imagery and iconography are products of age-old social processes that influence relationships across the socially constructed color line. Generally, racist images are constituted in the interrelated processes of *formulation, transformation,* and *redefinition.* First, there is the formulation of the white understanding of the white self that develops within the context of the long-term oppression of African Americans. Second, there is the perpetuation of the various prowhite and antiblack images and icons through the means of transformation and redefinition. These social processes enlarge and develop the "white" self and antiblack concepts, even as they provide a certain constancy over long periods of time. Across changing societal conditions, the racist imagery is central to the institutionalized rhetoric of racism and to the complex processes of legitimization of the white position in society. The racist images are continuously revised to maintain the balance between white society's understanding of "self" and "other."[34] Thus, the denial of racism imbedded in the claim "I'm not racist," and the white indication that what is in fact racist thought and behavior is normal or natural, are integral to the perpetuation of the racialized iconography and the racist system.

As we see it, those committed to antiracist thought and action, whatever their background or group, need to interfere regularly in the transmission and redefinition of this commonplace racist imagery and iconography—if it is to be started on the road to eradication. Our students often ask us what they can do as individuals to deal with the racist jokes, comments, and assertions made by those around them. Whether blatant or subtle, the racist understandings that are imbedded in daily life can be actively challenged every day. Only through verbal dissent and other active confrontation can the processes of racist transmission and redefinition be interrupted. The racist imagery will not disappear on its own; as Dr. Martin Luther King, Jr., once argued, "freedom is never given voluntarily by the oppressor; it must be demanded by the oppressed."[35]

Taking Action Against Racism: Problems and Prospects

On May 2, 1992, Nelson Mandela gave a speech celebrating the victory of black South Africans against a racial apartheid system. He noted, "This is one of the most important moments in the life of our country. I stand here before you filled with deep pride and joy—pride in the ordinary, humble people of this country. You have shown such a calm, patient determination to claim this country as your own, and now the joy that we can loudly proclaim from the rooftops—Free at last! Free at last!"[1]

In both South Africa and the United States the struggle of ordinary people to resist systems of oppression has been a recurring source of societal change. In the United States ordinary people, especially black Americans, have regularly challenged the ongoing racist regime. By doing so, they have enlarged the strategies and discourse of confrontation for all Americans.

Demands for *social justice* are central to three centuries of movements against antiblack racism in the United States. Courageous

Americans in these movements have made it clear to all that human freedom is unthinkable without equality and that freedom is impossible without social justice. In the past and the present, many white leaders, and much of the white population, have viewed social progress as continuing advancements in technology, as an expanding stock market and economy, or as the U.S. government becoming the dominant political power in a "new world order." In contrast, those in movements against racism have insisted that real social progress requires something else. It requires social justice and the implementation of full human rights for all Americans.

Ordinary black Americans rose in the 1960s in the Civil Rights Movement and, with support from other citizens of good will, brought major change to the United States and forced the passage of important civil rights laws. However, these civil rights laws have often been weakly enforced and, even when enforced, show themselves as incapable of overcoming much racial inequality and institutional racism. Richard Delgado has argued that the United States has two basic forms of racism: substantive and procedural. Substantive racism involves openly treating blacks as inferior to whites through legal segregation and other openly racist practices. More recently, however, a "procedural" racism has emerged, with less emphasis on black inferiority and more on white-established rules that invalidate or limit black opportunities and interests. "We erect difficult-to-satisfy standing requirements for civil rights cases, demand proof of intent, and insist on tight chains of causation. . . . . We insist that remedies not endanger white well-being. . . . . We elevate equality of opportunity over equality of result and reject statistical proof of all of the former."[2] Procedural racism assigns black demands for racial justice a low priority on the national political agenda. Delgado articulates his Law of Racial Thermodynamics: Racism is never destroyed but always comes back in new forms. For this and other reasons, some analysts and civil rights activists have argued that no further racial change will occur in the United States until powerful people again come to fear the possibility of major societal upheaval like that which took place in the 1960s—and take remedial action.

Legal and institutional challenges to white racism, and protests by thousands of Americans of all backgrounds, brought major civil rights advances and the legal desegregation of many U.S. institutions in the 1960s and 1970s. Today, through continuing antiracist discussions and movements, Americans in various racial-ethnic groups not only challenge racial inequality and institutional racism but also continually challenge themselves—and remind themselves that the civil rights movement did not end in the 1970s, but remains a commitment for the twenty-first century.

We are cautiously optimistic about the nation's future because we believe that Americans of many backgrounds will continue to confront white racism. We have learned from previous antiracism efforts what does not work. The liberal notion of one-way integration, of people of color assimilating to a white or white-Anglo-Protestant culture, will not heal the racial divide. This ideal of one-way integration assumes a divided America, with one side mighty and central and the other side weak in resources and vulnerable: If the latter is to survive, it must melt into the stronger side. However, in our view only a mutual integration of equals—an integration that recognizes the democratic principle that all groups must have equal respect and opportunity, that all Americans have a common destiny—can bring black and non-black Americans together to create a unified nation that can survive the twenty-first century.[3] In this chapter we draw out ideas from the case studies and interviews of previous chapters in order to help move the nation toward viable solutions to our wasteful racial divide.

Rethinking White Racism

Eric Nordlinger has written: "The history of ethnic conflicts suggests that they may be reduced if the stronger group is willing to make major concessions."[4] Will whites forsake their material and psychological privileges out of the goodness of their hearts or because they accept the American equality creed at an abstract level? Nonetheless, the argument for ending white racism does not rest exclusively on the moral weight of the American creed. As we have documented, racism is extremely expensive and wasteful for all Americans, as individuals and collectively. The eradication of racism is vital not only to the interests of African Americans and other Americans of color but also to the long-term interests of all white Americans: A system that is oppressive to one is oppressive to everyone.

In our view strengthening the struggle against white racism demands a reorientation in regard to how it is conceptualized and analyzed. As we have made clear, we see racism as the catastrophic collective waste of human time, energy, and resources. For centuries white American society has been obsessed with material profit, private property, and white dominance. To fulfill these obsessions, white Americans secured human beings from Africa and dehumanized their captives as racially different "others." White entrepreneurs bought African slaves to work on plantations and dictated laws to keep them chained, unlanded, and unschooled; such enslavement guaranteed that much of what Africans might have contributed to the new nation would be lost. Implementing slavery and, later on, maintaining legal segregation and informal patterns of discrimination dissipated much human creativity and energy. White America's black victims often survived slavery, but their lives were distorted and their humanity denied by the practices and rationalizations of the slaveholding class and its minions. Today black lives continue to be distorted, and black humanity continues to be denied by white racism. In addition, the great waste of talent, energy, and resources of the black targets of discrimination requires an extravagant and wasteful expenditure of talent, energy, and resources by the white perpetrators. In the long run, such brutal and profligate practices benefit nobody, regardless of power position; historically, similarly wasteful practices have brought down entire societies.

White rationalization of costly racist rites is based on basic social constructions—what we have termed sincere fictions of the white self and its "natural" privileges. Racist mythology involves abstract notions concerning human nature, the pace of historical change, and what might happen if traditional privileges are abandoned. White society has followed discriminatory courses of action supported by ideological constructions taken as acts of faith. This discriminatory system involves well-developed rituals with central officiants, acolytes, and passive participants. In previous chapters we observed white individuals and groups expressing themselves in hostile, often ritualized antiblack actions. We saw that racist acts are frequently perpetrated by "normal" white individuals who belong to families, churches, schools, political parties, and work groups.

In most cases the white actions carried the mark of the perpetrator's racial, gender, and class position. As a rule, the central officiants in most racial rituals were white men, with white women typically playing a lesser but still significant acolyte or passive participant role. In addition, we saw that racist actions cut across the class structure of white America. Class position can shape the character of racist action. The cross-burnings and other violence against Dubuque's black population and the Skinhead killing were mostly the work of less-educated whites, including some blue-collar workers. Yet the petitions against the Dubuque recruitment plan were signed by middle-class whites as well. Among the reported discriminators in the restaurant industry are white executives and managers. The Amadou Diallo shooting, the Rodney King and Abner Louima beatings, and the racial hoaxes involved actions taken by white police officers, other government officials, and whites in the mass media. White police officers and other government officials do much of the racial profiling, the euphemism used to cover the practice of considering people of color to be suspects for crimes merely because of their racial appearance. The Olivet College incidents involved white students carrying out their racial hostility toward black students in verbal and physical attacks. The creators of the "Willie" Horton and Sister Souljah icons were the well-educated advisers and campaign managers of presidential candidates and the candidates themselves. The character of racial practices is influenced by the social, economic, and political resources at the discriminator's command.

The varied manifestations of wasteful racist action have led many observers to think of them as distinctly different or isolated events rather than as *interrelated parts* of the same societal phenomenon. The white employer who passes over a black person for a job and the white contractor who excludes black construction workers do not consider themselves in the same category as whites burning crosses. Yet their covert and subtle discriminatory actions differ only in the weapons being used.

In addition to the white officiants and acolytes in racist rituals, there are many passive observers. The brutal and costly rituals of everyday racism in the United States are witnessed by millions who participate primarily as spectators. They watch racist practices in the workplace, in the streets, in public accommodations, in schools and colleges, and through the mass media. The passive participation of these whites reassures the direct perpetrators of the legitimacy of their actions. White officiants and onlookers doubtless have different degrees of consciousness and commitment to racist intervention and overt action. The degree of hostile fixation on black people can vary from a periodic commitment to a serious phobia. For the active perpetrators or for the spectators, the psychological orientation can vary from a sense of personal inferiority to envy to great fear and loathing. Yet in all cases the anti-other feelings reveal a breakdown of human empathy across the color line. For some whites, participation in the rituals of racism is an all-consuming matter; for others, it is of little consequence or interest; for yet others, watching the racist rituals is painful and brings a sense of shame. But so long as they remain silent, they become part of the problem that shames them.

The Costs of Racism for White Americans

From the perspective of society as a whole, the human time and energy expended in planning, staging, and implementing racist actions is extremely wasteful. The case studies show the huge costs for people of color of white stereotyping and discrimination. The civil rights laws passed in the 1960s made many formal acts of discrimination illegal, but because of weak enforcement they have not ended the broad array of blatant, subtle, and covert racism in police practices, in jobs, in housing, in education, and in political campaigns. Today the majority of black children still attend de facto segregated schools. Most black families live in more or less segregated residential areas, and many black families seeking housing face informal discrimination by white bankers, real estate agents, landlords, and homeowners. The majority of black defendants are tried by all-white juries from which blacks have been excluded, directly or indirectly, in the selection process. Most black workers, both blue collar and white collar, face covert and subtle, if not blatant, discrimination in the job market, including hiring and promotion barriers. Today racial discrimination is, as Justice William O. Douglas put it in the late 1960s, a "spectacle of slavery unwilling to die."[5]

In the past most social science research on the impact of racism has focused on the consequences of racism for African Americans. In previous books we ourselves have provided extensive documentation of the extraordinary burdens and costs that white racism has placed on African American individuals and communities.[6] In this book, however, we have emphasized not only the very heavy material and psychological costs for African Americans but also the serious material, psychological, and moral costs for white Americans. Let us note the costs for whites in some detail.

Material Costs

Although there is not much white awareness of the fact, racism involves substantial material and economic costs *for whites*. Racist actions sometimes produce apparent economic benefits, such as the chasing away of potential black workers who might compete for jobs, as in Dubuque. But the racial prejudices and outbursts in Dubuque not only used up the energy of white opponents, which could have been better invested (as in more education), but also probably chased away new employers who might have provided jobs for whites. It is hard to see any net material benefits to the family restaurant chains from the racist practices reported there, for they lost talented black workers and black customers. Our case studies and interviews also reveal the range of material costs for individual whites.

In the organizational context, racism negates the rational principle that goals should be achieved by the most efficient means. Unions that exclude black workers are weaker in their struggles against employers for better working conditions. Organizations that exclude black employees or make them invisible lose valuable talents and resources that could be utilized to reach the organization's major economic or social goals. The abandonment of efficiency because of a racist mythology is thus highly wasteful in concrete material terms. In addition, all who invest in such inefficient corporations lose materially from racism.

The costs of U.S. racism can be viewed in a global perspective as well. Today, the fact that Americans live in a global economy has become such a cliché that its meaning is not fully realized. To take but one example, international market conditions, still growing in competitive intensity, have made current patterns of antiblack discrimination in employment (with the consequent loss of talent and abilities) costly for companies to maintain and wasteful for the U.S. economy as a whole. Moreover, the economy produces not only for its own population but also for other countries around the world, and what Americans consume, from clothing to computer chips, comes from around the globe.

Racist events in the United States, such as those in our case studies, are often publicized to the rest of the world. Many people around the world have heard the stories of "Willie" Horton, Sister Souljah, and other black victims of U.S. racial patterns. Many people of color overseas may identify with these targets of racism in the United States. Certainly, the racist treatment of people of color in the United States does not escape those who watch the U.S.-pervaded mass media abroad. Indeed, the label "Made in the USA" may now elicit from some people overseas reactions similar to those once produced in many parts of the world by the label "Made in South Africa."

Moral Costs

Few Americans fail to recognize at some level or to some degree the *moral costs* of racism. In the contemporary United States the equality principles of the Declaration of Independence, religious and

political commitment to human rights and liberty, and civil rights legislation leave little room for doubt about the evil of racial discrimination, at least at an abstract level of morality. (We are using morality
here in the sense of principles of "right and wrong.") Yet it is also the
case that few whites who engage in actual discrimination against
African Americans or other people of color see themselves as immoral
or even racist. Reconciling the large gap between our society's
abstract principles of equality, justice, and freedom and the reality of
everyday racism has been for centuries a great challenge to all those
concerned with the eradication of racism.

Ultimately, a nation's unity, strength, and well-being rest on its citizens' compliance with its laws. While this compliance can be brought
about through force and fear, in the contemporary United States obe-
dience to laws primarily rests on the citizens' belief in the legitimacy
of those laws and in the moral authority of the society's legal and political institutions. In philosophy and practice white racism undermines
the moral authority without which there would be no American
nation. Racism is contrary to the fundamental principle of "liberty and
justice for all."

Significantly, the moral and ethical costs of racism lie deep in the
white psyche. In *White Racism* Joel Kovel argued that in some ways the
white self has been created out of the violation of the black self.[7] We
have seen in our case studies numerous examples of the way in which
racial hostility directed at African Americans seems to buttress a white
sense of privilege and supremacy. In *Playing in the Dark*, Toni Morrison analyzes white characters in American fiction who derive their
sense of power from the fact that they, no matter how weak they may
otherwise be, can at least dominate black slaves and servants.[8] Whites'
strong sense of whiteness derives from denigration of blackness. In this
juxtaposition, what is lost is the sense of humanity as a whole.

Related to these moral costs are serious political costs. White
racism makes full-fledged democracy impossible for all Americans.
Racism wrests from the less powerful group a recognition of the rights
of the dominant group while denying a reciprocal recognition. Yet this
denial of full and equal rights for some Americans, and the tolerance

of violence against them, puts every person in the society at risk of the same treatment at some point in time. Everyday racism makes true democracy impossible. Thus, the nation as a whole has paid a major political price for racism. Jennifer Hochschild has cogently argued that racism is *not* an aberration in the United States but rather part of the "democratic" system crafted at the time of the establishment of the United States by a white elite that included a significant number of slaveholders: "Since the English settled Jamestown, our politics have simultaneously affirmed the natural rights of all persons and legitimated the oppression of non-Caucasians."[9] For centuries slavery, segregation, and other racist practices have distorted democracy in the United States. From a black perspective and from a general democratic perspective, whites currently in power in U.S. institutions are exercising *illegitimate* power.[10]

We have noted earlier the economic problems racism can create for American companies around the globe. The international context creates moral and political costs for the United States as well. For many across the globe U.S. support of democracy and human rights overseas is viewed as hypocritical in light of America's racism at home. For example, the *London Times* wrote this about the 1992 Los Angeles riot: "Such incidents fuel the anger of those elsewhere in the world grown tired of globe-trotting American politicians lecturing them on democracy and human rights. They will say: 'Look to your own back yard, America!'"[11] The London *Daily Mail* called the rioting a "volcanic reminder that racism is as American as apple pie."[12] An article in the Egyptian press stated that the riot revealed the "profound levels of frustration and anger at some of the injustices of U.S. social, economic, and cultural policy."[13] China's *People's Daily* called the Los Angeles riot "the evil consequence of racial discrimination" that showed "the irony in some Americans wielding the big stick of 'human rights' to interfere in other countries' internal affairs. The facts show that American society is definitely not this country of equality and freedom certain 'human rights defenders' brag about."[14] Iraqi officials called for an emergency meeting of the United Nations Security Council "to discuss the violation of human rights in Los Angeles."[15]

Some Costs to the White Psyche

It is clear from this analysis of material and moral costs that these costs of racism cannot be separated from the psychological costs. Thomas Pettigrew once estimated that a quarter of white Americans are antiracist and consistently support black rights. Among the rest of whites some 15 percent are so deeply racist that, according to Pettigrew, they should be viewed as seriously *mentally ill*. The remaining 60 percent of whites are racist in their views, but they are conforming racists—that is, their racist views and propensities are not so deeply rooted in their psyches that they could not change in an antiracist direction should the social situation warrant that change. Pettigrew has argued that most prejudiced whites are not seriously mentally ill in the sense that they function reasonably well in the rest of their lives. He prefers to speak of this majority of white Americans as "mentally unhealthy," for they are often conforming, ignorant, authoritarian, or lacking in introspection and empathy.[16] The white majority's mental unhealthiness is reflected in the acceptance of many of the racial fictions and myths described in earlier chapters. Nowhere is the psychological cost of racism seen more clearly than in white Americans' obsessive fear of black men as criminals. The "Willie" Horton ads were successful in part because they exploited this deep-seated obsession.

Most research on whites' racial attitudes is focused on how whites see "others." The question of how whites see themselves as they participate in a racist society has been neglected. One article in a leading counseling journal has criticized models of white racial identity, such as they are, for being based on minority models of racial identity.[17] While we do not underestimate the value of learning about others, we believe that one way to begin to address white racism in this society is to reorient social science research to a thorough investigation of whites' own self-definitions and self-concepts.

Our selves, our self-conceptions, are shaped in part by how others view and react to us, in terms of how conflict is articulated between self and the other. What we are includes how we believe others label us. White racism denies black others recognition as human; what blacks see emanating from racist whites is not a reflection of themselves as human beings but rather negative black images projected from the white person's mind. In addition, racist whites refuse to see the true reflections of themselves that emanate from black people.

Why is this the case? One reason is the difference in white and black Americans' experiences. Most blacks must deal with a number of whites daily in the nation's predominantly white workplaces, shopping centers, and business or government settings. To navigate the white world, blacks must learn to read accurately the white images of black people. Whites, in contrast, generally have much less contact with and experience in dealing with blacks. Most whites can live in worlds where there are few or no blacks and thus are not required by social contexts to consider black images of their whiteness. Whites' ability to refuse to see black images of whites is also enhanced by the greater relative power of whites in most social settings where there is interracial contact.

The persistence of antiblack rituals has been publicized in the United States, although the widespread character and significance of these rituals tend to be ignored or denied by whites. Confronted with incidents such as the cross-burnings in cities across the nation, many whites will admit that they were probably racially motivated. But the cognitive acknowledgment of the racist acts of other whites does not necessarily bring an empathetic understanding of the pain that such acts inflict on the black victims. Empathy is not the same as sympathy. Sympathy means feeling sorry for someone. Empathy involves identifying strongly with the circumstances and pain of another human being: "Viewing another person's situation from the perspective of that person, as well as understanding how the situation appears to that person and how that person is reacting cognitively and emotionally to the situation."[18]

Empathy involves the ability to recognize the other as "human like me." Everyday racism has a firm place in the way our society is organized, in its material and mental structures. For that reason, an act of daring and the courage to cross often forbidden social borders are necessary to exercise human empathy of this character. White racism indicates a massive breakdown in empathy across color lines. Whites who discriminate against a black person, or who stand by while other whites discriminate, reveal that they have given up the ability to take the black person's place and to imagine what it would be like to be in her or his situation. Furthermore, the lack of empathy and the inability to reflect deeply on this matter means that many whites do not understand their participation in acts of oppression.

White Empathy with the Black Condition

Empathy is an essential component of human social life. Empathy tells us that a child's cry means discomfort or hunger. Empathy allows us to relate pleasure to a smile and pain to lament. Empathy permits us to come together and communicate. Empathy requires personal effort. Most importantly for our arguments here, empathy is essential for the resolution of racial oppression and conflict. Empathy at the individual level can make real equality possible at the societal level.

The possibility of empathy and antiracist thought are reasons to be cautiously optimistic about the nation's ability to overcome the extreme racial divide. Over centuries some white Americans have managed to develop genuine empathy for the oppressed condition of African Americans. In *Killers of the Dream,* Lillian Smith, a liberal white southerner, recounts a discussion about black people with a white girl in the South during the legal segregation period:

> *White girl:* I wonder how the Negroes felt. I've never thought about it. But the children, how did it make them feel? I guess it is strange that I've never tried to imagine how they felt.
> *Smith:* I suppose there is no way you can feel it, truly, unless you live through it. We whites have a color glaze on our imaginations that makes it hard to feel with the people we have segregated ourselves from."[19]

How does such an empathetic orientation develop, and how can it be spread? What makes cross-racial understandings possible on the part of whites? Are some whites more likely than others to develop this empathy and take action based on it? Some of the practical solutions for white racism lie in the answers to these questions.

The Role of Experience

Experience with oppression seems to be one key to these puzzling and difficult questions. We suggest here that white Americans who have some comprehension of personal experiences of being exploited, discriminated against, or oppressed in everyday life are more likely than other whites to understand the situation of and empathize with African Americans. Such experience can be used in antiracist action.

Consider, for example, the case of white women in the United States. Historically, white women have had a singular position in the patterns of oppression, being both racial oppressors and being oppressed by gender discrimination. Gendered experience, some researchers have argued, has generated distinctive ways of knowing about oppressive and other social realities. What has been called "connected knowing"— a knowing that emphasizes subjective relationships rather than impersonal rules—has been found to be more characteristic of the way women think and know than of the way most men think and know.[20] While some critics caution about exaggerating the gender difference, one might conclude from this that women are more likely to make judgments connecting their own experiences to those of other people than men are; men are more likely than women to be oriented to socially distancing rules, norms, and authority concerns.

Working with us, researchers Tiffany Hogan and Julie Netzer have examined ways in which white women think about the discrimination faced by African Americans. They conducted in-depth interviews with ten white women to explore whether their experiences with sexism in the workplace and elsewhere helped them develop insights into the oppression experienced by African Americans. In this important exploratory work they found that just being female did not necessarily increase understanding of racial oppression, although sometimes it did. But white women who were socially stigmatized in additional ways (e.g., lesbians) were better able than other white women to empathize with the discrimination faced by African Americans. From this pioneering research Hogan and Netzer have developed the idea of "approximating experiences." They suggest three different ways white women can draw on experience to interpret or relate to black oppression: (1) "borrowed approximations," relying on stories that blacks tell to make sense of black experiences; (2) "global approximations," relying on general humanism and values of fairness to relate to black oppression; and (3) "overlapping approximations," relying on aspects of their own oppression to make sense of similar black experience.[21]

The use of borrowed approximations is illustrated in the account of a white woman who learned about racial discrimination from a black woman with whom she works:

> I always thought that Sally was totally accepted at work, ... and on the surface you don't see any problems. Everyone is friendly, everyone is nice. And Sally is just about the nicest person you would ever hope to find. . . . . I went to her hairdresser with her and I was the only white woman in the shop and she was talking with her girlfriend about work and alluding to the fact that she just really had a lot of barriers there and that some of the things that people said to her, not intentionally but the way that they said it, were really racist. [How did that make you feel?] It surprised me. It did surprise me. . . . . I know that it's happening, but here's a nice person [Sally] who is at work, and I figured that most of the other people, I thought that they would just feel like I do. When I look at her, I see her as a person, ... and I just think of her as one of my coworkers and a friend, not as a black person. And I just assumed that everybody else felt the same way. I couldn't imagine that some of the people that she was working with, that I consider to be very nice people, too, would think of her first as black and then think of her as a nice person.

Even though this respondent knew that racism existed, when she was confronted with a personalized instance, her first reaction was "surprise," a word she stressed. Her point that she saw her friend as a person, "not as a black person," acknowledges the stigma she attaches to being a black person. She affirms her black friend's moral worth by repeating the statement that her friend is a nice person. Racism and other systems of oppression are usually made to appear rational by challenging or diminishing their victims' moral worth. If victims of racism are "not nice," discrimination is rationalized as an earned punishment. Our American creed of equality, of course, proposes that all human beings are created of equal moral worth.[22] This white woman relates to black oppression through the borrowed experience of a black acquaintance. Her personal understanding is based on her ability to take her coworker's narrative as the truthful statement of a lived experience. Without empathy, she would have viewed her friend's account with disbelief.

The use of global approximations to understand racism is illustrated by another white respondent's answer to a question asking if being a woman gave her insight into what it feels like to be black:

> In one respect, especially, in that I don't feel like I can go outside safely and in that way, my rights as a human being are infringed on. I can't go where I want, whenever I want. And if you look at the other side of that in terms of racial discrimination, if you're not able to economically earn what you are due, if you are oppressed economically or socially, it's the same thing. You're still not able to develop your full potential. You've got this pressure on you.

This woman's ability to think about injustice and her belief in equality allow her to empathize with the black experience even without the testimony of a particular black person. She uses her experience as a woman to increase her understanding of racism's infringement on basic human rights. Further into her interview, she moved from analyzing the black experience in terms of abstract civil liberties to comparing the inequities in pay and promotions that both women and blacks face.

To some degree most of the women interviewed were aware of the gulf between them and black women in experiences with oppression. Those respondents who made use of overlapping approximations expressed an even deeper and more profound understanding of the black experience. Lesbian and Jewish women tried the hardest to understand the black experience by drawing on similar experiences of their own. One white woman, who is a professional and a lesbian, explained her ability to empathize with a black person:

> I think that anybody that has experienced oppression on some level and hatred and blatant hatred on some level . . . as you do as a woman or as you do as a lesbian, has insight as to how it must be to be another type of minority and experience oppression—and like sometimes when I feel like I can't be who I am all the time. Like I do to a certain extent have to censor who I am . . . so that I can work effectively with my daily patrons I get. And this is why I don't work in the [names place], because it was so oppressive, and homophobic, that I couldn't do it. . . . And I think about a black person in a white world, because usually it's one black person surrounded by a hundred white people in a job environment. So in that way, I get insights into it, I mean, how do they feel? About it, you know, they must feel like shit about the fact that they know that they could apply for a hundred jobs but most of the time they won't get them, because they are black.

This woman's provocative words extrapolate from her own life experiences and subsume her experiences and those of black people under the general categories of oppression and hatred. Her experiences with being different and a minority because of her sexual orientation allow her to understand and empathize to a substantial degree with the experience of blacks.

When asked whether being a woman gave her insight into antiblack discrimination, a heterosexual Jewish woman replied:

> I feel different because I'm Jewish, not because I'm a woman, and that gives me insight into what it would be like feeling any kind of different. . . . I guess people don't understand why you do things differently. They feel sorry for you. Like, [in condescending tone], "Oh, you don't celebrate Christmas? You don't have a tree?" Instead of realizing that you have your own thing that you do and that you don't feel sorry for yourself about it, that you like what you do. So, I guess being black, people might say, "Oh, they don't have the same opportunities and they grew up in a poor environment." You know, they would sort of look down on a black person and feel that they weren't as [good]. . . . When you're

black, it's real obvious. People can see it, and it limits you. You have to overcome that and show people that you have abilities that they might think you don't have because you are black.

The last two respondents show more than sympathy; both draw on their own experiences and their awareness of themselves as being oppressed or stigmatized in order to take the place of the other and understand the trials blacks face.

The views of these four white women are different from those of many of the white women and men whose comments we examined in Chapter 7. The four statements illustrate much connected knowing, the ability to use personal experiences with discrimination to empathize with discrimination against African Americans. Sadly, many white women, and perhaps most white men, do not reach any of the three levels of understanding discussed in this section. The possibility of developing empathy by approximating experiences is only that, *a possibility*. We do not wish to be misunderstood here. Throughout the history of racism in the United States white women have played an important role in creating and buttressing racism, sometimes as active participants and often as acolytes supporting male activists. Research on white supremacy organizations from the 1920s to the present has shown the critical role of white women in them. For example, in the 1920s the women's auxiliary of the Klan had about a half million members.[23] Today many white women are still affiliated with white supremacist organizations, and many others share at least some of the views espoused by these organizations.[24]

Still, it is possible that white women's experience with sexism, homophobia, and anti-Semitism can be used in the educational process by those concerned with eradicating antiblack racism. It may also be possible that the experiences of some white men who must deal with homophobia and anti-Semitism can be used in a similar educational process. In these interviews and those in Chapter 7, we see the integral role of emotions in the way whites relate to blacks. Racist or empathetic responses are not just elements of analytical models but rather are parts of whole persons, which include emotions, cognitions, judgments, memory, and physiology, holistically constituted. Most traditional educational remedies directed at removing prejudices transform the problem of racism into an artificially narrow cognitive issue. Realistic education must address both the affective and the intellectual dimensions of racial identity and racist thought and action.

Confronting One's Own Racism

Most white Americans have absorbed racist attitudes from parents, friends, or the mass media. In this sense, racist views are a "normal" part of being American. Yet all whites can confront their racist views and propensities and seek to become egalitarian and antiracist. To understand the processes and dynamics of such change we and our students have conducted in-depth interviews and focus groups with whites who have taken antiracist steps or positions. In these interviews, antiracist whites often acknowledge their own antiblack racism. The paradox of white antiracists openly acknowledging their personal racism is related to another paradox: that this realistic consciousness of a racist self makes them more empathetic to the experiences of black people.

We can draw here on the unpublished work of Holly Hanson on the racial attitudes of people working to overcome racism.[25] One of the white women Hanson interviewed was once tied up by black thieves who robbed a store she was in. Yet she has refused to stereotype black people in general. She explained:

> I had spent many years before the incident nurturing friendships with black friends. So by the time the incident occurred, I had many black friends with whom I could talk intimately and honestly about my feelings. . . . We have to insulate ourselves with healthy relationships with people of other races to protect ourselves from the racist thought that is all around.

This woman had not come to her views from a life of isolation. Rather, she and her husband have developed friendships across the color line, which have helped her to withstand the daily drumbeat of racism all around her.

The paradox that it is the antiracists who are most aware of their own racism and the racism of others can be seen in an answer this same respondent gave when she was asked if she considered herself colorblind:

[I am] definitely aware of color. I think it is a superficial, comfortable response to, to denying one's own racism, and the problem of racism in society, to say that one has become colorblind. . . . The analogy that I frequently use is that, when people say, "Well, I just treat everybody the same and na-na-na," I say, if you know that a woman has been raped, you are liable to be careful, speaking to her. You are liable to be some-what sensitive about how you approach certain things and really, when you think about it, your behavior at the end of your encounter with this woman probably is such that you should use it with everyone, you know, in a way. It is not ridiculous behavior. You are just going to be conscious of not wanting to put salt in wounds that you recognize probably are there because of that person's experience. . . . That is frequently the way I feel about interactions between blacks and whites in America. I think black people have been raped. I think they are raped, regularly, in a variety of ways.

Antiracist whites are not certain they can really understand the black experience, but they try to make an honest attempt. They admit that it is hard to understand the pain and anger. In another interview, a white male educator commented on the difficulty of understanding black anger:

I think, yes, it is easy to accept a certain amount of anger. . . . I'm trying to construct explanations that help me understand, but I don't presume to understand from the point of view of having experienced in the same way as certain blacks who are angry might have experienced. So in that sense, no, I don't think it is easy to understand. . . . It takes a lot of effort, and a lot of time, and a lot of self-criticism on the part of the nonblack person.

This educator considers self-criticism a crucial part of the process of understanding. It is never easy, but, as he went on to explain, without it one becomes prey to wrongheaded assumptions about what is natural: "I think people who are in positions of power who are white and who are male need to learn. . . . the subtle ways in which they convey messages of inequality and unequalness to others." Being white in this society almost by definition means rarely having to think about it. Whites must make a special effort to become deeply aware of their own and others' racism. This educator was the victim of violence at the hands of blacks when he was younger, yet, like the woman above, he was able to process those incidents so the skin color of his assailants did not tint his larger view of the racism that afflicts U.S. society.

How do antiracists come to recognize and understand their own racism? For many a critical event or experience seems to catapult the matter of racism to the front of their minds. In an interview conducted by Hanson, a white teacher talked about what happened when she realized she gave support and attention to Latino toddlers and not to black toddlers where she once worked:

> And it was like I got hit with a bucket of cold water. And I thought, "Replay that one, Susan." And I replayed it in my mind, and I started to cry. And I cried and I cried, because I realized that *I had a prejudice.* And I thought I was without it. . . . So I went back, and I picked him up, and I played with him. I don't know, I sat him on my lap, and we did these little cutey games, patty-cake or whatever. And I had to work myself into it, because it was hard to do. It wasn't just a mental decision, "O.K., now I'm not going to be prejudiced any more." I did make a very strong effort, a concerted effort, to interact equally with all the children there. But I had to do it, I had to *make myself* do it. Because not only was I aware that it wasn't easy to do, once I knew that I was acting in a way that was prejudiced, I had to work very hard to overcome that.

A single important incident had focused her analysis of her own racist practice.

We have explored these critical incidents and events in our own research on antiracist whites. For two focus-group interview sessions, we invited several whites who had participated in at least one antiracist protest event. They had marched against the Ku Klux Klan, demonstrated against apartheid and racism, or appeared before city and county commissions in support of ordinances and policies designed to further human rights. They had taken a public stand against racism. A common thread uniting the focus group participants appears at first paradoxical: At one time or another, they all had to face the fact that they were themselves racist in thought or action. Most of the focus group participants associated their internal confrontation with their own racism with a triggering event or series of events in their lives.

One young woman related that she was raised by a father who was an official in the Ku Klux Klan. Her mother's marriage to this man ended when she was young, but not before she had adopted many racial dogmas of her father's group. Then, while still a teenager, she became pregnant by a white boyfriend and found herself ostracized by her white friends. Ironically, only the black students at school would associate and sympathize with her. When school officials barred her from attending classes because of her pregnancy, her black friends brought their notes and homework so she could graduate. This white woman's approximating experience of being ostracized because of her pregnancy gave her not only some experience with the pain of the "other" but also information that refuted her negative learned notions about blacks. Some years later, these critical experiences led her to become an active antiracist.

The events that led another participant, also a white woman, to an awareness of her own racism occurred when, as the wife of a U.S. soldier, she lived in integrated housing for the first time in her life. She found a job in a place where most of the other workers were black. As a white southerner, these were dramatically new experiences for her. She developed a close relationship with her black neighbors and coworkers and came to know their pain from racial discrimination firsthand. She and her husband came to reflect on their role in inflicting pain on African Americans in the past. As a result, she became an antiracist activist.

All of these respondents belong to the group of whites who, having been able to empathize with African Americans, took proactive stances to confront their own internalized racism and the racist views and actions of other whites, whenever the opportunity arose. These whites often became active participants in organizations to promote equality and human rights.

Taking Antiracist Action

Those seeking to engage actively in antiracist action often face the critique that they are pursuing an impossible dream, that they are isolated from the realities of everyday life or are uninformed about human nature. White racism not only destroys communities of color in particular, but also works to demolish human dreams of a better society and better future for all. Racism distorts human vision and limits human possibilities. White racist ideology—with its so-called "realistic" view of the past, present, and future—proclaims an inevitability for racial inequality. Indeed, one articulation of this viewpoint includes a denial of the existence of white racism and its continuing savagery.[26]

Antiracist ideas and strategies are a way that whites and people of color have adopted of "talking back," of aggressively fighting racism. As bell hooks points out, this "talking back" involves an act of courage, an act of risk, a challenge to the suppression of voices.[27] Antiracist strategies strive to confront white racism as an ideology, as institutions, and as practices in everyday life. Antiracism requires that we talk back in order to become participants in building an alternative future. Antiracism is an active confrontation of racism by people of varied religious and political ideologies who wish to build a better society.[28] Talking back, being an interruptor of racist commentary, and developing interpersonal empathy are key steps in an antiracist strategy. For whites in particular, empathy is an integral element of antiracist action.

To a substantial degree, white racist action is undergirded, as W. E. B. Du Bois put it, by "unconscious acts and irrational reactions, unpierced by reason, whose current form depended on the long history of relation and contact between thought and idea."[29] Du Bois's insight regarding racism's perpetuation by cementing the connection between thought and action is a key to devising antiracist strategies. Present-day antiracist struggles need to maintain a consciousness of past struggles by people of color and their white allies and to develop new struggles drawing on the vast reservoir of knowledge and experience rooted in those earlier movements. Moreover, at some point antiracist efforts need to link to struggles against other major forms of oppression and hierarchy.[30] Conceptualizing antiracism within this larger context ultimately involves uniting all forms of struggle against systems of domination—for example, by linking the antiracism struggle to struggles against class exploitation, sexism, and homophobia.

Antiracist strategies clearly include an individual focus—dealing with one's own racism. In her study of antiracist activists, Eileen O'Brien found that both individual *and* collective acts of resistance to racism are integral to challenging racist systems.[31] While one can struggle alone, greater strength lies in group efforts. Thus, bell hooks argues that in a community oriented to ending racism "solidarity and trust are grounded in a profound commitment to a shared vision. . . . where borders can be crossed and cultural hybridity celebrated."[32] The source of strength can lie in a "beloved community" of ordinary people. This type of community made the difference for those who struggled against South African apartheid.

It was a similar community that gave coherency, vitality, and support to the U.S. Civil Rights Movement. Dr. Martin Luther King, Jr., in his writings and speeches, noted that the beloved community was central to the actions and goals of the Civil Rights Movement. He defined the Montgomery bus boycott as a collective action leading to the creation of the "beloved community," while the foundation of the Southern Christian Leadership Conference presented the opportunity to celebrate and pursue the goals of the beloved community. At the heart of the idea of the beloved community lies a vision of total interrelatedness in a society.[33] King's position is an insistence on a community of equals celebrating a shared vision, where existing differences are affirmed without fracturing antiracist thought and action.[34] As King wrote in a letter dated April 16, 1963, from a Birmingham, Alabama, jail: "I am in Birmingham because injustice is here. . . . I cannot sit idly by in Atlanta and not be concerned about what happens in Birmingham. Injustice anywhere is a threat to justice everywhere."[35]

Doing antiracism involves the transgression of strongly supported cultural norms. It requires challenging oneself, making connections that defy the ordinary, and a willingness to go into struggle and participate in communities of many kinds of people struggling against racism. There are already many antiracists in this country, but they are not always organized in ostensibly antiracist groups. Many are in a loose coalition of organizations that struggle for social justice and work to end racism. These include some of the people in our focus groups discussed earlier. All have worked for antiracist causes or participated in antiracist protests. Whether in protest demonstrations or in the workplace or neighborhood, such actions can mean risking one's privileges or resources. One of Hanson's white respondents described an incident at a store where she once worked:

> It was a simple matter of, well, I mean, it is my suspicion, that that is what happened. A black person was not hired for this job, and a white person was, and I challenged my boss about it because I was suspicious, and she said it was just schedules, it had nothing to do with that. But I noticed that in the next year she hired two black people whereas before that she had never hired anyone black before.

The willingness to risk one's job shows a strong commitment to a nonracist society. In another interview a white teacher discussed what whites should do for black coworkers who experience discrimination:

> The [black] social worker at the [social] services department that was my liaison person went through a real rough time, and I was an encourager, and I think a mentor, saying, "This is something that you do not have to just accept. You have options. Let's take a look at those options. Let's get as much information as we can." It is like, like a good friend, willing to advocate for justice, or rights, or what's best for the person.

One critical question is: How do we increase the number of these antiracists? Or, more generally, how do we go about getting rid of white racism in the United States? There are white Americans and black Americans currently working hard on these problems. For example, working with other antiracist activists, Nathan Rutstein, a white man, has set up more than one hundred local Institutes for the Healing of Racism. Rutstein utilizes a medical model in his work with community groups. He approaches racism as a white mental disease that leads to discrimination against people of color. Whites have a superiority complex covered up by denial and are afraid of exposing the deep prejudices most know are wrong. In his view whites are also victims of racism. Rutstein's approach emphasizes the oneness of all human beings. From this perspective every human being is in fact related to every other human being; each person is at least a fiftieth cousin of any other person on the globe. The way to make the dream of equality and social justice a reality is to envision the United States, and ultimately the globe, as a community of inclusion instead of exclusion. One major step forward in the antiracist cause is to integrate into all U.S. educational systems new courses on the oneness of all humankind.[36]

Another example is the student founded and run organization called *Promoting Equality And Community Everywhere* (P.E.A.C.E.). The goal of P.E.A.C.E. is to "unite young people to address issues of prejudice, discrimination and hatred. . . . to demystify 'otherness' through positive experiences by building memories, relationships, knowledge and understanding."[37] The organization has a three-part program: a mentoring project among students, an Equal Rights Awareness Day—which encourages antiracist activities at the high school, college, and community levels by connecting these levels—and the creation of an antiracist community centered around local P.E.A.C.E. chapter meetings and involving working with other antiracist organizations. The centerpiece of the organization is the mentoring project, which is designed to teach young people to build antiracist groups among themselves and to question systems of oppression in communities. By the early twenty-first century the P.E.A.C.E. mentoring project had involved thousands of students in its mentoring activities. For this project, elementary school students pair up with mentors from local high schools and colleges to develop mutually beneficial relationships in understanding, celebrating, and promoting diversity and confronting racism. The Equal Rights Awareness Day complements the mentoring program by providing a forum for all participants to come together.[38]

More Collective Action Against Racism

Effective action against racial discrimination and oppression is almost always group action. The display of harsh facts on racial and other social inequality alone will not change individual or group behavior. In a context where white racism *is* everyday life, antiracist strategies can only succeed by becoming a way of life for organized groups of many Americans. The changes can develop in individual minds and hearts, but they must also become manifest in actions in neighborhoods, grocery stores, schools, places of worship, workplaces, and government institutions if large-scale societal transformation is to take place.

Dr. Martin Luther King, Jr., had a vision of truly integrated America, one that still rings in the words of his famous March on Washington speech in August 1963: "I have a dream that one day on the red hills of Georgia the sons of former slaves and the sons of former slaveowners will be able to sit down at the table of brotherhood." However, this would not happen, in his view, without long and arduous struggles to overcome racial and class oppression on the part of many Americans. While King foresaw the daunting barriers in this struggle, he did not give up. The night before he was assassinated, he made a speech in which he said he had gone "up to the mountain. And I've looked over, and I've seen the promised land."[39]

To change, people, especially white people, must perceive that a new direction is becoming the accepted way of doing things. There are many possible strategies. Jeffrey Kelly, a professor of psychiatry who has worked with groups to get people to change their habits, has noted that it is not the knowledge of facts that alters behavior but rather changes in people's perceptions of what is possible.[40] Many analysts of racism argue that the case-by-case medical model of racial healing is not sufficient for a society in which racism has been the structural reality for centuries. Among many other analysts, Thomas Pettigrew advocates a *structural* approach to overcome America's racial divide. Not only do bigots need to be cured, but racist structures and institutions must be eradicated.[41] As we have seen throughout this book, white racism is much more than scattered individual beliefs. It is also an institutionalized system encompassing social, economic, and political inequality along racial lines.[42] Reviewing the public policy of desegregation, Jennifer Hochschild has argued that Myrdal was too optimistic when he suggested that all whites held the ideals of "liberty and justice for all" and that change was a matter of getting them to act on their principles. She argues that racism is in fact a fundamental social and material reality webbed into the basic institutions of the American system, not the anomaly that Myrdal suggested. Institutionalized racism has its own countervailing "principles." Looking at school desegregation, Hochschild has demonstrated that a white-controlled policy of incrementalism has not brought a permanent destruction of racial discrimination. She describes a "new American dilemma" of continuing racism, a dilemma that is solvable, but at a price most white Americans so far seem "unwilling to pay. If that is the case, we are a much less liberal and democratic society than we would like to think."[43] A major commitment must be made by white Americans, and indeed all Americans, if institutional arrangements are to be altered in fundamental ways.

If racism is to be eradicated, material inequality in the United States must be fundamentally changed. This will require large-scale action and organization for change. In *The Case for Black Reparations*, Boris Bittker has argued that economic and other discrimination targeting African Americans has been much more extreme, for a much longer period of time, than that faced by any other racial or ethnic group in the United States and that massive reparations are necessary to compensate for that racial oppression.[44] From the earliest days of abolitionist activity in the eighteenth and nineteenth centuries, African American leaders and some of their white allies argued that the abolition of slavery and the gaining of citizenship by African Americans were not enough. These leaders also called for redress in the form of significant grants of federal land—"forty acres and a mule"— to African Americans.

In recent years numerous black leaders have continued to press for substantial reparations. At one time or another, black leaders as diverse as Martin Luther King, Jr., Whitney Young, Jesse Jackson, and Louis Farrakhan have called for major compensation programs for African Americans. Each year since the late 1980s one black member of Congress, John Conyers of Michigan, has filed a bill calling for a major national study of reparations for antiblack discrimination. N'COBRA, the National Coalition of Blacks for Reparations in America, was recently formed to pursue the case for monetary and other redress for racial oppression. In Oakland, California, one group of black plaintiffs, some of whom belong to N'COBRA, filed suit in federal court asking for $380 million in reparations for themselves and for new social support programs in black communities. According to one plaintiff, "We're seeking reparations for our ancestors who aren't here to bear witness. . . . Nobody was paid 40 acres and a mule because Lincoln was assassinated before it could go through."[45] Other African Americans have filed or contemplated filing similar suits demanding monetary redress.

There will undoubtedly be much opposition to paying hundreds of billions of dollars in reparations to African Americans. Such an idea will be called "too radical." However, in recent years federal and state governments have strengthened the principle of just reparations for damages done by individual and government action, as, for example, in laws providing for the compensation of victims of crime, including the 1984 Victims of Crime Act and the 1994 Violent Crime Control and Law Enforcement Act. In addition, over the last two decades the U.S. government has provided some monetary compensation to other minority groups for the depredations of white Americans. The federal government has paid hundreds of millions of dollars in reparations to a number of Native American groups for lands taken in violation of treaties, and the survivors of the Japanese American concentration camps in the western states during World War II have recently, if belatedly, received modest reparations of $20,000 each to compensate for their illegal imprisonment.[46] The principle is simple enough; perpetrators of wrong should not benefit from their wrong-doing. This is why thieves are not allowed to keep the things they steal and German corporations that used the slave labor of Jews are paying reparations to compensate for the labor they stole.[47]

What would the payment of major reparations to African Americans accomplish? Robert Browne has summarized the major objectives: (1) to punish white Americans for the brutal enslavement of African Americans carried out by their ancestors; (2) to compensate the African American community for the unpaid labor of their slave forefathers and foremothers; (3) to provide African Americans with their fair share of the national wealth and income that they would have had if given the same opportunities and advantages white Americans secured over the last 375 years.[48] The redress envisioned by N'COBRA and others would mark a collective recognition by white Americans of the severity and consequences of racial oppression.

State, local, and federal governments could take many other actions to reduce racial oppression, beginning with the vigorous enforcement of existing civil rights laws. During the 1960s the Civil Rights Movement pressured Congress to pass legislation banning discrimination in employment, voting, and housing, and over the next decade some effort was put into government enforcement of these laws. Yet these civil rights advances were stopped by the racist backlash of the 1980s and 1990s. The Ronald Reagan administration destroyed or weakened federal civil rights enforcement agencies, and for the most part President George Bush continued this negative approach to civil rights. Both Reagan and Bush appointed conservative justices to the Supreme Court, and Court decisions in this period restricted discrimination victims' ability to sue for redress. In the late 1980s a new civil rights bill was proposed to overcome the limitations of these conservative Supreme Court decisions. Bush at first opposed the bill, but after a long congressional struggle and some weakening of the bill he finally signed the 1991 Civil Rights Act into law. Since the early 1980s, the aggressive pursuit of equality of opportunity appears to have slipped off the federal government's agenda.

Even strong civil rights laws do not guarantee real equality of opportunity in everyday settings. Few of the many millions of cases of racial discrimination perpetrated by white Americans each year against African Americans are countered by effective private or government remedies. Indeed, U.S. government agencies have neither the resources nor the staff to enforce antidiscrimination laws vigorously. Because of underfunding, federal agencies like the Equal Employment Opportunity Commission (EEOC) typically have such a large backlog of cases that most victims of discrimination cannot achieve timely remedies through the federal government.

The 1970s and 1980s also brought a collapse in critical civil rights coalitions that once included blacks and liberal whites. Today, the enforcement of civil rights laws and the impetus for advances in their content and scope lack the broad support of the old coalitions and are the source of dissent even among former allies. New coalitions that bind together various racial and ethnic groups are essential for future action to redress racism. Aggressive political action by these coalitions needs to be directed at expanding the staff and the funding of civil rights enforcement agencies.

While a major expansion of civil rights enforcement will be an important step in guaranteeing the principle of formal equal opportunity, that too is not sufficient, for the existing system of laws is itself grounded in a constitution that was not crafted in a democratic fashion. A new U.S. Constitution—and thus a new constitutional convention—is required if the United States is to be based on a truly democratic foundation. Periodically, some Americans have called for a constitutional convention to deal with issues of great national concern. The most recent attempt has focused on a proposed constitutional amendment mandating a balanced budget for the federal government, and a large number of states have passed the legislation necessary for such a convention. However, some black leaders and civil rights groups have opposed such a convention, fearing that the white majority might roll back hard-won civil rights gains.

We believe that a strong case can be made for calling a constitutional convention, but one quite different from the balanced-budget convention and even from the first constitutional convention. The constitutional convention in 1787 excluded three major groups— women, African Americans, and Native Americans—who collectively made up about two-thirds of the U.S. population at the time. In 1776, the year of the Declaration of Independence, Abigail Adams wrote to her husband, the revolutionary leader John Adams, about the new code of laws for the emerging United States:

> In the new code of laws which I suppose will be necessary for you to make, I desire you would remember the ladies and be more generous and favorable to them than your ancestors. Do not put such unlimited power into the hands of the husbands. Remember, all men would be tyrants if they could. If particular care and attention is not paid to the ladies, we are determined to foment a rebellion, and will not hold ourselves bound by any laws in which we have no voice or representation.[49]

John Adams rejected her request, explaining that women were only one of several dependent "tribes," which term included Indians, children, and black slaves. Counseling his wife to be patient, Adams told her that other issues were more important than women's rights.[50] Eleven years later not one of Adams' so-called "dependent tribes" was represented at the first constitutional convention, from which white men without property were also excluded. Representatives of less than 10 percent of the total population fashioned the document that, with some amendments, has governed this republic ever since. The foundation these propertied white males built reflected their own interests. While some of these interests encompassed the desires of all Americans to be free of the tyrannies of Europe (such as the prohibition of aristocratic titles, of a state religion, and of indefinite terms of office for politicians), it took strong protests in the colonies before even a Bill of Rights was added to the original document.

In the 1776 Declaration of Independence the young Thomas Jefferson penned the language, "We hold these truths to be self-evident, that all men are created equal and are endowed by their creator with certain unalienable rights. . . . Life, Liberty, and the pursuit of Happiness." He envisioned here not only legal rights but also the basic rights people have solely by reason of being human. He and his fellow revolutionaries declared that the American minority of the British empire had rights that did not derive from British law but rather from natural law. Ever since, these revolutionary ideas have inspired similar statements of basic human rights by many other groups, including those disenfranchised by the original U.S. Constitution.

One of the most important of these statements, the Universal Declaration of Human Rights passed by the United Nations in 1948, stipulates that "all human beings are born free and equal in dignity and rights" and that "all are equal before the law and are entitled without any discrimination to equal protection of the law." Article 8 of this international agreement asserts: "Everyone has the right to an effective remedy . . . for acts violating the fundamental rights," and Article 25 states that these rights extend to everyday life: "Everyone has the right to a standard of living adequate for the health and well-being of himself and his family, including food, clothing, housing."[51]

Gideon Sjoberg and Ted Vaughan have pointed out that the human capacity to "take the roles of others and to recognize another's humanity and commonality with oneself is an essential step in recognizing the rights of others."[52] A signal step in securing everyday equality for all Americans will be for more whites to develop the ability to empathize with Americans of color as equal human beings. Human beings have the ability to reflect critically on their behavior, a reflection that is essential if all Americans are to move beyond racist perspectives and practices. All the various declarations of human rights over the last two hundred years are predicated on the recognition that human beings can reflect on their behavior and can change it for the better.

The United Nations' Universal Declaration affirms that human beings have rights *independent* of the particular societal and governmental conditions in which they live, and it presses governments to incorporate all basic human rights into their legal and political systems. In the United States this comprehensive task remains to be accomplished, for the fundamental documents of this nation do not today adequately protect the lives and welfare of African Americans and other Americans of color.

Indeed, they do not secure certain basic human rights, such as the right to a decent standard of living, for any U.S. resident.

A new constitutional convention is not a particularly radical idea. The possibility was envisaged by the drafters of the Constitution when they established the mechanism for conventions to make constitutional amendments. A few even suggested that a new Constitution might need to be forged by later generations. We propose a thorough-going revision of the present Constitution, this time by representatives of all the people of the United States. This country has come to a stage of mature development where it can be faithful to the liberty-and-justice principles on which it is theoretically founded. Today there is a growing consensus in the United States and across the globe on what human rights are essential for the creation of a truly democratic society. The people of this nation are gradually learning that without respect for the plurality of U.S. cultures there can be no real security or democracy for anyone. The official call for a constitutional convention such as we propose should include a prior acceptance of the democratic ideals of liberty and justice already expressed in the Declaration of Independence and the Bill of Rights. A new constitution must be no less rooted in human rights than the existing constitution but should also incorporate the many additional rights specified in the United Nations' Universal Declaration of Human Rights. Convention discussions should be grounded in mutual respect for the plurality of U.S. cultures, heritages, and values. A new constitutional convention that builds on the bedrock of the present Bill of Rights has a chance to transform the United States into a truly free and just society.

In our view a new constitutional convention *must* include representatives, in proportional numbers, of all racial, ethnic, religious, class, and gender groups. Such a broadbased assembly would be the only framework that would ensure for the first time in history that the white majority encounters a discussion of and pressure for the constitutional interests and rights of all minorities. The constitutional convention process we envision could begin with a series of "town meetings" and similar collective dialogues in a variety of settings, including workplaces, neighborhoods, schools, colleges, unions, and city halls, in which diverse groups of people could work out procedures for incorporating essential human rights in a new constitution. Current media technology even makes possible simultaneous "town meetings" for large numbers of people across the nation. Developing consensus by means of broad community discussions is not a new idea. Indeed, the National Endowment for the Humanities has recently launched public forums across the nation and has distributed citizen information kits to facilitate the discussion of ethnic and cultural pluralism.[53]

For all its possible difficulties, a new constitutional convention seems required not only to address the basic human rights of previously excluded groups but also to ensure that the fundamental governing document of this democracy is actually produced by representatives of all Americans.

Conclusion

As we see in the South African example that opened this chapter, challenges to white racism are increasingly global. Ongoing antiracist strategies in the United States are grounded in strategies and a central discourse of human rights and democratic rights shared across the globe despite continuing opposition.[54] People of color are pressing whites to abandon racist systems in a growing number of countries.

Derrick Bell has argued for an interest-convergence hypothesis: Whites support the cause of equality and justice for blacks *only* when it is in *their interest* to do so.[55] The difficult and necessary task, in our view, is to bring whites to a recognition that the destruction of racism is in their interest. Meaningful solutions to racism involve making the waste caused by this racism painfully evident for white Americans and all Americans. The major advantage in starting from an excess-of-resources perspective rather than a scarcity perspective is that policies for remedying racism do not require the paralyzing calculations of zero-sum thinking. In our view a strong defense of antiracist education and public policies such as reparations must show white Americans that contemporary racism is a waste of energy for *everyone*. Whites must be confronted again and again with the enormous loss of life, talent, and energy of African Americans and other Americans of color.

White Americans as well as African Americans will receive moral, psychological, and material benefits from the eradication of racism. White Americans will achieve a moral victory when they actually live by the equality creed they profess. International observers will no longer be able to accuse the United States of hypocrisy. White Americans will realize psychological benefits when they no longer have obsessive fears of blacks or feel threatened by them. White energy and resources once devoted to suppressing African Americans will be available for creative and beneficial pursuits. White people will no longer be enslaved by stereotyped myths about African Americans.

The abolition of racism can bring real material benefits for all Americans, including white Americans. The eradication of racism in the job, educational, and housing sectors could over time provide a reasonable standard of living for all workers and their families and thus reduce much poverty and crime in rural and urban areas, thereby saving lives and billions of dollars in personal and property damage and law enforcement costs. The cost to whites of black anger over racism is great. The 1992 Los Angeles riot alone cost the nation many human casualties and a billion dollars, with much of the latter cost being borne by non-black business owners and Los Angeles taxpayers. It is also likely that improved black job and other opportunities will substantially increase the gross national product.

While Bell's argument regarding the role of group interest in whites' support for racial change is generally accurate, it is important to remember that what generated the U.S. Civil Rights Movement, and the movement against apartheid in South Africa, was the continuing and assertive *organization of ordinary people*. It was their belief in themselves, the conviction of their power to create a just society for all, that gave them strength to envision progress as equality and freedom for all—and to organize aggressively and effectively for major societal change. Today, these convictions about equality and social justice sustain the increasing number of people across the globe who continue to organize against white racism.

Notes

Preface

1. For details, see Randall Robinson, *The Debt: What America Owes to Blacks* (New York: Dutton, 2000), pp. 3–7.

Chapter 1: The Waste of White Racism

1. David Firestone, "46,000 March on South Carolina Capitol to Bring Down Confederate Flag," *The New York Times*, January 18, 2000, p. A14; David Firestone, "Unfurling a Battle Cry and Its Last Hurrah," *The New York Times,* January 23, 2000, section 4, p. 5.
2. The term *racism* first appeared in a 1933 German book by Magnus Hirschfeld, who sought to counter the European racists' actions and ideas grounded in notions of a biologically determined hierarchy of races. See Magnus Hirschfeld, *Racism* (London: Gollancz, 1938). The book was published in German in 1933–1934.
3. For more on this point, see Joe R. Feagin, *Racist America: Roots, Current Realities, and Future Reparations* (New York: Routledge, 2000).
4. Pinar Batur-VanderLippe, "On the Necessity of Antiracist Praxis: An Experience in Teaching and Learning," *Teaching Sociology* 27 (1999): 274–285.
5. See Joe R. Feagin and Melvin P. Sikes, *Living with Racism: The Black Middle Class Experience* (Boston Beacon, 1994); Ellis Cose, *The Rage of a Privileged Class* (New York: Harper Collins, 1993).
6. See Sut Jhally and Justin Lewis, *Enlightened Racism: The Cosby Show, Audiences, and the Myth of America's Dream* (Boulder, CO: Westview Press, 1992), p. 110.
7. Michael Omi, "Shifting the Blame: Racial Ideology and Politics in the Post-Civil Rights Era," *Critical Sociology* 18 (1991): 79.
8. Stanley B. Greenberg, *Report on Democratic Defection. Report Prepared for the Michigan House Democratic Campaign Committee* (Washington, DC: The Analysis Group, 1983), as quoted in Omi, "Shifting the Blame," p. 79.

9. Omi, "Shifting the Blame," p. 80.

10. Toni Morrison, *Playing in the Dark: Whiteness and the Literary Imagination* (Cambridge, MA: Harvard University Press, 1992), pp. 9–10.

11. Keith E. Sealing, "The Myth of a Color-Blind Constitution," *Washington University Journal of Urban and Contemporary Law* 54 (Summer 1998): 159.

12. *Ibid.*, p. 159.

13. Justice Marshall (concurring in part and dissenting in part), *Regents of the University of California v. Bakke*, 438 U.S. 387, as quoted in Sealing, "The Myth of a Color-Blind Constitution," p. 161.

14. See Philomena Essed, *Understanding Everyday Racism: An Interdisciplinary Theory* (Beverly Hills, CA: Sage, 1991); Feagin and Sikes, *Living with Racism;* Cose, *The Rage of a Privileged Class.*

15. Linda Diebel, "Darkest Iowa," *Toronto Star,* February 23, 1992, p. Fl; Aric Press and Vern Smith, "Going After the Klan" *Newsweek,* February 23, 1987, p. 29.

16. See James Ridgeway, *Blood in the Face: The Ku Klux Klan, Aryan Nations, Nazi Skinheads, and the Rise of a New White Culture* (New York: Thunder's Mouth Press, 1990).

17. "Tension Rises in New York in March over Black's Death," *Austin American-Statesman,* December 28, 1986, p. A3.

18. "FBI Issues First Data on Hate Crimes," *Race Relations Reporter,* March 15, 1993, p. 8; Bernard Debusmann, "Hate Crime Shocks Washington," Reuters News Service, March 4, 1992.

19. James Martinez, "Two Guilty in Racial Burning," *Gainesville Sun,* September 8, 1993.

20. FBI Hate Crime Statistics, 1997, Table 1, at www.fbi.gov/hc97all.pdf.

21. Lee Sigelman and Susan Welch, *Black Americans' Views of Racial Inequality* (Cambridge, England: Cambridge University Press, 1991), pp. 53–57.

22. Margery Austin Turner, Michael Fix, and Raymond J. Struyk, *Opportunities Denied: Discrimination in Hiring* (Washington, DC: Urban Institute, 1991).

23. See Feagin and Sikes, *Living with Racism.*

24. Andrew Hacker, *Two Nations* (New York: Scribner's, 1992), pp. 97–140.

25. U.S. Bureau of the Census, *The Social and Economic Status of the Black Population in the United States,* 1971 (Washington, DC, 1972), p. 52; U.S. Commission on Civil Rights, *Unemployment and Underemployment Among Blacks, Hispanics, and Women* (Washington, DC, 1982), p. 5; Bureau of National Affairs, "Economic Statistics," *Daily Report for Executives,* March 9, 1992, p. N1; Joe R. Feagin and Clairece B. Feagin. *Social Problems: A Critical Power-Conflict Perspective,* 4th ed. (Englewood Cliffs, NJ: Prentice-Hall, 1994), pp. 118–119.

26. U.S. Bureau of the Census, *Money Income of Households, Families, and Persons in the United States: 1992* (Washington, DC, 1993), p. xii; U.S. Bureau of the Census, *Poverty in the United States: 1992* (Washington, DC, 1993), p. xi; U.S. Bureau of the Census, *Household Wealth and Asset Ownership: 1988* (Washington, DC, 1990), p. 8.

27. Sidney Willhelm, *Black in a White America* (Cambridge, MA: Schenkman, 1983), p. 261.
28. *Ibid.*, p. 273.
29. Georges Bataille, *The Accursed Share: An Essay on General Economy*, vol. I, *Consumption* (New York: Zone Books, 1988), p. 21.
30. *Ibid.*, p. 23.
31. Lillian Smith, *Killers of the Dream*, rev. ed. (New York: W. W. Norton, 1961), p. 68.
32. See Suzanne Harper, "The Brotherhood: Race and Gender Ideologies in the White Supremacist Movement," unpublished Ph.D. dissertation, University of Texas, 1993.
33. Gunnar Myrdal, *An American Dilemma*, vol. 2 (New York: McGraw-Hill Paperback, 1964), p. 560–562; Joe R. Feagin and Clairece B. Feagin, *Racial and Ethnic Relations*, 4th ed. (Englewood Cliffs, NJ: Prentice-Hall, 1993), pp. 224–225.
34. H. Sitkoff, *A New Deal for Blacks* (New York: Oxford, 1978), p. 15.
35. Trudier Harris, *Exorcising Blackness* (Bloomington: Indiana University Press, 1984), p. 11.
36. *Ibid.*, p. 12.
37. Myrdal, *An American Dilemma*; see also Michael Banton, *Racial and Ethnic Competition* (Cambridge, England: Cambridge University Press, 1983); Phyllis A Katz and Dalmas A. Taylor, "Introduction," in *Eliminating Racism*, ed. Phyllis A. Katz and Dalmas A. Taylor (New York: Plenum, 1988), pp. 1–18.
38. Thomas Pettigrew, "Preface," in *Racial Discrimination in the United States*, ed Thomas Pettigrew (New York: Harper & Row, 1975), p. x.
39. Joe R. Feagin and Clairece B. Feagin, *Discrimination American Style: Institutional Racism and Sexism* (Englewood Cliffs, NJ: Prentice-Hall, 1978), pp. 20–21.
40. See Peter Russell, *The Global Brain* (Boston: Houghton Mifflin, 1983), pp. 115–118.
41. See Joel Kovel, *White Racism: A Psychohistory*, rev. ed. (New York: Columbia University Press, 1984), pp. xliv, 4.
42. Smith, *Killers of the Dream*, p. 96.
43. *Ibid.*, p. 27.
44. Leonard Berkowitz, "Some Effects of Thoughts on Anti- and Prosocial Influences of Media Events," *Psychological Bulletin* 9 (1984): 410–427.
45. George L. Stearns, ed., *The Equality of All Men Before the Law Claimed and Defended* (Boston, 1865), p. 38, quoted in Robert R. Dykstra, *Bright Radical Star: Black Freedom and White Supremacy in the Hawkeye Frontier* (Cambridge, MA: Harvard University Press, 1993), p. 269.
46. Ruth Frankenberg, *White Women, Race Matters* (Minneapolis: University of Minnesota Press, 1993), pp. 228–229.
47. *Ibid.*, p. 231.
48. Theodore W Allen, *The Invention of the White Race* (London: Verso, 1994), p. 21; David R. Roediger, *Towards the Abolition of Whiteness* (London: Verso, 1994), p. 12.

49. Allen, *The Invention of the White Race*, pp. 21–50.

50. W. E. B. Du Bois, *Black Reconstruction in America, 1860–1880* (New York: Atheneum, 1992 [1935]), p. 700.

51. *Ibid.*, p. 701.

52. David R. Roediger, *The Wages of Whiteness* (London: Verso, 1991), p. 13.

53. Kovel, *White Racism*, p. xl.

54. W. E. B. Du Bois, *Dusk of Dawn* (New Brunswick, NJ: Transaction, 1984 [1940]), p. 6.

55. Gordon H Bower, "Mood and Memory," *American Psychologist* 36 (February 1981): 129–148.

56. Joan Karp, "The Emotional Impact and a Model for Changing Racist Attitudes," in *The Impacts of Racism on White Americans*, ed. by Benjamin P. Bowser and Raymond G. Hunt (Beverly Hills, CA: Sage, 1981), pp. 87–96.

57. Kovel, *White Racism*, pp. xli-xlvii.

58. Larry J. Griffin, "Temporality, Events, and Explanation in Historical Sociology," *Sociological Methods and Research* 20 (May 1992): 405.

59. *Ibid.*, p. 413.

60. Nelson Mandela, *Long Walk to Freedom* (Boston: Little, Brown, 1994), pp. 539–540.

Chapter 2: Racism in Practice: Case Studies

1. Linda Chavez, "Affirmative Action: Programs Are a Minority Putdown," *The Denver Post*, February 23, 1995, p. B7.

2. Carl Rowan, "Rutgers President Clearly Doesn't Deserve Criticism," *Chicago Sun-Times*, February 26, 1995, p. 36. See also Joe Feagin, Hernan Vera, and Nikitah Imani, *The Agony of Education: Black Students at White Colleges and Universities* (New York: Routledge, 1996), p. ix.

3. W. E. B. Du Bois, *Dusk of Dawn* (New Brunswick, NJ: Transaction, 1984 [1940]), p. 6.

4. Early black residents included both free blacks and slaves. See Robert R. Dykstra, *Bright Radical Star: Black Freedom and White Supremacy* (Cambridge, MA: Harvard University Press, 1993), pp. 13–18.

5. Iowa Advisory Commission, *A Time to Heal: Race Relations in Dubuque, Iowa* (Washington, DC: U.S. Commission on Civil Rights, 1993), p. 1.

6. *Ibid.*, p. 2. According to the 1990 census there were also 370 Hispanics, 368 Asian Americans, and 69 Native Americans in Dubuque.

7. Chamber of Commerce, *Brief History of Dubuque* (Dubuque, IA 1991).

8. Roger Maiers, who chaired the Dubuque Human Rights Commission from July 1989 to July 1991, listed a number of antiblack and anti-Asian incidents between June 1982 and October 1989 in his presentation to the Human Rights Commission Training Seminar, Omaha, Nebraska, August 26–28, 1993.

9. Isabel Wilkerson, "Seeking a Racial Mix, Dubuque Finds Tension," *The New York Times*, November 3, 1991, section 1, p. 1.

10. James Harney, "Iowa City Confronts Racism, But Racism Refuses to Die," *USA Today,* November 18, 1991, p. 10A; "Racial Intolerance in America's Heartland," *Larry King Live,* CNN, November 15, 1991; see also Mohammad A. Chaichian, *Racism in the Heartland: Dynamics of Race and Class in Dubuque, Iowa, 1800–1993* (Champaign-Urbana: University of Illinois Press, forthcoming).

11. Both of the black residents were quoted on "Welcome to White America," *20/20,* ABC News, December 20, 1991; Times Wire Service, "Racial Tension Smolders in City Once Tagged 'Selma of the North,'" *Los Angeles Times,* November 24, 1991, p. A1.

12. Jon D. Hull, "Race Relations: A White Person's Town?," *Time,* December 23, 1991, p. 39; Times Wire Service, "Racial Tension Smolders in the City," p. A1.

13. Hull, "Race Relations," p. 39.

14. Iowa Advisory Committee, *A Time to Heal,* p. 13.

15. Linda Diebel, "Darkest Iowa," *Toronto Star,* February 23, 1992, p. F1.

16. The *Telegraph Herald,* on November 11, 1991, announced, "Because of the high number of letters to the editor submitted in reaction to the racial issue in Dubuque, the *Telegraph Herald* on Tuesday will present an additional page of commentary." We examined the letters that appeared between July 11, 1991, and January 31, 1992.

17. The poll is cited in Lorrin Anderson, "Crimes of the Heartland," *National Review,* February 17, 1992, p. 30.

18. Quoted in Hull, "Race Relations," p. 39.

19. Constructive Integration Task Force, "We Want to Change," mimeographed (Dubuque, IA, 1991), p. 2.

20. Quoted in Roger Worthington, "Hate Flares as Iowa City Courts Blacks," *Chicago Tribune,* November 17, 1991, p. C23.

21. Quoted in Wilkerson, "Seeking a Racial Mix, Dubuque Finds Tension," p. 1.

22. See the comment of Katherine Newman, a Columbia professor, in Worthington, "Hate Flares as Iowa City Courts Blacks," p. C25.

23. Quoted in Wilkerson, "Seeking a Racial Mix, Dubuque Finds Tension," p. 1.

24. Terrell Bell, *The Thirteenth Man: A Reagan Cabinet Memoir* (New York: Free Press, 1988), p. 104.

25. Quoted in Diebel, "Darkest Iowa," p. F1.

26. Anderson, "Crimes of the Heartland," p. 30.

27. Brady was quoted on "Welcome to White America," *20/20.*

28. Mary Cerney, "Many Dubuquers Afraid to Speak Out," letters, *Telegraph Herald,* August 20, 1991, p. 3A.

29. Wilkerson, "Seeking a Racial Mix, Dubuque Finds Tension," p. 1.

30. Diebel, "Darkest Iowa," p. F1.

31. Quoted in Hull, "Race Relations," p. 39; "Welcome to White America," *20/20.*

32. Quoted in Times Wire Service, "Racial Tension Smolders in City," p. A1.

33. "Man Indicted in Cross-Burning," UPI, BC Cycle, March 27, 1992; Stacey McKenzie, "Some Dubuque Residents Feel Hate Crime Convictions Will Help City," *Des Moines Register,* as cited in Gannett News Service, April 22, 1993.

34. Times Wire Service, "Racial Tension Smolders in City," p. A1.

35. Quoted in Hull, "Race Relations," p. 39.
36. Quoted in Times Wire Service, "Racial Tension Smolders in City," p. A1.
37. Quoted in Hull, "Race Relations," p. 39.
38. Quoted on "Welcome to White America," *20/20.*
39. *Ibid.*
40. Quoted in Diebel, "Darkest Iowa," p. F1.
41. Quoted in Times Wire Service, "Racial Tension Smolders in City," p. A1; see also Anderson, "Crimes of the Heartland," p. 30.
42. Anderson, "Crimes of the Heartland," p. 30.
43. Joe P. Bean, "Hate Politics: Iowa Town Finds Hope," *San Francisco Chronicle,* December 14, 1991, p. A18; "Anti-Klan Protestors Outnumber Ku Klux Klan at Rally," UPI, BC Cycle, May 30, 1992; Hull, "Race Relations," p. 39.
44. Peter Berger and Thomas Luckmann, *The Social Construction of Reality: A Treatise in the Sociology of Knowledge* (Garden City, NY: Anchor Books, 1967), pp. 138–139.
45. Letter to the authors from Professor Mohammad A. Chaichian, University of Iowa. November 16, 1993.
46. Henri Hubert and Marcel Mauss, "Essai sur la nature et la fonction du sacrifice," in Marcel Mauss, *Oeuvres* (Paris: Les Editions du Minuit, 1968), pp. 205–206.
47. See Ruth Marcus, "Supreme Court Overturns Law Barring Hate Crimes," *Washington Post,* June 23, 1992, p. A1.
48. Cited in David Roediger, *Towards the Abolition of Whiteness* (London: Verso, 1994), p. 10.
49. Immanuel Wallerstein, *Unthinking Social Science: The Limits of Nineteenth Century Paradigms* (Cambridge, England: Polity Press, 1991), p. 86.
50. *Ibid.,* p. 87.
51. John McCormick and Vern Smith, "Can We Get Along?" *Newsweek,* November 9, 1992, p. 71.
52. Debora Wiley, "Dubuque Still Trying to Get Rid of Stigma," Gannett News Service, January 28, 1993.
53. Isabel Wilkerson, "Racial Tension Erupts, Tearing a College Apart," *The New York Times,* April 13, 1992, p. A14; Ruth Sidel, *The Struggle for Identity and Community on College Campuses* (New York: Viking, 1994).
54. Lynne Duke, "Ugly Racial Melee Shakes Students, Officials at Small Michigan College," *Washington Post,* April 12, 1992, p. A3; Jerry Thomas, "Brawl May Empty College of All Blacks," *Chicago Tribune,* April 26, 1992, p. C23.
55. Duke, "Ugly Racial Melee Shakes Students," p. A3; Thomas, "Brawl May Empty College of All Blacks," p. C23.
56. Duke, "Ugly Racial Melee Shakes Students," p. A3.
57. Don Gonyea, "Olivet College Copes with Racial Tension," *All Things Considered,* National Public Radio, April 29, 1992.
58. Wilkerson, "Racial Tension Erupts, Tearing a College Apart," p. A14.
59. "Olivet Disciplinary Panel to Begin Investigation of Racial Brawl," UPI, BC cycle, April 15, 1992.

60. Elizabeth Atkins, "Today's Woman: College Leader Takes Stand for Multicultural Harmony," Gannett News Service, September 15, 1992.
61. Rick Pluta, "Regional News," UPI, BC cycle, April 26, 1992; Paul Leavitt, "Buffalo Faces 2nd Week of Protests," *USA Today*, April 27, 1992, p. 3A.
62. Thomas, "Brawl May Empty College of All Blacks," p. C23; Wilkerson, "Racial Tension Erupts, Tearing College Apart," p. A14.
63. Quoted in Gonyea, "Olivet College Copes with Racial Tension"
64. *Ibid.*
65. Quoted on *Both Sides with Jesse Jackson*, CNN, March 26, 1994.
66. Quoted in Duke, "Ugly Racial Melee Shakes Students," p. A3.
67. Quoted in Wilkerson, "Racial Tension Erupts, Tearing a College Apart," p. A14.
68. Quoted in Thomas, "Brawl May Empty College of All Blacks," p. C23.
69. Quoted in Atkins, "Today's Woman."
70. Gonyea, "Olivet College Copes with Racial Tension."
71. Quoted on *World News Tonight with Peter Jennings*, ABC News, April 15, 1992.
72. Quoted in Duke, "Ugly Racial Melee Shakes Students," p. A3.
73. Quoted in Wilkerson, "Racial Tension Erupts, Tearing a College Apart," p. A14.
74. Quoted in Thomas, "Brawl May Empty College of All Blacks," p. C23.
75. Wilkerson, "Racial Tension Erupts, Tearing a College Apart," p. A14.
76. Gonyea, "Olivet College Copes with Racial Tension."
77. James Harney, "Michigan College Probes Racial Brawl," *USA Today*, April 15, 1992, p. 3A; Pluta, "Regional News."
78. Harney, "Michigan College Probes Racial Brawl," p. 3A; Rick Pluta, "Racial Tensions Rise on Michigan Campuses," UPI, BC cycle, April 17, 1992.
79. See Joe R. Feagin and Harlan Hahn, *Ghetto Revolts* (New York: Macmillan, 1973).
80. Quote by Catherine Crier, on "A Right to Privacy?" *Crier & Company*, CNN, April 13, 1992.
81. *World News Tonight with Peter Jennings*, ABC News, April 15, 1992.
82. "Race Fear, and How to Avoid It," *The Economist*, April 18, 1992, p. 21.
83. *Ibid.*, p. 21.
84. "Valparaiso Students March to Protest Racism," UPI, BC cycle, April 16, 1992.
85. Christopher Shea, "Protests Centering on Racial Issues Erupt on Many Campuses This Fall," *Chronicle of Higher Education*, November 25, 1992, p. A23; also *Both Sides with Jesse Jackson*, CNN, March 26, 1994.
86. Wilkerson, "Racial Tension Erupts, Tearing a College Apart," p. A14.
87. Atkins, "Today's Woman."
88. Quoted in Jack Lessenberry, "Campus Journal: After a Racial Crisis, Some Painful Introspection," *The New York Times*, August 4, 1993, p. B9; see also Todd Schulz, "Martial Arts Veteran Takes Over Helm of Olivet School," AP State and Local Wire, December 6, 1999, BC cycle.
89. Du Bois, *Dusk of Dawn*, p. 6.
90. Stokely Carmichael, "Black Power," in *Black Protest: History, Documents and Analyses, 1619 to the Present*, ed. Joanne Grant (New York: Fawcett Premier, 1968), pp. 460–461.

Chapter 3: Ghosts of Segregation: Discrimination in Restaurants

1. David J. Carrow, *Bearing the Cross: Martin Luther King, Jr., and the Southern Christian Leadership Conference* (New York: Vintage Books, 1986), p. 127.
2. *Ibid.*, p. 128.
3. Conrad P. Kottack, "Rituals at McDonald's," *Natural History* 87 (1978): 75.
4. Richard Martin, "Foodservice's Changing Face: Still Grappling with Diversity," *Nation's Restaurant News,* September 20, 1993, p. 1.
5. Calvin W. Rolark, "Let's Talk: Restaurant Justice Is Needed," *Washington Informer,* July 28, 1993, p. 12.
6. Martin, "Foodservice's Changing Face," p. 1.
7. The New York Times News Service, "Transformation: Settlement Commits Shoney's to Top-to-Bottom Restructuring," *Dallas Morning News,* February 1, 1993, p. D1; Joan Oleck, "Shoney's Angles for Settlement," *Restaurant Business,* September 20, 1992, p. 26.
8. Darryl Fears, "Shoney's Agrees to Extend Minority Business Investments," *The Atlanta Journal and Constitution,* June 3, 1993, p. G1.
9. *Ibid.*, p. 1; The New York Times News Service, "Transformation," p. D1.
10. Oleck "Shoney's Angles for Settlement," p. 26.
11. Quoted in Steve Watkins, "Racism du Jour at Shoney's," *Nation,* October 18, 1993, pp. 426–427.
12. Martin Dyckman, "Lawyers Can Be Heros Too," *St. Petersburg Times,* April 11, 1993, p. 3D.
13. "Shoney's Co. Founder Quits Board, Sells Stock After Multimillion Bias Decision," *Jet,* March 29, 1993, p. 4; Ronald Smothers, "$105 Million Poorer Now, Chain Mends Race Policies," *The New York Times,* January 31, 1993, section 1, p. 16.
14. Watkins, "Racism du Jour at Shoney's," pp. 426–427.
15. *Ibid.*, pp. 426-427.
16. See Blair S. Walker and Judith Schroer, "Paralyzing Prejudice: Minority Customers Still Shut Out," *USA Today,* June 11, 1993, p. B1.
17. Watkins, "Racism du Jour at Shoney's," p. 427.
18. Dyckman, "Lawyers Can Be Heros Too," p. 3D.
19. Fears, "Shoney's Agrees to Extend Minority Business Investments," p. 1.
20. *Ibid.*, p. 1.
21. *Chicago Tribune* wire service, "Shoney's Stock Falls on News of Shakeup," *Chicago Tribune,* December 22, 1992, p. C3.
22. The New York Times News Service, "Transformation," p. D1.
23. *Ibid.*, p. D1; "Shoney's Ex-Chairman Danner Quits Board," Reuters Limited, BC cycle, June 30, 1993.
24. Clarence Page, "Paying the Price for Racism," *Chicago Tribune,* February 7, 1993, p. C3.
25. Martin, "Foodservice's Changing Face," p. 1.
26. Joe R. Feagin and Clairece B. Feagin, *Racial and Ethnic Relations,* 4th ed. (Englewood Cliffs, NJ: Prentice-Hall, 1993), pp. 232–233.

27. Jerry Thomas, "NAACP's Army Thins as Its Battles Multiply," *Chicago Tribune,* September 27, 1993, Zone N, p. 1.
28. The 1991 Civil Rights Act was designed to countermand these Supreme Court decisions. Congress was more liberal than the court and President Bush were.
29. Margery Austin Turner, Michael Fix, and Raymond J Struyk, *Opportunities Denied: Discrimination in Hiring* (Washington, DC: Urban Institute, 1991); James E. Ellis, "The Black Middle Class," *Business Week,* March 14, 1988, p. 65.
30. "Restaurants Ordered to Change Name," UPI, March 18, 1981, BC cycle; Cheryl Devall, "African-Americans Still Suffer Bias When Eating Out," *Weekend Edition,* National Public Radio, May 29, 1993.
31. Calvin Sims, "Giving Denny's a Menu for Change," *The New York Times,* January 1, 1994, section 1, p. 43; Jim Doyle, "32 Blacks Sue Denny's for Bias," *San Francisco Chronicle,* March 25, 1993, p. A17.
32. Doyle, "32 Blacks Sue Denny's for Bias," p. A17.
33. James Vicini, "Denny's Restaurants Settles Race-Bias Charges," *Reuters Asia-Pacific Business Report,* March 26, 1993, BC cycle.
34. Sims, "Giving Denny's a Menu for Change," p. 43; Robin Schatz, "Denny's and Others Stumble on Racism Charges," *Newsday,* August 8, 1993, p. 84.
35. Schatz, "Denny's and Others Stumble on Racism Charges," p. 84.
36. Jay Mathews, "Denny's Tackles a Stained Image: Fighting Bias Charges, Chairman Forges Links with Rights Leaders," *Washington Post,* August 1, 1993, p. H1.
37. Susan Christian, "Denny's Hires San Diego Consultant for Civil Rights Job, Liaison," *Los Angeles Times,* July 28, 1993, p. D1.
38. Mark J. McGarry, "Denny's to Spend $1 Billion to Do the Right Thing," *Newsday,* July 2, 1993, p. 47.
39. Mathews, "Denny's Tackles a Stained Image," p. H1.
40. Quoted in Andrea Adelson, "Denny's Parent Vows Larger Role for Blacks," *The New York Times,* July 2, 1993, p. D2.
41. *Ibid.,* p. D2.
42. Sandra Clark, "Denny's Campaigns to Counter Charges," *Plain Dealer,* July 20, 1993, p. F2.
43. Bruce Vielmetti, "More Saying Denny's Discriminates," *St. Petersburg Times,* June 17, 1993, p. A1.
44. Robert L. Jackson, "Denny's Breaks Bias Vow on Day of Accord," *Los Angeles Times,* May 22, 1993, p. A1; Doyle, "32 Blacks Sue Denny's for Bias," p. A17.
45. "Not Yet Free from Racism," *Metro Reporter,* January 26, 1992, p. 3; Chuck Hawkins, "Denny's: The Stain That Isn't Coming Out," *Business Week,* June 28, 1993, p. 98; "New Race Bias Charges Against Denny's Restaurants," *San Francisco Chronicle,* June 17, 1993, p. A19.
46. Quoted in William D. Murray, "Denny's Charged with Discriminating Against Blacks," UPI, BC cycle, March 24, 1993.
47. Quoted in Calvin Sims, "Restaurant Chain Settles Charges of Racial Bias," *The New York Times,* March 26, 1993, p. A14.

48. Quoted in Murray, "Denny's Charged with Discriminating Against Blacks."

49. "Class Action Suit," *Sacramento Observer,* March 31, 1993, p. F1.

50. Quoted in Mathews, "Denny's Tackles a Stained Image," p. H1.

51. Reynolds Farley, Howard Schuman, Suzanne Blanchi, Diane Colasanto, and Shirley Hatchett, "Chocolate City, Vanilla Suburbs," *Sociology and Social Research* 7 (1978): 335–336.

52. *Washington Post* wire services, "Turning Up Heat on Denny's," *Houston Chronicle,* June 17, 1993, p. A10.

53. "New Race Bias Charges Against Denny's Restaurants," p. A19.

54. Quoted in Mathews, "Denny's Tackles a Stained Image," p. H1.

55. Jerry Thomas, "Invisible Patrons Demand to Be Seen," *Chicago Tribune,* June 10, 1993, Zone N, p. 1; Mathews, "Denny's Tackles a Stained Image," p. H1.

56. Quoted in Thomas, "Invisible Patrons Demand to Be Seen," p. 1.

57. Quoted in Devall, "African-Americans Still Suffer Bias When Eating Out."

58. Schatz, "Denny's and Others Stumble on Racism Charges," p. 84.

59. Quoted in Jackson, "Denny's Breaks Bias Vow on Day of Accord," p. A1.

60. Bureau of National Affairs, "Discrimination: Denny's Restaurants to Pay $46 Million, Provide 'Sensitivity Training' to Employees," BNA Management Briefing, May 26, 1994.

61. "Denny's Does Some of the Right Things," *Business Week,* June 6, 1994, p. 42.

62. "Denny's, Blacks Settle Suits: Company to Pay $547 Million," *Orlando Sentinel,* May 25, 1994, p. A1.

63. Rupert Cornwell, "Rocketing Cost of Race Bias in the U.S." *The Independent,* May 28, 1994, p. 8.

64. "Justice Department News Conference with Deval Patrick, Assistant Attorney General, Civil Rights Division," Federal News Service, May 24, 1994.

65. David Segal, "Denny's Serves Up a Sensitive Image; Restaurant Chain Launches PR Drive to Show Minorities It Has Changed Its Ways," *Washington Post,* April 7, 1999, p. E1.

66. *Ibid.,* p. E1.

67. Thomas, "Invisible Patrons Demand to Be Seen," p. 1.

68. Walker and Schroer, "Paralyzing Prejudice," p. B1.

69. Bill Carlino, "IHOP OKs Settlement in Racial Bias Suit," *Nation's Restaurant News,* January 18, 1993, p. 3.

70. Joan Oleck, "Hearings Set in IHOP Discrimination Suit," *Restaurant Business,* October 10, 1992, p. 22.

71. "Pizza Franchise Must Serve Black Beach," *Atlanta Journal and Constitution,* February 14, 1998, p. 7B.

72. Hawkins, "Denny's: The Stain That Isn't Coming Out," p. 98.

73. *Ibid.,* p. 98.

74. Quoted in Schatz, "Denny's and Others Stumble on Racism Charges," p. 84.

75. Paul Claudel, *The Structures of Everyday Life* (New York: Harper & Row, 1981), p. 208.

76. *Ibid.,* p. 186.

77. Calvin Sims, "Giving Denny's a Menu for Change," *The New York Times,* January 1, 1994, p. 43.
78. Segal, "Denny's Serves Up a Sensitive Image."
79. "Denny's Pact Combats Racism," *Chicago Sun-Times,* May 30, 1994, p. 17.
80. James Lawson, "Student Nonviolent Coordinating Committee, Statement of Purpose," *Black Protest: History, Documents, Analyses,* ed. Joanne Grant (New York: Ballantine, 1991), p. 290.

Chapter 4: Racism and Murder: The Cases of Boston, Portland, and Jasper

1. An Ohio survey found that 82 percent of white respondents statewide considered racism to be a big or somewhat of a problem in the U.S. today. However, 75 percent thought that the problems African Americans face are not caused primarily by whites. See the survey, "Race Relations Attitudes/Differences Survey Report," prepared for The Franklin County (OH) United Way Race Relations Vision Council, by Paul J. Lavrakas and Clarence N. Wood in March 1999; www.uwaycolumbus.org/critical.race/report/atrrrdno.html.
2. Gordon Allport, *The Nature of Prejudice* (New York: Addison-Wesley, 1979), p. xvi.
3. Patricia J. Williams, *The Alchemy of Race and Rights: Diary of a Law Professor* (Cambridge, MA: Harvard University Press, 1991), p. 6.
4. Quoted in Peter J. Howe, "From Nightmare to Reality, a City Is Reeling," *Boston Globe,* January 7, 1990, Metro/Region, p. 1. The paragraph draws on this source.
5. Montgomery Brower, Dirk Mathison, and S. Avery Brown, "A Dark Night of the Soul in Boston: The Murderous Assault on a Pregnant Woman and Her Husband Hits a Nerve of Deep Fear in a Divided City," *People,* November 13, 1989, p. 52.
6. Michael Rezendes, "Mayor's Reputation as Racial Healer Gets Some Tarnish," *Boston Globe,* September 10, 1991, Metro/Region, p. 1.
7. Quoted in Brower et al., "A Dark Night of the Soul in Boston," p. 52.
8. Joe Sharkey, *Deadly Greed: The Riveting True Story of the Stuart Murder Case That Rocked Boston and Shocked the Nation* (New York: Prentice-Hall, 1991), pp. 143–145.
9. Jerry Thomas, "Mission Hill Wants Action Over Searches," *Boston Globe,* February 9, 1990, Metro/Region, p. 1.
10. Steve Marantz and Elizabeth Neuffer, "Flynn Resists Calls to Open Report on Stuart Case Leaks," *Boston Globe,* July 12, 1990, Metro/Region, p. 25; Margaret Carison, "Presumed Innocent," *Time,* January 22, 1990, p. 10.
11. Carison, "Presumed Innocent," p. 10.
12. Thomas Palmer, "Stuart Killing Haunts Courts, Lives," *Boston Globe,* August 11, 1991, Metro/Region, p. 1.
13. Peter S Canellos, "Car Linked to Stuart Is Found," *Boston Globe,* May 2, 1992, Metro/Region, p. 21.

14. Peter J. Howe, "Probers Say Disclosures Would Have Made Difference; Many Kept Clues About Stuart to Themselves," *Boston Globe,* January 9, 1990, Metro/Region, p. 1.

15. Doris Sue Wong, "Stuart Probe to Subpoena Bennet," *Boston Globe,* September 21, 1991, Metro/Region, p. 25.

16. Chris Reidy and Doris Sue Wong, "A Tearful Stuart Admits His Guilt, Gets 3 to 5 Years," *Boston Globe,* November 3, 1992, p. 1.

17. Sean P. Murphy, "From Mission Hill to Revere, Repercussions Still Felt," *Boston Globe,* November 3, 1992, Metro/Region, p. 16.

18. "Boston's Stuart Murder/Suicide Case," *Nightline,* ABC News, January 8, 1990.

19. Sharkey, *Deadly Greed.*

20. *Ibid.,* p. 81.

21. *Ibid.,* p. 82. The rest of the paragraph draws in part on data in this book.

22. See *Nightline,* "Boston's Stuart Murder/Suicide Case."

23. *Ibid.*

24. Associated Press, "FBI Checks Boston Police Over Probe of Stuart Case," *Orlando Sentinel,* February 24, 1990, p. A11.

25. "Misconduct by Cops," *Newsday,* August 20, 1992, p. 14.

26. Elizabeth Neuffer, "U.S. Attorney Ends Misconduct Probe in Stuart, Case," *Boston Globe,* July 4, 1991, Metro/Region, p. 1.

27. Brower et al., "A Dark Night of the Soul in Boston," p. 52.

28. Quoted on *Nightline,* "Boston's Stuart Murder/Suicide Case."

29. Jerry Thomas, "Mission Hill Wants Action Over Searches," p. 1; Philip Bennett and Adrian Walker, "Scars Still Visible in Mission Hill," *Boston Globe,* September 27, 1991, Metro/Region, p. 1.

30. UPI, "DiMaiti Honored with 1,000 Points of Light," August 7, 1990.

31. Rezendes, "Mayor's Reputation as Racial Healer Gets Some Tarnish," p. 1.

32. Quoted on *Nightline,* "Boston's Stuart Murder/Suicide Case."

33. Quoted in Fox Butterfield and Constance L. Hays, "A Boston Tragedy: The Stuart Case—A Special Case," *The New York Times,* January 15, 1990, p. A1.

34. On racial bias in media accounts, see Doris A. Graber, *Crime News and the Public* (New York: Praeger, 1980).

35. Sander L Gilman, "Black Bodies, White Bodies: Toward an Iconography of Female Sexuality in Late Nineteenth-Century Art, Medicine, and Literature," *Critical Inquiry* 12 (Autumn 1985): 209.

36. See Thomas F. Gossett, *Race* (New York: Schocken Books, 1965), pp. 42–43.

37. John Dollard, Caste and Class in a Southern Town, 3rd ed. (New York: Doubleday Anchor Books, 1949 [1937]), pp. 162–166.

38. "Charges Considered Against Man in Wife's Stabbing," "Regional News," UPI, April 27, 1992; Roger Worthington, "After Claiming Attack, Man Charged in Wife's Stabbing Death," *Chicago Tribune,* April 29, 1992, p. C18.

39. Quoted in "Charges Considered Against Man in Wife's Stabbing"; on the trial, see Associated Press, "Man Who Killed Wife, Blamed Blacks, Gets 60 Years," *Chicago Tribune,* September 30, 1992, p. M3.

40. "Road to Judgement," *Newsweek*, August 7, 1995, p. 20.

41. Katherine K. Russell, *The Color of Crime: Racial Hoaxes, White Fear, Black Protectionism, Police Harassment and Other Macro Aggressions* (New York: New York University Press, 1998), p. 77.

42. James Willwerth, "Making War on WAR," *Time*, October 22, 1990, p. 60; "The Great Debate: Pulling the Strings of Hate," *20/20*, ABC News, January 11, 1991.

43. Elinor Langer, "The American Neo-Nazi Movement Today," *Nation*, July 16, 1990, p. 82; Rick Mofina, "The Racist Underground," *Calgary Herald*, February 9, 1992, p. B1.

44. Langer, "The American Neo-Nazi Movement Today," p. 82.

45. Joel Kotkin, "California Klansman Nominated for Congress as Democrat," *Washington Post*, June 8, 1980, p. A4.

46. We are indebted to Suzanne Harper for this information.

47. James Quinn, "School to Rebut Racist Flyers with Survivors," *Los Angeles Times*, January 18, 1985, part 2, p. 6.

48. Quoted in Langer, "The American Neo-Nazi Movement Today," p. 82; see also Darlene Himmelspach, "Younger Metzger Is Denied Entry into Germany, Returned to U.S.," *San Diego Union-Tribune*, April 14, 1994, p. 3.

49. Associated Press, "Democrats Disavow Nominee from Klan," *The New York Times*, June 6, 1980, p. A17; Langer, "The American Neo-Nazi." p. 82.

50. "General News," UPI, November 4, 1980; "Regional News," UPI, February 4, 1982; "Klansman Loses Senatorial Bid," UPI, AM cycle, June 9, 1982.

51. Quoted in Richard A Serrano, "Affidavit Links Metzger to Killing," *Los Angeles Times*, February 22, 1990, p. B1.

52. Willwerth, "Making War on WAR," p. 60.

53. Quoted in Don Duncan, "Racial Rhetoric Fills Courtroom as Trial Opens," *Seattle Times*, October 10, 1990, p. F1.

54. Quoted on "The Great Debate: Pulling the Strings of Hate," *20/20*.

55. Serrano, "Affidavit Links Metzger to Killing," p. B1.

56. *Ibid.*, p. B1; Don Duncan, "Skinhead Who Once Idolized Metzger Testifies Against Him," *Seattle Times*, October 13, 1990, p. A14.

57. Mazzella was quoted on, "The Great Debate: Pulling the Strings of Hate," *20/20*.

58. *Ibid.*

59. Langer, "The American Neo-Nazi Movement Today," p. 82; Serrano, "Affidavit Links Metzger to Killing," p. B1.

60. John M. Glionna, "Metzger Rejects Deal to Let Him Remain in Home," *Los Angeles Times*, November 15, 1990, p. B1.

61. Michael Granberry, "Film Spurs Review of Metzger's Probation," *Los Angeles Times*, June 5, 1992, p. B1.

62. The data in this paragraph are from Langer, "The American Neo-Nazi Movement Today," p. 82; Curtis Wilkie, "Lawsuits Prove to Be a Big Gun in Anti-Klan Arsenal," *Boston Globe*, June 17, 1993, p. 1; Michael Barkun, "Reflections After Waco: Millenialists and the State," Christian Century, June 2, 1993, p. 596. The list in the paragraph draws in part on Langer.

63. James Ridgeway, *Blood in the Face: The Ku Klux Klan, Aryan Nations, Nazi Skinheads, and the Rise of a New White Culture* (New York: Thunder's Mouth Press, 1990), p. 164.
64. "General News," UPI, October 23, 1980.
65. *Chicago Tribune* wire services, "KKK Establishing Chapters in Germany," Chicago Tribune, August 14, 1992, p. C12.
66. "Bonn Says German Far-Right as Dangerous as Far-Left," *Reuters Library Report,* July 29, 1992; Deidre Berger, "Right-Wing Extremists in U.S. Helping German Neo-Nazis," National Public Radio, January 3, 1994.
67. Ben Barber, "Shattering the Silence," *Calgary Herald,* September 6, 1992, p. B10.
68. Sue Fishkoff, "Geraldo, a 'Golani Kind of Jew' vs. Neo-Nazis," *Jerusalem Post,* September 11, 1992.
69. Houston Chronicle News Services, "National Briefs," *Houston Chronicle,* January 15, 1994, p. 18; Andrea Stone, "2 Plead Innocent in Los Angeles Race War Case," *USA Today,* August 3, 1993, p. 9A.
70. Tom Laceky, "When Hatemongers Came for Minorities, Town Said No," Los Angeles Times, March 6, 1994, p. B4; "An Antidote to Hate," *St. Louis Post-Dispatch,* March 9, 1994, p. 6B.
71. Sarah Henry, "Marketing Hate: The Church of the Creator Has Sold Violent Racism as Religion for 20 Years," *Los Angeles Times Magazine,* December 12, 1993, p. 18.
72. *Ibid.,* p. 18.
73. Pam Belluck, "Hate Groups Seeking Broader Reach," *The New York Times,* July 7, 1999, p. A16.
74. Paul Duggan, "Tearing Down a Fence and More; Racist Killing Forces Jasper, Tex., to Look Hatred in the Eye," *The Washington Post,* January 26, 1999, p. A3.
75. Sue Anne Pressley, "Disabled Man Dragged to Death: Three Whites Charged with Murder; FBI Probes for Racial Motive," *The Washington Post,* June 10, 1998, p. A3.
76. David Firestone, "A Life Marked by Troubles, but Not Hatred," *The New York Times,* June 13, 1998, p. A6.
77. "Second Man on Death Row in Dragging of Black Man," *The New York Times,* September 24, 1999, p. A14.
78. "Second Man Convicted in Dragging Death," *The New York Times,* September 21, 1999, p. A18.
79. Blaine Harden, "Giuliani Suspends 2 N.Y. Firemen for 'Display of Racism' at Parade: Participants Mocked Dragging Death of Black Man in Texas," *The Washington Post,* September 12, 1998, p. A6.
80. Ridgeway, *Blood in the Face,* p. 8.
81. Jo Thomas, "A City Takes a Stand Against Hate," *The New York Times,* September 21, 1999, p. A18.
82. Christopher Edley, Jr., "Racist Media, Politicians Sustained Boston Hoax," *Manhattan Lawyer,* March 1990, p. 18.

83. Thomas, "A City Takes a Stand Against Hate."

84. *Ibid.*

Chapter 5: The Racial Profile of Police Brutality

1. Toni Morrison, "Introduction, Friday on the Potomac," in *Race-ing Justice, Engendering Power: Essays on Anita Hill, Clarence Thomas, and the Construction of Social Reality,* ed. Toni Morrison (New York: Pantheon Books, 1992), pp. vii–xxx.

2. Lou Waters, "News Conference with Rodney King," CNN News Live Report, May 1, 1992.

3. Ashley Dunn and Andrea Ford, "The Man Swept Up in the Furor; Friends, Family Say King Was Sometimes Lost But Never Violent," *Los Angeles Times,* March 17, 1991, p. B1.

4. Dunn and Ford, "The Man Swept Up in the Furor," p. B1; in the civil trial attorneys for the city of Los Angeles brought up other entries in King's criminal record.

5. *Ibid.,* p. B1.

6. *Ibid.,* p. B1.

7. Seth Mydans, "Friend Relives Night of Police Beating," *The New York Times,* March 21, 1991, p. B1.

8. *Primetime Live,* ABC News, April 18, 1991.

9. *Ibid.;* "The Case of CA v. Powell," Magnum Court Video, 1992.

10. Linda Rapattoni, "Companion of Victim in Police Beating Sues," UPI, March 21, 1991.

11. *Ibid.*

12. Seth Mydans, R. W. Stevenson, and T. Egan, "Seven Minutes in Los Angeles—A Special Report," *The New York Times,* March 18, 1991, p. A1; Richard A. Serrano, "Police Documents Disclose Beating Was Downplayed," *Los Angeles Times,* March 20, 1991, p. A1.

13. Interview with Steve Lerman, *Nightline,* ABC News, April 18, 1991.

14. Interview with George Holliday, *Nightline,* ABC News, April 18, 1991

15. Mydans et al., "Seven Minutes in Los Angeles," p. A1.

16. *Primetime Live,* ABC News, April 18, 1991.

17. Lynne C. Shifflett, "King Beating Trial: The Blue Code Is Broken," *The Ethnic Newswatch,* April 8, 1992, p. A1. Throughout this discussion of events we draw on the trial videotape, "The Case of CA v. Powell."

18. *Primetime Live,* ABC News, April 18, 1991.

19. Reynolds Holding, "Dramatic Start to Second Trial in King Beating," *San Francisco Chronicle,* February 26, 1993, p. A1.

20. Quoted in James Baker, Linda Wright, Nadine Joseph, and Peter Katel, "Los Angeles Aftershocks," *Newsweek,* April 1, 1991, p. A1.

21. Ted Rohrlich, "The Times Poll: Majority Says Police Brutality Is Common," *Los Angeles Times,* March 10, 1991, p. A1.

22. Sheryl Stolberg, "The Times Poll: 31% of Angelenos Say Gates Should Quit Now," *Los Angeles Times,* March 22, 1991, p. A1.

23. Serrano, "Police Documents Disclose Beating Was Downplayed," p. A1.

24. Richard A. Serrano, "Officers Claimed Self-Defense in Beating of King," *Los Angeles Times,* March 30, 1991, p. A1.

25. Quoted in *Ibid.,* p. A1.

26. Richard W Stevenson, "Tape Forever Ties Victim to Beating," *The New York Times,* March 20, 1991, p. A19.

27. Andrea Ford, "King Lawyer Says Police Used Slurs," *Los Angeles Times,* May 4, 1991, p. B1.

28. Mydans, "Friend Relives Night of Police Beating," p. B8.

29. Dunn and Ford, "The Man Swept Up in the Furor," p. B1; Pat Morrison and Sheryl Stolberg, "Anger Against Gates Boils Over at Public Hearing," *Los Angeles Times,* March 15, 1991, p. A3.

30. Mydans et al., "Seven Minutes in Los Angeles," p. A1.

31. Joe Davidson, "Have the Police Declared War on Blacks?" *Emerge* (May 1993): 30.

32. Anne Kornhauser, "Civil Rights Commission Seeks Direction During Mid-Life Crisis," *The Recorder,* July 5, 1991, p. 1.

33. Mydans et al., "Seven Minutes in Los Angeles," p. A1.

34. *Ibid.,* p. A1. All statistical data are from Daniel B. Wood, "L.A. Beating Bares Racism Problem," *Christian Science Monitor,* March 11, 1991, p. 1. For further data see reference in note 38.

35. Leslie Berger, "Crisis in the LAPD: The Rodney King Beating Suit Charges Powell Used Force in '89," *Los Angeles Times,* April 20, 1991, p. B1. Officer Briseño, one of the four officers tried for the beating, is a light-skinned man of South American background.

36. Marc Lacey, "Two Men Killed by Officer Were Shot 20 Times," *Los Angeles Times,* March 11, 1991, p. B1; "Violence and Justice: A Record of Police Brutality in LA," *Boston Globe,* March 17, 1991, p. 45; George Will, "L.A. Police Department Badly in Need of Leadership," *The Atlanta Journal and Constitution,* March 14, 1991, p. 15; George Will, "L.A. Police: Time for an Accounting," *Washington Post,* March 13, 1991, p. A17.

37. Mydans et al., "Seven Minutes in Los Angeles," p. A1.

38. Data are from Ted Rohrlich and Victor Merina, "Racial Disparities Seen in Complaints to LAPD," *Los Angeles Times,* May 19, 1991, p. A1.

39. See David Freed, "Police Brutality Claims Are Rarely Prosecuted," *Los Angeles Times,* July 7, 1991, p. A1.

40. See Neil A. Lewis, "Police Brutality Under Wide Review by Justice Department," *The New York Times,* March 15, 1991, p. A1.

41. Warren Christopher et al., *Report of the Independent Commission on the Los Angeles Police Department,* Los Angeles, July 9, 1991; Ruth Marcus, "History of Mistrust May Have Contributed to Riots. Experts Say Los Angeles's Minorities Have Long Been Critical of 'Hard-Nosed' Police," *Washington Post,* May 2,

1992, p. A18; Tracy Wilkinson, Andrea Ford, and Tracy Wood, "Panel Urges Gates to Retire; Report on Police Cites Racism, Excess Force," *Los Angeles Times,* July 10, 1991, p. A1.

42. Cecilia Rasmussen, "Facts, Figures and Reactions: The Computer Messages," *Los Angeles Times,* July 10, 1991, p. A15; John L. Mitchell and Shawn Hubler, "King Gets Award of $3.8 Million; Trial: The City Will Pay Compensatory Damages and Lost Income from 1991 Police Beating; Jury Will Consider Punitive Amount," *Los Angeles Times,* April 20, 1994, p. A1.

43. "Urgent Call for Reform That Los Angeles Must Not Ignore: Christopher Panel Proposes Major Changes for the Troubled Police Department," *Los Angeles Times,* July 10, 1991, p. B6.

44. Richard R. Serrano, "LAPD Holds Back Black Officers, State Says," *Los Angeles Times,* January 24, 1991, p. B1.

45. There were ten whites, one Filipino, and one Latino on the jury.

46. Andrea Ford and Darryl Kelley, "King Case to Be Tried in Ventura County," *Los Angeles Times,* November 27, 1991, p. A3.

47. Adrienne Goodman, "NAACP Head Criticizes Site of King Trial," *Los Angeles Times,* December 5, 1991, p. B1.

48. Much of the discussion that follows is based on a court videotape of portions of the trial: "The Case of CA v. Powell."

49. "The Case of CA v. Powell." Freddie Helms, the other passenger of the car, died in June 1991 in an unrelated car accident.

50. *Ibid.*

51. *Ibid.*

52. *Ibid.*

53. *Ibid.*

54. *Ibid.*

55. D. M. Osborne, "Reaching for Doubt," *The American Lawyer* (September 1992): 62.

56. *Ibid.,* p. 62.

57. *Ibid.,* p. 62.

58. *Ibid.,* p. 62.

59. *Ibid.,* p. 62.

60. *Ibid.,* p. 62.

61. *Ibid.,* p. 62.

62. *Ibid.,* p. 62.

63. *Ibid.,* p. 62.

64. See Joe R. Feagin and Harlan Hahn, *Ghetto Revolts: The Politics of Violence in American Cities* (New York: Macmillan; 1973), pp. 6–13.

65. "LA Is Burning," *Frontline,* Public Television, April 24, 1993. In contrast, many of the Latino rioters were not native born.

66. See Charles Leerhsen, "LA's Violent New Video," *Newsweek,* March 18, 1991, pp. 33, 53.

67. *Congressional Record,* 102nd Cong., 1st Sess., March 18, 1991, H17R5, Vol. 137, No. 46.
68. *Congressional Record,* 102nd Cong., 1st Sess., May 7, 1992, H3081, Vol. 138, No. 62.
69. *Congressional Record,* 102nd Cong., 1st Sess., March 22, 1991, E1136, Vol. 137, No. 50.
70. *Congressional Record,* 102nd Cong., 1st Sess., March 14, 1991, H1762, Vol. 137, No. 44.
71. *Congressional Record,* 102nd Cong., 1st Sess., March 18, 1991, H1776, Vol. 137, No. 46.
72. *Congressional Record,* 102nd Cong., 1st Sess., March 18, 1991, H1780, Vol. 137, No. 46.
73. Susan N. Herman, "Justice Sees Through a Glass, Darkly," *Newsday,* May 4, 1992, p. 37.
74. "Making His Case," *MacNeil/Lehrer News Hour,* March 11, 1993.
75. Rogers Worthington, "Patrol Officer Says She Didn't Aid King for Fear of Heckling," *Chicago Tribune,* March 30, 1993, p. N4.
76. Lou Cannon, "Ruling in King Case Hinders Prosecution: Jury Won't Hear Officer's Racial Phrase," *Houston Chronicle,* March 26, 1993, p. A5; Greg LaMotte, "Judge Rules 'Mandingo' Reference 'Inflammatory,'" *CNN News,* March 26, 1993.
77. Stacey C. Koon, *Presumed Guilty: The Tragedy of the Rodney King Affair* (Washington, DC: Regnery Gateway, 1992), p. 33.
78. *Ibid.,* p. 220.
79. *Ibid.,* pp. 86–87.
80. Jim Newton, "Koon, Powell Denied Bail During Appeal," *The New York Times,* August 31, 1993, p. A1.
81. Neil A. Lewis, "A.C.L.U. Opposes Second Trial in Beating Case," *The New York Times,* April 5, 1993, p. A10.
82. Quoted in Norma Meyer and Gale Holland, "2 Cops get $2\frac{1}{2}$ Years in King Case," *San Diego Union-Tribune,* August 5, 1993, p. A1.
83. Isabel Wilkerson, "King Case Touches Middle-Class Blacks," *Dallas Morning News,* May 5, 1993, p. 47A.
84. Seth Mydans, "Rodney King Is Awarded $3.8 Million," *The New York Times,* April 20, 1994, p. A14; William Hamilton, "King Is Awarded $3.8 Million in Los Angeles Police Beating," *Washington Post,* April 20, 1994, p. A1.
85. Seth Mydans, "King Hit in Head, Officer Testifies; 'Hit Him!' Rookie Says Sergeant Urged," *Houston Chronicle,* April 23, 1994, p. A2.
86. Gale Holland, "King Case Officer Tells of Ostracism by Peers After Trial Testimony; Teary-Eyed Briseño Says He Is an Outcast After Opposing Beating," *San Diego Union- Tribune,* April 27, 1994, p. A3.
87. Norma Meyer, "Judge Drops Gates from King Lawsuit; Four Officers Who Viewed Beating Also Let Off," *San Diego Union-Tribune,* May 10, 1994, p. A3.

88. Christopher et al., *Report of the Independent Commission on the Los Angeles Police Department;* Sam Walker, "Pro-White Rally in Boston Prompts Little Sympathy," *Christian Science Monitor,* May 9, 1994, New England Section, p. 8; Chris Black, "City Puts $350,000 Price Tag on Parade Protection Services," *Boston Globe,* May 11, 1994, Metro/Region, p. 27.

89. Andy Furillo and Brad Hayward, "Denny Pair Innocent on Key Counts," *Sacramento Bee,* October 19, 1993, p. A1. For the perspective of the jurors, see Ted Koppel, *Nightline,* ABC News, October 27, 1993.

90. Carla Rivera, "The Times Poll: Majority Say Denny Verdicts Too Lenient," *Los Angeles Times,* October 26, 1993, p. A1.

91. Samuel Francis, "Black Civil Rights, White Civil Rights," *Washington Times,* October 22, 1993, p. A27; see also Richard Cohen, "Balkan Justice in LA," *Washington Post,* October 26, 1993, p. A17.

92. See Kim Lersch, "Current Trends in Police Brutality: An Analysis of Recent Newspaper Accounts," unpublished master's thesis, Gainesville, University of Florida, 1993.

93. David B. Oppenheimer, "The Movement from Sympathy to Empathy, through Fear; The Beatings of Rodney King and Reginald Denny Provoke Differing Emotions but Similar Racial Concerns," *The Recorder,* June 9, 1992, p. 14; see also Joe R. Feagin and Clairece B. Feagin, *Racial and Ethnic Relations,* 4th ed. (Englewood Cliffs, NJ: Prentice-Hall, 1993).

94. David Rohde, "A Brush with the Law Increasingly Ends with a Night in Jail," *The New York Times,* February 6, 2000, p. A29.

95. "Relative: Woman Shot by Police Was Unconscious," *The Atlanta Journal and Constitution,* December 30, 1998, p. 4A.

96. Martin Luther King, Jr., *Why We Can't Wait* (New York: Penguin, 1963), p. 77.

97. David Theo Goldberg, "Racism and Rationality: The Need for a New Critique," *Philosophy of Social Sciences* 20 (1990): 317–348.

98. See Freed, "Police Brutality Claims Are Rarely Prosecuted," p. A1.

99. David Kocieniewski, "Minority Drivers Tell of Troopers' Racial Profiling," *The New York Times,* April 14, 1999, p. B1.

100. Richard Weizel, "Policing the Police: On Racial Profiling," *The New York Times,* July 26, 1998, section 14, p. 1.

101. "Racial Profiling in New Jersey," *The New York Times,* April 22, 1999, p. A30.

102. Amy Waldman, "The Diallo Shooting: The Overview: 4 Officers Enter Not-Guilty Pleas to Murder Counts in Diallo Case," *The New York Times,* April 1, 1999, p. A1.

103. David Herszenhorn, "Capital Demonstration Widens Support for Diallo Rallies," *The New York Times,* April 4, 1999, p. 22.

104. Joseph Fried, "Louima Jury Hears Officer Describe Bloody Gloves," *The New York Times,* May 18, 1999, p. B8.

105. Amy Waldman, "The Louima Case: The Officer; Unremarkable Past and Unspeakable Act," *The New York Times,* May 26, 1999, p. B9.

106. David Barstow, "Volpe's Father Says Warlike Stress Led to Violent Outburst," *The New York Times,* June 2, 1999, p. B1.
107. David Barstow, "The Louima Case: The Overview; Officer, Seeking Some Mercy, Admits to Louima's Torture," *The New York Times,* May 26, 1999, p. A1.
108. John J. DiJulio, "White Lies about Black Crime," *The Public Interest* 118 (1995): 31.
109. *Ibid.,* p. 32.
110. See Katheryn K. Russell, *The Color of Crime* (New York: New York University Press, 1998), pp. 26–36; Joe R. Feagin and Clairece B. Feagin, *Social Problems: A Critical Power-Conflict Perspective* (Upper Saddle River, NJ: Prentice-Hall, 1997), chapter 8.
111. "Where was the D.A.?" *Los Angeles Times,* March 23, 2000, p. B8; "Deepening Stain in LAPD," *Los Angeles Times,* September 17, 1999, p. B6.
112. "Where Was the D.A.?," p. B8; Associated Press, "Highlights of Los Angeles Police Corruption Scandal," February 23, 2000.
113. Wilkinson, Ford, and Wood, "Panel Urges Gates to Retire; Report on Police Cites Racism, Excess Force," p. A1.
114. *Ibid.,* p. A1.
115. Brenda Grinston, "Why Minority Cops Are Afraid to Speak Out: Police: It's the Code of Silence, Enforced by Fear and Conditioning, Says a Black, Female Former Officer," *Los Angeles Times,* July 2, 1991, p. B7.
116. Pierre Bourdieu, *Outline of a Theory of Practice,* trans. Richard Nice (Cambridge, England: Cambridge University Press, 1977), p. 190.
117. King, *Why We Can't Wait,* p. 79.

Chapter 6: Racism in the Halls of Power: The Texaco, "Willie" Horton, and Sister Souljah Cases

1. "Foot-in-Mouth Disease," *Gannett News Service,* February 9, 1990.
2. Peter Ross Range, "What We Say, What We Think, " *U.S. News & World Report,* February 1, 1988, p. 27.
3. "Baseball Committee Formed to Investigate Racist, Ethnic Remarks Made by Cincinnati Reds Owner," *Ethnic NewsWatch,* December 9, 1992, p. 1.
4. David Casstevens, "Schott Case a Bad Lesson in Hypocrisy," *Arizona Republic,* February 5, 1993, p. F1.
5. Ruth Rovner, "Novel Idea: A Desire to Produce His Own Book and Promote Social Responsibility Led Charles Powell Out of Corporate World and into His Own Publishing Venture," *Focus,* June 5, 1991, section 1, p. 10; Charles Powell, *Servants of Power* (Philadelphia: Quantum Leap Press, 1990).
6. See Joe R. Feagin and Melvin P. Sikes, *Living with Racism: The Black Middle Class Experience* (Boston: Beacon, 1994), Chapters 4–5.
7. Dennis Duggan, "New York's 'Incivility Factor,'" *Newsday,* August 4, 1991, p. 43. For harsh oppposition to multiculturalism, see Rush Limbaugh, *The Way Things Ought to Be* (New York: Pocket Star Books, 1993), pp. 206–220.

8. Paul Harvey, "America: An Overloaded Lifeboat," as reprinted in NAAWP *News*, (1982): 11.

9. James J. Kilpatrick, "Whites Have Civil Rights Too," as reprinted in NAAWP *News*, (1984): 14.

10. Sharon Walsh, "Chairman Says Texaco Is Battling Racial Bias," *Washington Post*, July 30, 1997, p. D9.

11. Courtland Milloy, "Texaco Taps a Deep Well of Racism," *Washington Post*, November 10, 1996, p. B1.

12. Kurt Eichenwald, "Texaco's Tale of the Tape," *The New York Times*, November 10, 1996, section 4, p. 2.

13. Kurt Eichenwald, "The Two Faces of Texaco," *The New York Times*, November 10, 1996, section 3, p. 1.

14. Linda Yglesias, "Shame of Texaco: Racist Tapes No Shock: Plaintiffs," *Daily News*, November 10, 1996, p. 46; see also Bari-Ellen Roberts, *Roberts v. Texaco: A True Story of Race and Corporate America* (New York: Avon Books, 1998), p. 1 and passim.

15. Linda Yglesias, "Tapes No Shock: Plaintiffs," *Daily News*, November 10, 1996, p. 46.

16. *Ibid.*

17. Eichenwald, "The Two Faces of Texaco"

18. Carol Memmott, "Author Offers Ugly Account of Texaco Lawsuit," *USA Today*, April 13, 1998, p. 6B.

19. David Ivanovich, L. M. Sixel, and Chris Woodyard, "Oil Industry Struggling with Diversity; Minority Applicants Are Rare, Compounding Problem," *Houston Chronicle*, November 17, 1996, p. A1.

20. Elsa Brenner, "Blacks See Texaco Victory as a Start," *The New York Times*, December 1, 1996, section 13, p. 1.

21. "Ads Say Texaco Dumped Toxic Waste in Rain Forest," *Houston Chronicle*, September 24, 1999, p. 3.

22. Quoted in Laura Westra and Peter Wenz, eds, *Faces of Environmental Racism: Confronting Issues of Global Justice* (London: Rowman & Littlefield, 1995), p. xvi.

23. *Timothy C. Pigford et al. v. Dan Glickman, Secretary, The United States Department of Agriculture*, United States District Court for the District of Columbia, Civil Action No. 97-1978 (PLF).

24. The last two paragraphs draw on a summary of research by Phyliss Craig-Taylor. See her *Open Door Days on the Last Plantation*, unpublished research manuscripts, University of Florida, 1999.

25. Tim Cox, "Rights Groups Cautious About 'Odd Couple' Appearances,'" *UPI*, November 22, 1988.

26. "News Digest," *NAAWP News* 20 (1982): 3.

27. Paul Walker, "Clinton Country: 1992 Arizona Political Races," *National Review*, November 2, 1992, p. NRW6.

28. Raymond Means, "Minorities Demand INS Commissioner's Firing," UPI, AM cycle, September 23, 1987.

29. David DeVoss, "Glendale Jurist Stunned by His Fall from Grace," *Los Angeles Times,* August 31, 1987, part 5, no 1.

30. Andrew Kopkind, "Buchanan: We'd Rather Be Right," *Nation,* January 6, 1992, p. 1.

31. Quoted in an unsigned editorial, "Buchanan Campaign Rhetoric," *Boston Globe,* January 12, 1992, p. 68.

32. "Big Business," *Financial Times,* January 3, 1991, p. 12.

33. Steven Neal, "D-e-a-v-e-r Spells Insensitivity," *Chicago Tribune,* May 9, 1985, Zone C, p. 19.

34. Terrel Bell, *The Thirteenth Man* (New York: Free Press, 1988), pp. 104–105.

35. *Ibid.,* p. 103.

36. Quoted in Ernest Furgurson, *Hard Right* (New York: Norton, 1986), p. 219.

37. *Ibid.,* p. 219.

38. Priscilla Painton, "Quota Quagmire," *Time,* May 27, 1991, p. 20; "The 1990 Elections State by State," *The New York Times,* November 8, 1990, p. B8.

39. Quoted in Ross K. Baker, "The G. in G.O.P. is 'Gaffe,'" *The New York Times,* September 24, 1983, section 1, p. 23.

40. Ted Koppel, *Nightline,* ABC News, May 16, 1994.

41. *Ibid.*

42. Lou Cannon and David S. Broder, "GOP Debaters Restate Basic Positions: Seven Republicans Restate Their Basic Positions in N.H. Debate," *Washington Post,* February 21, 1980, section 1, p. A1.

43. Roger Simon, "Virulent Foot-in-Mouth Disease Strikes Again," *Los Angeles Times,* April 1, 1990, p. E7.

44. Anthony Ramirez, "Word for Word/Asian Americans," *The New York Times,* March 5, 2000, section 4, p. 7.

45. Stephen Engelberg, "Bush, His Disavowed Backers and a Very Potent Attack Ad," *The New York Times,* November 3, 1988, p. A1.

46. Bruce Buchanan, *Electing a President: The Markle Commission Research on Campaign 1988* (Austin: University of Texas Press, 1991), pp. 161–162; Kathleen Hall Jamieson, *Dirty Politics: Deception, Distraction, and Democracy* (New York: Oxford University Press, 1992), pp. 17–23.

47. Jeffrey M. Elliot, "The Man and the Symbol: The 'Willie' Horton Nobody Knows," *Nation,* August 23/30, 1993, pp. 201–202.

48. Jamieson, *Dirty Politics,* p. 19; Marshall Ingwerson, "Campaigns That Stoop to Conquer," *Christian Science Monitor,* October 29, 1992, p. 14.

49. Retha Hill, "Bush Aide Denounces Maryland Letter," *Washington Post,* October 31, 1988, p. A1.

50. Samuel Perry, "Dukakis Counters Bush Campaign of Fear and Smear," *Reuters Library Report,* October 22, 1988.

51. Robert K. Dornan, *Congressional Record*—House, 102nd Cong., 2nd Sess., 1992, H9434, Vol. 138, No. 132.

52. David R. Runkel, ed., *Campaign for President: The Managers Look at '88* (Dover, MA: Auburn House Publishing, 1989), pp. 113–114.

53. *Ibid.*, p. 116.

54. *Ibid.*, p. 119.

55. Thomas B. Edsall, "Race: Still a Force in Politics; GOP Stronger Among Whites in Heavily Black States," *Washington Post,* July 31, 1988, p. A1.

56. Runkel, *Campaign for President,* p. 120.

57. Lee Atwater, with Todd Brewster, "Lee Atwater's Last Campaign," *Life,* February 1991, p. 58.

58. David Nyhan, "2 Men, 2 Destinies," *Boston Globe,* October 13, 1988, p. 15.

59. Jamieson, *Dirty Politics,* p. 128.

60. *Ibid.*, p. 129.

61. Elliot, "The Man and the Symbol," p. 204.

62. See Chris Black, "Campaign 88: Amid More Charges of Lies, a Look for the Truth," *Boston Globe,* October 26, 1988, p. 17; Jamieson, *Dirty Politics,* p. 130.

63. Jamieson, *Dirty Politics,* p. 22.

64. *Ibid.*, p. 22.

65. E. J. Dionne, Jr., "Democratic Strength Shifts to West," *The New York Times,* November 13, 1988, p. 32.

66. Jeffrey M. Elliot, "A Few Words from Willie Horton," *Playboy,* December 1989, p. 166.

67. Christine M Black and Thomas Oliphant, *All by Myself: The Unmaking of a Presidential Campaign* (Chester, CT: Globe Pequot Press, 1989), p. 208.

68. Elliot, "A Few Words from Willie Horton," p. 166; Elliot, "The Man and the Symbol," pp. 201–205.

69. Elliot, "The Man and the Symbol," pp. 202–203.

70. Elliot, "A Few Words from Willie Horton," p. 166.

71. *Ibid.*, p. 166.

72. Quoted in Stephen Kurkjian, "President Defends 1988 Campaign's Use of 'Willie Horton' Ad," *Boston Globe,* July 11, 1991, p. 8.

73. Major R. Owens, *Congressional Record*—House, 102nd Cong., 2nd Sess., 1992, H3667, Vol. 138, No. 71.

74. Bill Bradley, *Congressional Record*—Senate, 102nd Cong., 1st Sess., 1992, S10465, Vol. 137, No. 111.

75. *Ibid.,*

76. See Feagin and Sikes, *Living with Racism,* Chapter 2; Doris A Graber, *Crime News and the Public* (New York: Praeger, 1980); Dennis B. Roddy, "Perceptions Still Segregate Police, Black Community," *Pittsburgh Press,* August 26, 1990, B1.

77. U.S. Department of Justice, *Criminal Victimization in the United States,* 1991 (Washington, DC: 1992), p. 61.

78. For a critique of this idea see Nathan Rutstein, *Healing Racism in America: A Prescription for the Disease* (Springfield, Mass: Whitcomb Publishing, 1993), p. 54.

79. Winthrop Jordan, *The White Man's Burden: Historical Origins of Racism in the United States* (New York: Oxford University Press, 1974), p. 80.

80. Quoted in Rutstein, *Healing Racism,* p. 59.

81. Joel Kovel, *White Racism: A Psychohistory*, rev. ed. (New York: Columbia University Press, 1984).

82. David Mills, "Sister Souljah's Call to Arms: The Rapper Says the Riots Were Payback: Are You Paying Attention?" *Washington Post*, May 13, 1992, p. B1.

83. Quoted by Jackie Judd, *World News Saturday*, ABC News, June 13, 1992.

84. Carleton R. Bryant, "Sister Souljah Makes Most of Clinton's Ire," *Washington Times*, June 16, 1992, p. A1.

85. James T. Jones IV, "Sister Souljah: Clinton Gave Me a Bad Rap," *USA Today*, June 17, 1992, p. 1D.

86. Jeffrey Stinson, "Clinton Has Light Schedule, Working on Acceptance Speech," Gannett News Service, June 13, 1992.

87. Jeffrey Stinson, "Clinton Needs to Stick to His Old Character," Gannett News Service, June 17, 1992.

88. Quoted in Ron Howell and Timothy Clifford, "Jackson: It's Clinton Scheme," *Newsday*, June 21, 1992, p. 6.

89. *Crier & Company*, CNN, July 2, 1992.

90. "Sister Souljah: In the Eye of the Storm," *Larry King Live*, CNN, June 19, 1992.

91. Quoted in "Rap's Sister Souljah Raps Clinton's Rebuke," UPI, June 16, 1992.

92. "Sister Souljah: In the Eye of the Storm," *Larry King Live*.

93. Mills, "Sister Souljah's Call to Arms," p. B1.

94. David Mills, "Out on the Edge: Political Hip-Hop," *Washington Post*, April 5, 1992, p. G1.

95. *Ibid.*, p. G1.

96. *Ibid.*, p. G1.

97. Quoted in Michael Posner, "Jesse Jackson Hints He Might Not Back Clinton," *Reuters Library Report*, June 17, 1992.

98. *Crier & Company*, CNN, August 26, 1992.

99. "Sister Souljah: In the Eye of the Storm," *Larry King Live*.

100. Quoted in "Inside Politics," *Washington Times*, June 21, 1992, p. A4.

101. Senator Robert Byrd, "Sister Souljah's Statement Challenged," *Congressional Record*—Senate, 102nd Cong., 2nd Sess., June 15, 1992, S8159, Vol. 138, No. 85.

102. Robert K Dornan, "Violence Against American Youth," *Congressional Record*—House, 102nd Cong., 2nd Sess., June 25, 1992, H5188, Vol. 138, No. 93.

103. Jonathan Alter, "Clinton's Challenge," *Newsweek*, November 30, 1992, p. 26.

104. "Clinton and Jackson: Sound and Fury Signifying . . . Something?" American Political Network, *The Hotline*, June 22, 1992.

105. Colman McCarthy, "For Grim Rapper, Hatred Is a Cash Crop," *Washington Post*, June 23, 1992, p. C10.

106. *Ibid.*, p. C10.

107. Nickie McWhirter, "Try a Rap Against All Killing," Gannett News Service, June 23, 1992.

108. Jack E. White, "Sister Souljah: Capitalist Tool," *Time*, June 29, 1992, p. 88.

109. *Ibid.*, p. 88.

110. Bill Strauss and Neil Howe, "Enter the Boomers," *Vancouver Sun,* January 16, 1993, p. A16.

111. Quoted in Sam Fulwood III, "Clinton Carves New Strategy with Double-Edged Sword," *Los Angeles Times,* June 16, 1992, p. A20.

112. Quoted in John Gilardi, "Dinkins Says Clinton Should Have Handled Race Remarks Better," Reuters, June 20, 1992.

113. Derrick Z. Jackson, "Rap's Primal Scream," *Boston Globe,* June 21, 1992, p. 83; see also Darrell Dawsey, "Dawsey: Taking the Wrong Rap," Gannett News Service, June 29, 1992.

114. David Garrow, " Lani Guinier," *The Progressive,* September 1993, p. 28.

115. Quoted in Lori Rodriguez, "In the Defense of Cheated Nominee," *Houston Chronicle,* July 24, 1993, p. A27.

116. See, for example, Lani Guinier, "The Triumph of Tokenism: Voting Rights Act and the Theory of Black Electoral Success," *Michigan Law Review* 89 (March 1991): 1077.

117. William E. Forbath, "Civil Rights, Economic Justice and the Meaning of the Guinier Affair," *Legal Times,* June 28, 1993, p. 21; Michael Isikoff, "Readings in Controversy: Guinier's Pivotal Articles," *Washington Post,* June 4, 1993, p. A10; Lani Guinier, *The Tyranny of Majority: Fundamental Fairness and Representative Democracy* (New York: Free Press, 1994).

Chapter 7: Sincere Fictions of the White Self

1. Howard Schuman, Charlotte Steeh, and Lawrence Bobo, *Racial Attitudes in America* (Cambridge, MA: Harvard University Press, 1985), pp. 139–162.

2. National Opinion Research Center, "1990 General Social Survey." Tabulations by the authors.

3. Anti-Defamation League, *Highlights from an Anti-Defamation League Survey on Racial Attitudes in America* (New York: Anti-Defamation League, 1993), p. 10.

4. Schuman et al., *Racial Attitudes in America,* pp. 86–125.

5. National Opinion Research Center, "1990 General Social Survey."

6. Louis Harris Associates and NAACP Legal Defense and Educational Fund, *The Unfinished Agenda on Race in America* (New York: NAACP Legal Defense and Educational Fund, 1989), pp. 6–10.

7. National Opinion Research Center, "1991 General Social Survey." Tabulations by the authors.

8. Joe R. Feagin, *Subordinating the Poor: Welfare and American Beliefs* (Englewood Cliffs, NJ: Prentice-Hall, 1975).

9. National Opinion Research Center, "1991 General Social Survey." Tabulations by the authors.

10. John B. McConahay and Joseph C. Hough, "Symbolic Racism," *Journal of Social Issues* 32 (1976): 38.

11. Most respondents agreed to be interviewed on condition of anonymity; changes have been made in the quotes to protect their anonymity and, occasionally, to edit lightly for grammar and to eliminate filler words such as "uh." We are indebted to

Peggy Moore, Debra Van Ausdale, Katherine Dube, Mark Dulong, Kim Lersch, John Talmadge, Brian Fox, E. J. Brown, Kay Roussos, and several other students for allowing us to quote from interviews they conducted. We are indebted to Susana McCollom and Debra Van Ausdale for conducting our own interviews. The format of the interview schedules varied but in each case included a range of questions about white attitudes toward racial relations and African Americans. The interviews were transcribed by the interviewers or by Kevin Knapke.

12. Robert W. Terry, "The Negative Impact on White Values," in *Impacts of Racism on White Americans,* ed. Benjamin P. Bowser and Raymond G. Hunt (Beverly Hills, CA: Sage, 1981), p. 119.

13. For evidence on this, see Joe R. Feagin and Melvin P. Sikes, *Living with Racism: The Black Middle Class Experience* (Boston: Beacon Press, 1994).

14. Bob Blauner, *Black Lives, White Lives: Three Decades of Race Relations in America* (Berkeley: University of California Press, 1989), p. 259.

15. Margaret A. Moore, "The Paradox of Egalitarianism and the Denial of Racism," unpublished research paper, University of Florida, December 9, 1992.

16. Gunnar Myrdal, *An American Dilemma* (New York: Harper & Row, 1944).

17. S. L. Gaertner, "The Role of Racial Attitudes in Helping Behavior," *Journal of Social Psychology* 97 (1975): 95–101.

18. Erving Goffman, *The Presentation of Self in Everyday Life* (Garden City, NY: Anchor Books, 1959).

19. Sally Jacobs, "The Put-Upon Privileged Ones: Feelings Wounded, White Men Complain Society Stereotypes Them as Boring Jerks," *Boston Globe,* November 22, 1992, p.1.

20. Jacobs, "The Put-Upon Privileged Ones," p.1.

21. Frederick R Lynch, *Invisible Victims: White Males and the Crisis of Affirmative Action* (New York: Greenwood Press, 1989); see also Rush H. Limbaugh, *The Way Things Ought to Be* (New York: Pocket Star Books, 1993).

22. Thomas Dye, *Who's Running America?* 4th ed. (Englewood Cliffs, NJ: Prentice-Hall, 1986), pp. 190–205.

23. Studs Terkel, *Race: How Blacks and Whites Think and Feel About the American Obsession* (New York: The New Press, 1992), p.289.

24. Joel Kovel, *White Racism: A Psychohistory,* rev. ed. (New York: Columbia University Press, 1984), p. xliv.

25. Joe R. Feagin and Clairece B. Feagin, *Social Problems,* 4th ed. (Englewood Cliffs, NJ, 1994), pp. 96–97.

26. See Feagin, *Subordinating the Poor.*

27. See Suzanne Harper, "The Brotherhood: Race and Gender Ideologies in the White Supremacist Movement," unpublished Ph.D. dissertation, University of Texas, 1993.

28. Mark R. Rank, *Living on the Edge: The Realities of Welfare in America* (New York: Columbia University Press, 1994); see also Charles M. Madigan, "Welfare Finger–pointing: Society Often Determines Stereotypes," *Chicago Tribune,* February 20, 1994, p. C1.

29. Limbaugh, *The Way Things Ought to Be,* p. 219.
30. See the surveys cited in "You Ain't the Right Color, Pal: White Resentment of Affirmative Action," *Policy Review,* Winter 1990: 64.
31. See Jonathan Leonard, "Employment and Occupational Advance Under Affirmative Action," *Review of Economics and Statistics* 66 (August 1994): 377–385; Margery A. Turner, Michael Fix, and Raymond J. Struyk, "Opportunities Denied," Urban Institute Research Report, Washington, DC, 1991.
32. Richard Delgado, *The Rodrigo Chronicles: Conversations about America and Race* (New York: New York University Press, 1995), p. 6.
33. Derrick Bell, *Faces at the Bottom of the Well: The Permanence of Racism* (New York: Basic Books, 1992), pp. 7–8.
34. John VanderLippe, "Racism and International Relations: Stereotypes and the Making of American Policy Towards Turkey," *The Global Color Line: Racial and Ethnic Inequality and Struggle from a Global Perspective,* ed. Pinar Batur-VanderLippe and Joe Feagin (Stanford, CT: JAI Press, 1999), pp. 47–63.
35. Martin Luther King, Jr., *Why We Can't Wait* (New York: Penguin, 1963), pp. 80–81.

Chapter 8: Taking Action Against Racism: Problems and Prospects

1. Nelson Mandela, *Long Walk to Freedom* (Boston: Little, Brown, 1994), pp. 539–40.
2. Richard Delgado, "When a Story Is Just a Story: Does Voice Really Matter?" *Virginia Law Review* 76 (February 1990): 105.
3. For an excellent discussion of this point, see Lani Guinier, *The Tyranny of the Majority: Fundamental Fairness and Representative Democracy* (New York: Free Press, 1994).
4. Eric Nordlinger, "Containing the Ethnic Conflict," as reprinted in the *Congressional Record,* 103rd Cong., 1st Sess., March 4, 1993, S2447, Vol. 139, No 25.
5. William O. Douglas, "Concurring Opinion: *Jones et ux. v. Alfred H. Mayer Co.*" (1968), 392 U.S. 445.
6. See Joe R. Feagin and Melvin P. Sikes, *Living with Racism: The Black Middle Class Experience* (Boston: Beacon Press, 1994).
7. Joel Kovel, *White Racism: A Psychohistory,* rev. ed. (New York: Columbia University Press, 1984), p. xliii.
8. Toni Morrison, *Playing in the Dark: Whiteness and the Literary Imagination* (Cambridge, MA: Harvard University Press, 1992).
9. Jennifer L. Hochschild, *The New American Dilemma: Liberal Democracy and School Desegregation* (New Haven, CT: Yale University Press, 1984), p. 1.
10. This flaw has led the United States to create unsavory political alliances, such as its long-term alliance with the racist Union of South Africa.
11. "Flames of Racial Rage," *London Times,* May 1, 1992.
12. When the Melting Pot Boils Over," *Daily Mail,* May 1, 1992, p. 6.
13. Al-Ahram, "Choosing the Right Type of Capitalism for Egypt," Middle East News Network, June 4, 1992.

14. Quoted in "China Again Slams U.S. Human Rights After L.A. Riots," Agence France Presse, May 4, 1992.

15. Insight/Middle East Update, "Iraq Wants UN to Discuss Los Angeles Riot," Middle East News Network, May 5, 1992.

16. Thomas Pettigrew, "The Mental Health Impact," in *Impacts of Racism on White Americans*, ed. Benjamin Bowser and Raymond G. Hunt (Beverly Hill, CA: Sage, 1981), p. 117.

17. Wayne Rowe, Sandra K. Bennet, and Donald Atkinson, "White Racial Identity Models: A Critique and Alternative Proposal," *The Counseling Psychologist* 22 (January 1994): 129–146.

18. Kent L. Granzin and Janeen E. Olsen, "Characterizing Participants in Activities Protecting the Environment: A Focus on Donating, Recycling, and Conservation Behaviors," *Journal of Public Policy & Marketing* 10 (Fall 1991): 1. See also C. Daniel Batson and Jay S. Coke, "Empathy: A Source of Altruistic Motivation for Helping?" in *Altruism and Helping Behavior: Social, Personality, and Developmental Perspectives*, ed. J. Philippe Rushton and Richard M. Sorrentino (Hillsdale, NJ: Lawrence Erlbaum, 1981), pp. 157–187; Daniel Batson and Katherine McDavis, "Empathic Mediation of Helping: A Two-Stage Model," *Journal of Personality and Social Psychology* 36 (July 1978): 752–766; and Dennis Krebs, "Empathy and Altruism," *Journal of Personality and Social Psychology* 32 (December 1975): 1134–1146.

19. Lillian Smith, *Killers of the Dream*, rev. ed. (New York: W. W. Norton, 1961), pp. 68–69.

20. See Deborah Tannen, *You Just Don't Understand: Women and Men in Conversation* (New York: Ballantine Books, 1990), pp. 148–175; and Mary F. Belenky, Blythe M. Clinchy, Nancy R. Goldberger, and Jill M. Tarule, *Women's Ways of Knowing: The Development of Self, Voice, and Mind* (New York: Basic Books, 1986), pp. 112–113.

21. Some portions of their innovative research were presented in Tiffany L. Hogan and Julie K. Netzer, "Knowing the Other: White Women, Gender, and Racism," unpublished paper presented at the annual meeting of the American Sociological Association, Miami Beach, Florida, August 1993.

22. See John L Hodge, "Equality: Beyond Dualism and Oppression," in *Anatomy of Racism*, ed. David Theo Goldberg (Minneapolis: University of Minnesota Press, 1990), pp. 89–107.

23. Kathleen Blee, *Women of the Klan: Racism and Gender in the 1920s* (Berkeley: University of California Press, 1991), pp. 2–3.

24. See Suzanne Harper, "The Brotherhood: Race and Gender Ideologies in the White Supremacist Movement," unpublished Ph.D. dissertation, University of Texas, 1993.

25. We are indebted to Holly Hanson for permission to use excerpts from interviews she conducted (in the Northeast and the Southeast) for her work on the racial attitudes of people working to overcome racism.

26. Pinar Batur-VanderLippe, "On the Necessity of Antiracist Praxis: An Experience in Teaching and Learning," *Teaching Sociology* 27 (1999): 274–285.

27. bell hooks, *Talking Back: Thinking Feminist, Thinking Black* (Boston: South End, 1989), p. 5.

28. Pinar Batur-VanderLippe, "Centering on Global Racism and Anti-Racism: From Everyday Life to Global Complexity," *Sociological Spectrum* 19 (1999): 467–84.

29. W. E. B. Du Bois, *Dusk of Dawn: An Essay Toward an Autobiography of a Race Concept* (New Brunswick, NJ: Transaction Books, 1984 [1940]), p. 6.

30. Pinar Batur-VanderLippe and Joe Feagin, "Racial and Ethnic Inequality and Struggle from the Colonial Era to the Present: Drawing the Global Color Line," in *The Global Color Line: Racial and Ethnic Inequality and Struggle from a Global Perspective,* ed. Pinar Batur-Vanderlippe and Joe Feagin, volume 6 in the series *Research in Politics and Society* (Greenwich, CT: JAI Press, 1999), pp. 3–21.

31. Eileen O'Brien, "Mind, Heart and Action: Understanding the Dimensions of Antiracism," *The Global Color Line,* pp. 305–321.

32. bell hooks, *Killing Rage: Ending Racism* (New York: Henry Holt and Company, 1995), p. 272.

33. Kenneth Smith and Ira Zepp, *Search for the Beloved Community: The Thinking of Martin Luther King, Jr.* (Valley Forge, PA: Judson Press, 1974), pp. 117–120.

34. hooks, *Killing Rage,* pp. 263–272.

35. Martin Luther King, Jr., *Why We Can't Wait* (New York: Mentor, 1964), p. 77.

36. Nathan Rutstein, *Healing Racism in America* (Springfield, MA: Whitcomb Publishing, 1993), pp. 1–51, 121–129.

37. Pinar Batur-VanderLippe, " On the Necessity of Antiracist Praxis: An Experience in Teaching and Learning," *Teaching Sociology* 27 (1999): 279.

38. *Ibid.*

39. Emily Morison Beck, ed., *John Bartlett's Familiar Quotations,* 15th ed. (Boston: Little, Brown, 1980), p. 909.

40. Quoted in David Gelman, "The Young and the Reckless," *Newsweek,* January 11, l992, p. 61.

41. Pettigrew, "The Mental Health Impact," p. 117.

42. Gunnar Myrdal, *An American Dilemma,* vol. 1 (New York: McGraw-Hill, 1964), p. 24; and Joe R. Feagin, *Racist America: Roofs, Current Realities and New Reparations* (New York: Routledge, 2000).

43. Hochschild, *The New American Dilemma,* p. 12.

44. Boris Bittker, *The Case for Black Reparations* (New York: Random House, 1973).

45. Stephen Magagnini, "Descendants Suing U.S. over Slavery," *Sacramento Bee,* April 14, 1994, p. A1.

46. See John Woolfolk, "Seeking Redress for Slavery's Scars: Foster City Woman Leads Campaign to Force U.S. to Pay Reparations," *San Francisco Chronicle,* February 22, 1994, p. A13.

47. See Roy Brooks, editor, *When Sorry Isn't Enough: The Controversey over Apologies and Reparations for Human Injustice* (New York: New York University Press, 1999).

48. Robert S. Browne, "The Economic Basis for Reparations to Black America," *Review of Black Political Economy* 21 (January 1993): 99.

49. *John Bartlett's Familiar Quotations,* 15th ed., p. 392.

50. Alice S. Rossi, ed., *The Feminist Papers* (New York: Bantam Books, 1974), pp. 10–15.

51. "United Nations Universal Declaration of Human Rights," in *The Human Rights Reader,* Walter Laqueur and Barry Rubin, rev. ed. (New York: New American Library, 1989), pp. 197–202.

52. Gideon Sjoberg and Ted R. Vaughan, "The Ethical Foundations of Sociology and the Necessity for a Human Rights Perspective," in *A Critique of Contemporary American Society,* ed. Ted R. Vaughan, Gideon Sjoberg, and Larry Reynolds (New York: General Hall, 1993), p. 135. Italics added.

53. Griff Wigley "Can Citizen Dialogues Forge National Identity? National Endowment for the Humanities Launches Discussion Forums," *Utne Reader,* (May/June 1994): pp. 36–37.

54. Etienne Balibar, *Masses, Classes, Ideas: Studies on Politics and Philosophy Before and After Marx,* translated by James Swanson (New York: Routledge, 1994), p. 210; see also Batur-VanderLippe, "Centering on Global Racism and Antiracism."

55. Derrick Bell, *"Brown v. Board of Education* and the Interest-Convergence Dilemma," *Harvard Law Review* 518 (1980): 93.

Index